P9-CBH-101

A HISTORY OF
THE IRISH SETTLERS
IN NORTH AMERICA,

FROM THE EARLIEST PERIOD TO THE
CENSUS OF 1850

By
THOMAS D'ARCY McGEE

CLEARFIELD

Reprint of the 1852 edition

Genealogical Publishing Co., Inc.
Baltimore, 1974

Reprinted for
Clearfield Company, Inc. by
Genealogical Publishing Co., Inc.
Baltimore, Maryland
2003

Library of Congress Catalogue Card Number 74-2606
International Standard Book Number 0-8063-0618-1

Reprinted from a volume in
the George Peabody Branch,
Enoch Pratt Free Library,
Baltimore, Maryland
1974

Made in the United States of America

TO

MY EMIGRANT COUNTRYMEN

IN

THE UNITED STATES AND CANADA,

AS

AN ACKNOWLEDGMENT OF THE MANY KINDNESSES RECEIVED DURING MY

SECOND RESIDENCE AMONG THEM,

This Volume

IS AFFECTIONATELY DEDICATED.

CONTENTS.

1*

CHAPTER IX.

CHAPTER X.

CHAPTER XI.

CHAPTER XII.

CHAPTER XIII.

CHAPTER XIV.

CHAPTER XV.

CHAPTER XVI.

CHAPTER XVII.

CHAPTER XVIII.

CHAPTER XIX.

CHAPTER XX.

CHAPTER XXI.

CHAPTER XXII.

CHAPTER XXIII.

CHAPTER XXIV.

CHAPTER XXV.

CHAPTER XXVI.

INDEX.

INTRODUCTION.

EUROPE AND AMERICA.

THE fifteenth century in Spain (the point from which the discovery of America emanated) was marked by the cessation of the Crusades, by treaties, made between the Moors and Christians of Spain and France, the Porte and Venice, of amity and commerce. Asiatic arts and luxury, Asiatic idols, and Asiatic valor, had made deep and sensible impressions upon Christendom. The schools of Cordova, the chivalry of Grenada, the galleys of Fez, the grandeur of the Soldan, exercised a moral despotism throughout Europe. What Russian power and Russian pretensions are to Europe to-day, the Ottoman empire was to the Christian Europe of Columbus' youth.

The exact sciences were, as yet, in a rude and chaotic state. Astrology, alchemy, and both magics had professors and postulants. Medicine was little better than herbal traditions, or a litany of incantations. Amulets blest by conjurers were worn, and the stars believed in by the highest intellects. It was then, — when star-gazers advised kings to peace or war, when brazen heads were fabricated by Albertus Magnus and Friar Bacon, when Aldrovandus had to dissect his own child, fearing to touch another human body, — with Fatalism enthroned in

Asia, and Credulity in Europe, — it was then, that Columbus turned his piercing vision towards the West.

Domestic slavery existed very generally through Europe. The lords of the soil exacted the services, lives, and the very honor, of their serfs. The serf was chained to his district and predestined to his profession. There was no freedom of will, or mind, among the populace. A few trading towns had, indeed, wrung chartered privileges from their sovereigns, but these privileges were confined to the class of master workmen, who held in servitude the great body of the citizens and apprentices.

Chivalry had lost its charm, and was obsolete. The age of Commerce, which was felt to be approaching, was looked for exclusively in the East; so that, even in the knowledge of its own wants, Europe was in error.

Two great facts of this century precede Columbus, and only two. The science of government was being studied carefully in Italy, France, and Spain, and the science of reasoning in the great colleges, since called universities. The fall of Constantinople, in 1453, sent the learned of the East for refuge into Italy, and new classic schools began to assume a regular existence at Rome and Florence, Bologna and Ferrara.

While these mental possessions were beginning to accumulate in Europe, in the wisdom of Providence, a New World was about to become a sharer in their diffusion.

Let us be just to the European thinkers of those days. With much that seems absurd in the " schoolmen," and

much that was ephemeral, there is combined the vital principle of all human history, — Does man, under God, suffice for himself? Can he justify his own intellect? — can he self-govern his own life? — this was their great problem through all their studies. Doubtless, they did not know whither their own theories ultimately led; doubtless, they, too, attempted to set limits to faith and to science; but, with all that can be said against them, there they stand, — the ferrymen plying between ancient and modern civilization, bringing over to us the most precious products of distant times, and teaching us how to start in our new career.

The long and painful preparatory efforts of Columbus to interest the old world in his project, would seem almost to be permitted, in order to prove the inefficiency of the age he was to electrify on his return from the first voyage.

He besought Genoa and Venice for a ship or two, to find his world, and they refused him; he petitioned the wise kings of Portugal and England, and they refused to risk a single sail in such a quest; he sojourned long about the courts of France and Spain, appealing to the wisdom of the wise, the judgment of the learned, the ambition of the brave, and the avarice of the acquisitive; but he argued, appealed, petitioned in vain! No one believed in his theory, or hoped in his adventure. Nay, the wise smiled scornfully, the learned laughed in their academic sleeves, and even the brave had no stomach for battling the tempest, or for planting their banners in the wide sea-field.

Besides, was he not a common sailor? He had, indeed, commanded some merchant ships, and had an uncle an admiral. His name, some said, was noble; but of this there was no proof. The age that believed in the Divine right of the blood royal, and the sovereign inheritance of the blood noble, could not conceive of a mere sailor achieving a conquest, which princes and grandees could not so much as imagine, after all his arguments.

Where, then, did Columbus and his theory find believers? Who were his first converts and first assistants? A woman, a sailor, and a monk, are the three by whom the curtain of the Atlantic is raised, and America pointed out afar off. Before the dense curtain of that grandest scene of all human history, they stand, — the woman, the sailor, and the monk. Columbus converted the prior of La Rabida, the prior converted the queen of Castile, and so the armament did sail, after all, in quest of the New World in the West.

That is a noble group, and deserves long contempla-tion. The woman personifies gentleness, the monk, faith, the sailor, courage. Faith, gentleness, and cour-age are thus confederated to find the New World, and claim it for their own!

Columbus sailed, and, except by a very few, was soon forgotten. The prior may have prayed for him; the queen may have sometimes asked news of him; Paulo Toscanelli, the map-maker, in his Florentine study, may have cast his eye over the conjectural track of the two Spanish carvels, to the ideal shore of Saint Brendans, land; but great, gross Europe sleeps, eats, and drinks, just as if no apostle of the Future was laboring through the shoreless ocean. The capture of Grenada, with its half million Moors, no doubt, seemed to all the wise heads of Europe incomparably the greatest act that century could see. The Genoese sailor and his New World are hidden, for the time, by that cloud of turbans, with its pale, disastrous crescent still visible, though eclipsed.

What a month that must have been in Europe, when Columbus returned with his plants and minerals, and his men, red and naked as the sun! The telegraph of rumor proclaimed his success from Lisbon to Madrid, and from Madrid to Rome, Venice, Antwerp, Paris, and London. What wild tales are told and swallowed, — what a crying curiosity thrusts out its ears from every corner of Europe, — what sudden new light breaks in on the learned, — what passion for ocean adventure seizes on the brave, — what visions of mountains of gold and valleys of diamonds drive away sleep from the couches of the avaricious!

In this age of inferior "excitements," we can hardly imagine what Europe felt in that day; though, if the "sensation" can be imagined anywhere, 't is here. It must have been something incomparably more intense than the "California fever." "A New World found!" was the trumpet-blast which rung from end to end of Europe. Europe, that yesterday considered the fall of Gren-

2

ada the greatest of facts, has already almost forgotten Grenada! Europe, that began to smile at the crusade, grasps again the banner of the Cross, to plant it, not on Saint Sophias, or Mount Calvary, but to plant it on the further verge of the ocean, bordered with illimitable lands! Europe, in the hour of Columbus' arrival, attained her majority, began to act and think for herself, and, ceasing to be a child, to cast away the things of her child-hood.

On the authentication and details of the discovery there is no need to pause. On the names of the new chivalry of the ocean we need not linger. Cabot, Cartier, Americus, Verrazzini, Hudson, Raleigh, Drake, Balboa, Cortez, Pizarro, — America knows them all. They developed the idea of the great sailor. They found the western way to India. They demonstrated the rotundity of the earth. They are the true experimental philosophers, to whom Bacon, Descartes, Linnæus, and Gassendi, were but the amanuenses. They will be forever honored among men, — the graduates of the universe! — the alumni of the ocean!

When Columbus, ill-requited by Spain, and weary of life, felt his end approach, he desired, as his last request, that it might be engraven on his tomb, " *Here lieth Christopher Columbus, who gave to Castile and Arragon a New World.*" If this was meant as a reproach to Ferdinand, it was a magnificent reproach. If it was meant as a lasting definition of his own act, it is miserably deficient. What he actually did, is, indeed, insignificant, compared to what he was the cause of being done; but, even from his death-bed, that clear-sighted man must have foreseen that not to Fedinand and Isabella was his New World given; not to Spain, nor even to Europe; but rather that it was given to all humanity, for the remainder of time to come.

Three hundred years and more have passed over the grave of Columbus. In his cathedral tomb, at Havana, he sleeps within the circle of the greatest exploit of modern men, — the civilization of America, — which he most heroically began. All the races of Europe have contributed workmen to the work, who, amid much " confusion of tongues," are rearing it heavenward, day by day, in hope and harmony, and, let us trust, with all due reverence and humility of spirit.

Columbus has been justified; so has Spain. The shares of France, England, Holland, Sweden, and Germany, in civilizing America, have been all recorded, in the works of sympathetic and laborious historians.

And now, also, Ireland advances her claim to respect and remembrance as a contributor to this world's work. She also has helped to reclaim the land from barrenness, and to liberate it from oppression. Her sons have made many a clearing, found many a ford, worked out many a noble plan, fighting stoutly for their new country, on land and sea, when so required. Ireland, which has furnished actors to every great act of civilization, since Dathi died at Sales, following in the track of Brennus and Alaric, was also, as we shall see, represented here, from the beginning, by able and useful men. It is of these Irish settlers in America, this book is written; and, while looking over its brief chapters, I cannot suppress a sigh, that much greater books have been written of men who did not deserve the honor one half so well.

The following pages, dear reader, were filled up after many interruptions and under many distractions; therefore, have mercy in your judgment of the work. I venture it into print with the hope that the whole subject may come, ere long, under the hands of a master, who can make of it a story both Europe and America would love to listen to.

Boston, Saint Patrick's Day, 1851.

A HISTORY

OF THE

IRISH SETTLERS IN NORTH AMERICA.

CHAPTER I.

THE LEGEND OF "GREAT IRELAND" AND OF SAINT BRANDAN — NORWEGIAN ACCOUNT — IRISH ACCOUNT — ITALIAN AND SPANISH ACCOUNTS.

IT is uncertain whether Christopher Columbus was the first European who saw America.   A general tradition of its existence was widely received before his birth, and we cannot reject, as entirely incredible, the repeated allusions to this tradition, contained in the early chronicles of the northern nations of the old world.   To the Genoese belongs the glory of disenchanting the Ocean, — of bringing two hemispheres into contact separated from the beginning, — of leaving a land of refuge accessible to humanity, and of opening the history of its population, by one of the most glorious examples of patience, fortitude, and courage, ever exhibited by man.   Who could wish his glory greater or less ?

The Scandinavians count three several precursors of Columbus — Ari Marson, whose voyage took place in 983 ; Biorn, a later adventurer, and Gudlief, son of Gudlang, who, towards the middle of the 11th century, followed the track of, and conversed with, Biorn, in Huitramannaland, or *Irland it Mikla*, beyond the Atlantic. The account of Ari in the Landnamabock is short, but perfectly intelligible.   It says : —

" Ulf the Squinter, son of Hogni the White, occupied the whole of *Reykianess*, (south-west promontory of Ice-

2*

land,) between Thorskafiord and Hafrafell. He had a wife named Biorg, the daughter of Eyvind the East-countryman. They had a son named Atili the Red, who married Thorkotu, daughter of Hergil. They had a son named Ari, who was driven by a tempest to Huitraman-naland, (white man's land,) which some call Irland it Mikla, (Great Ireland,) *which lies in the western ocean, near to Vinland the Good, west from Ireland,"* — by a number of days' sail, which is uncertain, some error hav-ing crept into the original in these figures. "Ari was not permitted to depart, but was baptized there."

Of the second and third voyages, the same Landna-mabock (compiled in the 13th century) relates : —

"So Rafn, the Limerick merchant, first stated, who lived for a long time in Limerick, in Ireland." Rafn was kinsman to Ari Marson, and lived at the beginning or middle of the eleventh century. "So also Thorkel, the son of Geller, (grandson of Ari Marson,) says that certain Icelanders stated, who heard Thorfinn, Jarl of the Ork-neys," — also kinsman to Ari Marson, and born 1008, died 1064, — "relate that Ari had been seen and known in Huitramannaland, and that, although not suffered to depart thence, he was there held in great honor.

"Ari had a wife named Thorgerd, daughter of Alf of Dolum. Their sons were Thorgils, Gudlief, and Il-lugi ; which is the family of Reykianess." Then fol-lows a passage which shows that Eirck the Red was connected with the family of this Ari Marson, and which it may not be amiss to repeat, as all these historical allusions afford corroboration of the authenticity of dif-ferent narratives. "Jorund was the son of Ulf the Squinter. He married Thobiorg Knarrarbring. They had a daughter, Thjodhild, whom Eirck the Red mar-ried. They had a son, Leif the Lucky, of Greenland." It is worthy of remark, that the writer of this account was Ari the Learned, born 1067, who flourished at the end of the eleventh century, and who therefore lived within a century after Ari Marson's departure from Ire-land. He was immediately descended from Ari Marson, and would, of course, be anxious and careful to obtain the most accurate accounts of his ancestors. It is to be observed the situation of Huitramannaland is here stated, "In the western ocean near Vinland, and west of Ireland." It points, of necessity, to that portion of the country now known as the midland or southern States of the Union.*

The *Irland it Mikla*, or Great Ireland, is frequently alluded to in the Northern Sagas. They describe the route towards it, from the North of Europe, thus : —

" To the South of habitable Greenland there are uninhabited and wild tracts, and enormous icebergs. The country of the Skrælings lies beyond these ; Markland beyond this, and Vinland the Good beyond the last. Next to this, and something beyond it, lies Albania, that is, Huitramannaland, whither, formerly, vessels came from Ireland. There, several *Irishmen* and *Icelanders* saw and recognized Ari, the son of Mar and Kotlu, of Reykianess, concerning whom nothing had been heard for a long time, and who had been made their chief by the inhabitants of the land."

In this vague sketch, modern antiquarians have labored hard, and not unsuccessfully, to identify the country of the Skrælings as the Esquimaux coast, Markland as Labrador, Vinland as New England, and Huitramannaland as the country " further southward, beyond the Chesapeake Bay."†

" The Skrælinger," says Humboldt, " related to the Northmen settled in Vinland, that further southward, beyond the Chesapeake Bay, there dwelt ' white men, who clothed themselves in long, white garments, carried before them poles to which clothes were attached, and called with a loud voice.' This account was interpreted, by the Christian Northmen, to indicate processions in which banners were borne accompanied by singing. In the oldest Sagas, the historical narrations of Thorfinn

* Smith's " Northmen in New England." Boston: Hilliard & Grey, 1839.
† Humboldt's " Cosmos."

Karlsefne, and the Icelandic Landnammabock, these
southern coasts, lying between Virginia and Florida, are
designated under the name of the *Land of the White
Men.* They are expressly called Great Ireland, (*Irland
it Mikla*,) and it is maintained that they were peopled
by the Irish. According to testimonies which extend to
1064, before Lief discovered Vinland, and probably about
the year 982, Ari Marson, of the powerful Icelandic race
of Ulf the Squint-eyed, was driven in a voyage from
Iceland to the South, by storms, on the coast of the Land
of the White Men, and there baptized in the Christian
faith ; and, not being allowed to depart, was recognized
by men from the Orkney Islands and Iceland." *

The volumes in which these corroborative accounts are
recorded were compiled in the North, three centuries before the birth of Columbus, and, evidently, represent the
then prevailing belief in a " Great Ireland " beyond the
western sea.

The Irish Annals themselves make special mention of
the same fact. They credit the first voyage westward to
Saint Brandan, patron of Clonfert and Ardfert on the
south-west coast. It is recorded that he flourished from
the year A. D. 550 till the beginning of the following
century, and that his voyages in search of the promised
land, were two ; after which he returned no more. The
precise point of departure, — " the foot of Brandon
Mountain," now Tralee Bay, — is stated ; his sea store
consisted of live swine, his companions of monks, and
his first voyage, of course, abounded in adventures. The
dates in these legends are well fixed, whatever else may
be dubious ; and we do not feel at liberty to reject facts
which an Usher and a Humboldt long pondered over, and,
at last, set down with reverence. †

The voyages of Saint Brandan were received traditions
in France, the Netherlands, Spain, and Italy, soon after
the Northern Chroniclers had written their memoranda

* Humboldt's " Cosmos," vol. i.
† Usher's Antiq. of British Churches ; Usher's Epistles of the Irish
Saints.

concerning *Irland it Mikla*. Old metrical romances, in the French and Dutch languages, give a world of details about them, — some credible, and some absurd enough.* But, what is more to our purpose, Jacobus Voraginius, Provincial of the Dominicans and Bishop of Genoa, (the native city of Columbus,) gave St. Brandan's land special prominence in the 13th century, in his " Golden Legend,"† and the Italian geographers set it down, on their conjectural charts, opposite " Europe and Africa, from the south of Ireland to the end of Guinea." In the map made for Columbus previous to setting out on his first voyage, by Paulo Toscannelli, of Florence, the customary space was occupied by " Saint Borondon's, or Saint Brandan's land."

In the letters of Columbus to his sovereigns, it is notable that the " singing of the birds," and " the greenness of the vegetation," so much dwelt on in " the Golden Legend," are frequently mentioned. The phrase " Promised Land" also occurs, in the mystical sense in which it is employed by Bishop Jacobus.

Even after the voyage of Columbus, so strong was the belief in St. Brandan's, that various expeditions were sent to explore it, as appears from depositions taken before the Grand Inquisitor of the Canaries, Pedro Ortez de Funez, and from other Portuguese and Spanish accounts. The last of these voyages was undertaken as late as 1721, by " Don Gaspar Dominguez, a man of probity and talent. As this was an expedition of solemn and mysterious import, he had two holy friars as apostolical chaplains. They made sail from the island of Teneriffe, toward the end of October, leaving the populace in an indescribable state of anxious curiosity. The ship, however, returned from its cruise as unsuccessful as all its predecessors."‡

---

* See Notices of some of these old Poems in Appendix No. I.

† Voraignus died A. D. 1298.

‡ Nunez, *Conquist de la Gran Canaria;* Viera *Hist. Isl. Can.;* Irving's Life of Columbus, vol. i.

Although these reports were not justified by the facts, yet it would be unwise to confound the early belief with the modern illusion, since the latter did not and could not beget the former, though they have obscured and almost hidden it from our sight.

There is quite sufficient reason to infer that the ancients believed in the existence of a Great Ireland in the West, before Columbus' discovery; and assuredly, if they were mistaken, we are in a fair way to see the doubtful vision of their days become a reality. The dates and details we must leave to the antiquarians, while we endeavor to show what modern emigration has done to accomplish the legend of *Irland it Mikla*.

CHAPTER II.

THE FIRST IRISH EMIGRANTS, — IN BARBADOES — IN PENNSYLVANIA — IN NEW YORK — IN MARYLAND — IN VIRGINIA — IN THE CAROLINAS — IN KENTUCKY — ADVENTURE OF SIMON BUTLER IN DELAWARE.

THE half century after the voyage of Columbus was spent in exploring the harbors, rivers, and coasts of the "New World." Colonization followed, — the Spanish nation still leading. In 1565, the Spaniards founded St Augustine, in Florida; in 1562, the French had built a Fort in Carolina, and in 1608, they founded Quebec; in 1585, Raleigh settled 180 emigrants at Roanoke; in 1606, Jamestown was begun; in 1629, Plymouth, and in 1634, Baltimore. These are the first authentic dates of North American settlements.

The first Irish people who found permanent homes in America, were certain Catholic patriots, banished by Oliver Cromwell to Barbadoes, in 1649. After the failure of the confederation formed in that year, 45,000 Irishmen were transported beyond the seas, some to France and Spain, and several ship-loads to Barbadoes. In this island, as in the neighboring Montserat, the Celtic language was commonly spoken in the last century, and, perhaps, it is partly attributable to this early Irish colonization, that Barbadoes became "one of the most populous islands in the world." At the end of the 17th century, it was reported to contain 20,000 white inhabitants.

During the last quarter of the 17th century there does not appear to have been any considerable emigration from Ireland. After the Restoration of Charles II., in 1660, the influence of the Duke of Ormund procured letters patent suspending the Navigation Laws, so as to allow Ireland comparative freedom of trade. From this, manufactures flourished, and there was no "surplus population" left. The French Refugees, who fled from the Revocation of the Edict of Nantes, in 1685, contributed their manufacturing skill still further to enrich the country, which certainly enjoyed, in the interval from the Restoration to the Revolution, unusual prosperity.

The revolution of 1688 marks a new and less prosperous era for the Mother Country. William and Mary, in the first year of their reign, were called, by both Houses of Parliament, to discourage the manufactures of Ireland which competed with those of England, which they complacently consented to do. By this invidious policy, according to Lord Fitzwilliam, "100,000 operatives" were driven out of Ireland. "Many of the Protestants," says an historian of Irish trade, "removed into Germany," — "several Papists at the same time removed into Spain." Another cotemporaneous writer speaks of multitudes having gone to America from Ireland "in consequence of the rack rents there." A cotemporary account estimates that 3000 males left Ulster yearly for the colonies.* And we hear, at intervals, amid the confusion of this panic flight, the stern accents of Swift, upbraiding the people with their submission, and reproaching the aristocracy with their suicidal impolicy, in cultivating cattle and banishing men.

In the Colony of Pennsylvania one of the earliest settlements of Irishmen was made. In 1699, James Logan, of Lurgan, and others, accompanied William Penn to his new plantation, and were most heartily welcomed. Logan became one of the most considerable men in the colony, which he governed for two years after the death of Penn, and whose capital he enriched by bequeathing to it the most considerable library hitherto opened to its inhabitants. He was, for that age, a most tolerant man, — even more so than his Quaker friend, Penn, who writes him from London, in 1708 : "There is a complaint against your government, that you suffer public Mass in a scandalous manner. Pray send the matter of fact, for ill use

---

* Dobbs on "Irish Trade:" Dublin, 1729.

is made of it against us here."* This charge reflects honor now where it shed suspicion then The name of Logan is honorably identified with the city in which he exercised his beneficent authority.

Attracted by this precedent, others followed the emigrants of 1699, chiefly from the North of Ireland. In the interior of the State we find townships called Derry, Donegal, Tyrone, and Coleraine, so early as 1730. The arrivals at the port of Philadelphia, for the year ending December, 1729, are set down as —

English and Welsh, . . .	267
Scotch, ...	43
Palatines, (Germans,) . . .	343
Irish, ...	5655†

Or, a proportion of ten Irish emigrants to one from all other nations in Europe. And this constant influx, though not in so great disproportion to other arrivals, recurred annually at the same port, till the close of the century.

In 1729, several families from Longford took shipping at Dublin, with a Captain Rymer, for Pennsylvania. He appears to have been one of those brutal mariners still to be met with in the emigrant trade. Although they made the coast of Virginia, and saw land for several days, he would not land them, until he had extorted an extra payment, and his officers were in such awe of him, they dare not remonstrate. At length he landed them at Cape Cod, whence some of them moved to the banks of the Hudson. Of these was Charles Clinton, who had then three children of Irish birth, destined to become historical men in the annals of New York.‡

The Colony of Maryland, founded by Roman Catholics, held out special attractions to the first emigrants of that denomination. The Irish rising of 1641, it is thought, "affected the population of the province."§

* Watson's Annals of Philadelphia, p. 290.
† Holmes' Annals of America, vol. i.
‡ Hoozack's Life of DeWitt Clinton.
§ Bozman's Maryland, vol. i.

The Carrols emigrated to the colony about 1689, and were, in common with the other Catholic settlers, disfranchised by the Protestant Revolution of 1688. Thus, by a singular reverse, the descendants of those who were the first to proclaim complete freedom of conscience in the New World, were for near a hundred years deprived of it by the children of the fugitives to whom they had first afforded the protection elsewhere denied them.

The Irish population in Virginia began about the year 1710, and chiefly settled along the Blue Ridge, in what are now the counties of Patrick and Rockbridge. The McDowells, Breckenridges, McDuffies, McGruders, and others, were of this colony, and the two rivers Mayo, as well as the localities called McGaheysville, Healys, Kennedys, McFarlands, Lynchburgh, and Kinsale, are evidently of Irish origin.

In 1737, a considerable Irish colony obtained a township on the Santee River, in South Carolina, in the district called, from its Indian proprietors, the Waxhaws. Williamsburg, on the Black River, was entirely peopled by our race in 1734, as was Camden, on the Wateree. "Of all other countries," says the historian of that State, "none has furnished the province with so many inhabitants as Ireland. Scarce a ship sailed from any of its ports for Charleston, that was not crowded with men, women, and children." One of our settlements in that colony was peculiarly unfortunate. "The Council having announced, in England and Ireland, that the land of the ejected Yemassees would be given to the actual settlers, five hundred persons from Ireland transported themselves to South Carolina, to take the benefit of it. But the whole project was frustrated by the proprietors, who claimed those lands as their property, and insisted on the right of disposing of them as they saw fit. Not long afterwards, to the utter ruin of the Irish emigrants, and in breach of the provincial faith, these Indian lands were surveyed, by order of the proprietors, for their own use, and laid out in large baronies." "Many of the unfortunate Irish emigrants," adds the historian, "having spent the little money they brought with them, were reduced to misery and famished. The remainder removed to the northern colonies."[*] Among the Irish settlers in the Waxhaws, we notice the now famous names, Rutledge, Jackson, and Calhoun.

After the Williamite war, in Ireland, several emigrant Irish families arrived in North Carolina, and settled there. Of these, the most active and distinguished was Governor James Moore, who headed the revolution of 1705, which converted the province from a proprietary to a popular government, elective from the people. He held out against all the force and power of the proprietors, and was the first people's Governor of Carolina. He transmitted his spirit and his influence to a succession of eminent descendants. He claimed relationship to the Drogheda family of the same name, and probably was a native of that vicinity.

In 1746, the settlement of Kentucky was commenced under the intrepid Daniel Boone, by whose side, also, we find Irishmen. The historian of Kentucky observes, " for enterprise and daring courage none transcended Major Hugh McGrady.[†] A Harland, a MacBride, and a Chaplain, deserve also to be mentioned." The second Kentucky settlement was formed, in 1773, by James and Robert McAfee, and the third, in 1775, by Benjamin Logan, an Irish Pennsylvanian. Simon Butler, McLellan, and Hogan, all Irishmen, were also pioneers of Kentucky, and among the first to explore the country beyond the Ohio.[‡] The same hardy race of backwoodsmen also sent out the first successful pioneers of popula-

---

[*] Ramsay's South Carolina.

[†] In Ireland there was a famous family of this name, near Mayo, whose decay an Irish bard of the Jacobite era pathetically laments : —

> " 'T is my grief that Patrick Loughlin is not
>   Earl in Erris still ;
> That Brian Duff no longer rules as
>   Lord upon the Hill ;
> That *Colonel Hugh McGrady* should
>   Be lying stark and low, —
> And I sailing, sailing swiftly
>   From the County of Mayo."
>   *McCarthy's " Book of Irish Ballads.*

[‡] Marshall's Hist. of Kentucky, chap. iii. vol. i.

tion on the greater current of the Mississippi, to mark along its banks the sites of future settlements. As a specimen of what the Irish pioneer then endured, we give the following stirring episode in the early history of Kentucky : —

"Simon Kenton, alias Butler, who has been heretofore noticed, now claims further attention, as connected with the occurrences of this year. His active and enterprising spirit had induced him to join Colonel George Rogers Clark, and he was with him at the capture of Kaskaskias. After the fall of that place, Butler, with others, was sent to Kentucky with despatches. On their way they fell in with a camp of Indians with horses. They broke up the camp, took the horses, sent them back to Kaskaskias, and pursued their route by post to St. Vincennes. Entering that place by night, they traversed several streets, and departed without discovery, or alarm, after taking from the inhabitants, who were hostile, two horses for each man. When they came to White River, a raft was made on which to transport the guns and baggage, while the horses were driven in to swim across the river. On the opposite shore there lay a camp of Indians, who caught the horses as they rose the bank.

" Butler and his party, now finding themselves in the utmost danger, permitted the raft to float down the stream, and concealed themselves till night ; when they made another raft, at a different place, on which they crossed the river, returned safe to Kentucky, and delivered the letters, as they had been directed. Some of them were intended for the seat of government.

"This part of his duty being discharged, Butler made a tour to the northern part of the country, and in the same year was made prisoner by the Indians. They soon after painted him black, and informed him that at Chillicothe, where they were going, he should be burned. Nor were they willing to permit him to pass the interim without adding to his mental pains those of the body. Not more to torture him than to amuse themselves, they mounted him on an unbroke and unbridled horse ; tied his hands behind his body, and his feet under the animal; and then let him loose to run through the bushes.

"This he did, capering and prancing through the worst thickets, thereby to discharge his load, but in vain. There is no means of checking the horse, or of guarding the body, or face, or eyes, from the brush. This rends the clothes, and almost tears the flesh from the bones, — to the very great amusement of the savages, and to the equal danger of the rider's life.

"The horse at length worries himself, becomes gentle, and rejoins the cavalcade, which now approaches within a mile of Chillicothe. The Indians halt, dismount their prisoner, and prepare the stake. At this they kept him tied and standing for nearly twenty-four hours, with what sensations, can better be imagined than expressed. From the stake, however, he was not released by fire, but taken by the Indians to run the gauntlet. At this place there were assembled five or six hundred Indians, of all ages, sexes, and conditions. These were armed with switches, sticks, and every kind of hand-weapon known to savages, and formed into rows, reaching to the council-house, distant nearly one mile. Butler was now told that he was to run between those files to the drum, which was beaten at the council-house door; and that, if he could get into the council-house, he should be cleared, but that he was to expect a blow from each Indian as he passed. Next, he was placed between these ranks, and put into motion, by an order and a blow. In a little time he broke through one of the files, before he received many blows, and continued running for the council-house door, which he had nearly gained, when he was knocked down by a warrior with a club. Here he was severely beaten, and again taken into custody.

"In this distressed and miserable condition, when life had become burthensome, and death would have been relief, was he marched from town to town, often threatened to be burned at the stake, and frequently compelled to run the gauntlet.

3*

" On one of these occasions he broke the rank, determined, at the risk of his life, to make his escape ; and had actually gained a considerable advantage of his foot pursuers, when he was met by some Indians coming to town on horseback, and compelled to surrender.

" At thirteen towns he ran the gauntlet, and was certainly to have been burned at the Lower Sandusky ; but an accident suspends his progress, and seems to change his destiny.

"At the Upper Sandusky resided Simon Girty, who had just returned from an unsuccessful expedition against the frontiers of Pennsylvania, and in very bad humor. Hearing that there was a white prisoner in town, he sought him, fell upon him, threw him on the ground, and, to color his violence, accused him of stealing the Indians' horses. Butler, recognizing Girty, made himself known. They had been comrades and friends. Girty is astonished to find him in such a situation ; relents, raises him from the ground, offers him his hand, promises to save him from further injury, and to obtain his release from captivity.

" The horrors of his mind now yielded to the cheering prospects of hope and better fortune, and the little life which yet languished in his bruised and emaciated body became an object of his solicitude.

"A council was called, the case stated, and Girty's influence obtained a decree of liberation in his favor. Girty now took him to his house, bestowed on him the rites of hospitality, washed his wounds, and dressed him in a new suit of clothes.

" For five days he was at liberty, and felt himself recovering both strength and spirits. But such is the instability of a disorganized democracy, and the spirit of ferocity in uncivilized man, that the chiefs of several neighboring towns, hearing that the white prisoner was set free, now became dissatisfied, and, repairing to Sandusky, demanded another council. This was accordingly held, and the former decree in favor of Butler, notwithstanding all Girty's exertions, promptly reversed. He is once more reduced to the condition of a prisoner, and his former sentence of death renewed against him. Girty was now compelled to give him up, and he was marched away to Lower Sandusky, to be burned. At this place he met with Peter Drewyear, Indian Agent from Detroit. Drewyear, from motives of humanity, interceded with the council, and obtained permission to take Butler with him on his return home. At Detroit, he was given up to the British governor, and paroled, with orders to appear at nine o'clock, each day, when the drum beat for parade.

"This partial freedom was solaced with joy by meeting with Jesse Coffer, Nathaniel Bullock, and others, from Kentucky, who had been taken prisoners by the Indians, and found safety for their lives at a British garrison.

"In some short time, Butler and the men just named found means of escape, and, in 1779, returned to Kentucky, after a march of thirty days through the woods."*

Romance has nothing equal to this simple story. It wants nothing of the grandeur of "Mazeppa," but the Polish fore-ground, which encloses so well that kindred legend of the wilderness.

The State of Delaware, originally disputed between certain Connecticut settlers and Pennsylvania, became, shortly before the Revolution, the home of several Irish families. In the contests of the two parties of settlers, Colonel Plunkett, an Irishman, commanded what is called "the Pennyite" force, and Colonel Zebulon Butler "the Yankees." Among those who fell in this contest, special mention is made of "Thomas Neill, an Irishman of middle age, and the most learned man in the valley." He joined the Yankees because, as he said, "they were the weakest side." His captain, McKarrachan, killed in the Wyoming massacre, was also an Irishman. He emigrated from Belfast, in 1764, and was a magistrate of Westmoreland County, before the war.

* Marshall's Kentucky, vol. i.

It was a strange chance, in that memorable massacre, that the British commander was Colonel John Butler, a remote relative of the American defender, Colonel Zebulon Butler. If the Indian slaughter at that siege has aspersed with blood the name of the one, it has covered with glory that of the other.*

This family of Butler, destined to give so many distinguished names to America, originated in Kilkenny. The founder of the Pennsylvania house of that name emigrated as Agent for Indian Affairs, towards the close of the 17th century. Attracted, probably, by his example or advice, other cadets of the Ormond stock had settled in Carolina and Kentucky, from whom many generals and senators have been furnished to the Union.†

* The historian of Wyoming tells a pleasant anecdote of an Irish settler, — " an old man named Fitzgerald. The Indians and their allies placed him on a flax-brake, and told him he must renounce his rebel principles and declare for the king, or die. ' Well,' said the stout-hearted old fellow, ' I am old, and have little time to live any how, and I had rather die now a friend of my country, than live ever so long, and die a Tory.' They had magnanimity enough to let him go." — *Miner's Hist. of Wyoming*, p. 200.

† The present General William O. Butler, of Kentucky, and Pierce Butler, Senator for South Carolina, are of this family.

CHAPTER III.

In the Colony of Massachusetts Bay, prejudices against natives of Ireland existed from the beginning. At a meeting held in 1725, at Haverhill, for settling the town of Concord, it was resolved, " That no alienation of any lot should be made without the consent of the community." " The object of this regulation," says Mr. Moore, " undoubtedly was to exclude Irish settlers, against whom a strong national prejudice existed, heightened, perhaps, by zeal in differing religious opinions."* And these were not individual prejudices, for the General Court of the colony, claiming jurisdiction over the neighboring territory, resolved, in 1720 : — " Whereas, it appears that certain families recently arrived from Ireland, and others from this province, have presumed to make a settlement," &c., &c., — " that the said people be warned to move off within the space of seven months, and if they fail to do so, that they be prosecuted by the attorney general, by writs of trespass and ejectment.'" The Irish settlers would not be moved off, and it does not appear that the attorney general ever tried his writs. upon them.

In the capital of New England, (as the eastern colonies began to be called,) some Irish settlers had early homes. In 1737, forty " gentlemen of the Irish nation," residing at Boston, adopted the following programme of association : —

" Whereas, several gentlemen, merchants, and others, of the Irish nation, residing in Boston, in New England,.

* Jacob B. Moore's Sketch of Concord, N. H., Hist. Collections of N. H., p. 155.

from an affectionate and compassionate concern for their countrymen in these parts, who may be reduced by sickness, shipwreck, old age, and other infirmities and unforeseen accidents, have thought fit to form themselves into a Charitable Society, for the relief of such of their poor, indigent countrymen, without any design of not contributing towards the provision of the town poor in general, as usual."

The names of the twenty-six original members of this Society are as follows : —

" Robert Duncan, Andrew Knox, Nathaniel Walsh, Joseph St. Lawrence, Daniel McFall, William Drummond, William Freeland, Daniel Gibbs, John Noble, Adam Boyd, William Stewart, Daniel Neal, James Maynes, Samuel Moor, Phillip Mortimer, James Egart, George Glen, Peter Pelham, John Little, Archibald Thomas, Edward Alderchurch, James Clark, John Clark, Thomas Bennett, and Patrick Walker."

In 1737, William Hall was President; in 1740, Robert Achmuty ; in 1743, Neil McIntire ; in 1757, Samuel Elliot; in 1784, Moses Black ; in 1791, Thomas English ; in same year, General Simon Elliot, Jr., was elected ; in 1797, Andrew Dunlap ; and in 1810, Captain James McGee.

At the period of the foundation of the Charitable Society, the Irish in Boston were chiefly Protestants, and the 8th Article of the Constitution declared that none but Protestants were eligible to its offices or committees. The most absurd ideas of Irish inferiority prevailed. In 1752, an Irish servant was openly " sold for four years." Catholics, however, were " tolerated," and, at the period of the Revolution, there were several Catholic families in Boston, after which they rapidly increased.*

In 1636, the *Eagle Wing*, with 140 passengers, sailed

---

* The following letter from Concord, Mass., furnishes some interesting particulars about a good man, one of the first settlers of that town : —

" With some difficulty, I found the last resting-place of our countryman, HUGH CARGILL. It is from the grave I write. It is marked by a plain slab, surmounted by an urn in relievo, on which is inscribed the initials of

from Carrickfergus to found a colony on the Merrimack. This vessel having put back by stress of weather, the project was, for many years, abandoned. Towards the end of the 17th century, it was again revived, and " the Londonderry settlement" was formed in the spring of 1719. It began with but sixteen families, who gave the name of their native home to their new abode. They were all Presbyterians in religion, and of that Celtic stock, first planted in Scotland from Ireland, then re-naturalized in the parent land, previous to its deportation to the sterner, but more independent, soil of New England. Few settlements were more prosperous, or productive of great men, than this. " In process of time," says Barstow, " the descendants of the Londonderry settlers spread over Windham, Chester, Litchfield, Manchester, Bedford, Goffstown, New Boston, Antrim,

the deceased. The inscription is nearly defaced, but, after hard rubbing, I made out the following :

' Here lies interred the remains of HUGH CARGILL, late of Boston, who died in Concord, January 12, 1799, in the 60th year of his age. Mr. Cargill was born in Ballyshannon, in Ireland ; came to this country in the year 1774, destitute of the comforts of life ; but, by his industry and good economy, he acquired a good estate ; (demised ?) to his wife, Rebecca Cargill ; likewise, a large and generous donation to the town of Concord, for benevolent purposes.'

" Further down on the stone are the following lines :

' How strange, O God that reigns on high,
    That I should come so far to die !
And leave my friends where I was bred,
    To lay my bones with strangers dead !
But I have hopes, when I arise,
    To dwell with them in yonder skies.'

" I find, in the statistics of the town, the following additional facts :

' Mr. Hugh Cargill bequeathed to the town the *Stratton Farm*, so called, which was valued, in 1800, at $1300, to be improved as a poor-house ; and the same to be improved by and for the benefit of the poor, and to be under the special direction of the town of Concord for the time being, and for the purpose aforesaid, forever.

' This farm is now the pauper establishment. He also gave several other parcels of real estate, valued at $3720, the income of which is solely to be applied for the benefit of the poor.' — *Hist. of the Town of Concord.*

" It is also said he gave the ground to build the Orthodox meeting-house, but I could not find for certain if this is so.

" He was present on the memorable 19th of April, 1775, at the first battle for American liberty, and rendered good service, together with one Bullock, in saving the town records from the ravages of the brutal soldiery.

" There was another eminent Irishman, about the same time, in *Acton*. If I find anything about him, I will send it along.

" Yours, very truly,   JOHN GRAHAM."

Peterborough, and Ackworth, in New Hampshire, and
Barnet, in Vermont. They were also the first settlers of
many towns in Massachusetts, Maine, and Nova Scotia.
They are now, to the number of 20,000, scattered over
all the States of the Union."* Cherry Valley, in New
York, was also in part peopled from Londonderry.†

In the year 1723, the Irish settlement of Belfast was
established in Maine, by a few families. Among these
was a Limerick schoolmaster, named Sullivan, who, on
the outward voyage, had courted a female fellow-passen-
ger, a native of Cork, to whom he was married some time
after his arrival in America. This gentleman had two
sons, John and James, whom the father and mother lived
to see at the summit of civil and military authority. In
1775, James Sullivan founded in the same State the township called Limerick, from which city several of its first
settlers were brought over.

At Wellfleet, Cape Cod, and at Saybrook, Conn., we
find some Longford emigrants, — Higginses and Reillys.
One of the earliest settlers at Plymouth was the founder
of the Higgins family, now so numerous in New England ; and the first deed of record in Hampden County,
Mass., is an Indian transfer of land to one of the Reillys.

---

* Barstow's New Hampshire, p. 130. It may not be out of place to
append here what I have been obliged to establish in detail elsewhere, — the
inaccuracy of certain New Hampshire orators and others, in inventing a
mixed race, whom they call " Scotch-Irish." To each of them we may say,
as we have said to one of their best men : — " When you assert that the
McClellands, Campbells, McDonalds, Magills, Fergusons, McNeils, Mc-
Gregors, &c., of Ulster, Scotland, and New Hampshire, are of a race
' entirely distinct' from the O'Flings, Sullivans, and Murphys, of the
same or adjoining settlements, you are, I repeat it, in error. We are the
same people. Our original language is the same. Our fathers, speaking a
common Gaelic tongue, fought, intermarried, and prayed together. The
' Mac' is our joint inheritance, as the Norman prefix ' de,' or the Saxon
affix ' son.' Time and ignorance have obscured the early connexion of
the two nobler kingdoms ; and, I grant you, it is more flattering to New
England pride to claim kin with Bruce and Burns, whom they do know,
than with Brian and Carolan, whom they as yet know not. If, indeed, a
' Wizard of the West' should arise, like him of the North, to throw enchantment round Ireland's illustrious names, I have no doubt they also would
find many anxious to claim kindred with them."

† McKensie's Remarkable Irishmen, Part I., where one of the Cherry Valley families, named Campbell, is particularly noticed.

The name of Ireland Parish, under Mount Holyoke, still shows the place of their settlement.

Some Irish families also settled early at Palmer and Worcester, Mass. On a tombstone, in the old burial place of the latter town, are the names of John Young, a native of Derry, who died in 1730, aged 107; and David Young, a native of Donegal, who died in 1776, aged 94 years.

In 1761, 200 Irish emigrants settled in Nova Scotia. The town of Londonderry and County of Dublin were probably named by them. After the peace of 1763, a large number emigrated to the same colony, where, under the distinguished Irish Bishop, Dr. Burke, the diocese of Halifax was founded, in 1802.

One of the most interesting episodes in the early annals of our predecessors here, is the voyage of Berkely to New England, to found his long-projected college of Saint Paul's, for the civilization of the red men. George Berkely was a native of Kilkenny, born near Thomastown, in 1684. His "Theory of Vision," composed in his twentieth year, made his name familiar in Europe. After travelling through France and Italy, he was promoted to the rich deanery of Derry. In the year 1725, his mind became fully impressed with the project of founding a college for the conversion of the red race, which he broached the same year, in a pamphlet entitled "A Proposal for converting the savage Americans to Christianity, by a college to be erected in the Summer Islands, otherwise called the Isles of Bermuda." After great exertions, certain lands in the West Indies, and an instalment of £10,000, were voted to him by the English Parliament, to be paid over as soon as the project went into operation. He at once resigned his deanery, stipulating for a yearly salary of £100, and "seduced some of the hopefullest young gentlemen" of Dublin University to accept professorships in the future Saint Paul's, at £40 per year.* In January, 1729, Berkely and his

* Swift's Letter to Lord Cartaret; Swift's Works.

companions arrived at Newport, R. I., after a long and stormy voyage. Here, the inconstancy of courts pursued him. He was kept in waiting three years for the money voted him by Parliament, and finally assured by Walpole that there was no prospect of its ever being paid. In these three years he was not inactive. He had a farm of ninety acres near Newport, where " Whitehall," the house he inhabited, still stands. Tradition points out his favorite retreat for reading, among the rocks that project over the deep waters of Narraganset Bay. Here his son was born, here his " Minute Philosopher" was composed, and here, also, he wrote those grand lines, so poetical in conception, —

> " Westward the star of Empire takes its way, —
> The three first acts already past ; *
> The fourth shall close it with the closing day, —
> Earth's noblest empire is the last."

When about to return to Ireland, in 1732, he bequeathed his farm to Yale College, then in its infancy. He also presented it with " the finest collection of books that ever came at one time into America."† Thus, though his first design in favor of civilization was defeated, these private benefactions went far to supply its place ; and the historian of art in America will yet take pleasure in recording that the first organ which hymned the praise of God in New England, and the first artist that had dwelt amid its woods, were brought hither by the illustrious Bishop of Cloyne. This artist was the architect of Faneuil Hall, as first built, and the teacher of Copley, the first considerable native painter, produced in the American Colonies.‡

---

* " The three first acts," — Asia, Africa, and Europe.
† Baldwin's Annals of Yale College, p. 417.
‡ The artist's name was Smibert ; his picture of the Berkely family is in Yale College, Connecticut.

CHAPTER IV.

THE EMIGRANTS IN ARMS — ADVENTURE OF JOHN STARK — THE IRISH BRIGADE IN CANADA — INDIAN WARS — PEACE OF 1763 — DAWN OF THE REVOLUTION.

FRANCE and England had early laid claim to the same American territory. France claimed through Cartier's discovery; England through Cabot's. France possessed the Gulf of St. Lawrence, (excepting Newfoundland,) the banks of the Kennebec, the St. Lawrence, St. John, and Ottawa, Lakes Champlain and Ontario, and had its forts on the present sites of Detroit, Pittsburgh, and St. Louis. French adventurers had sketched a magnificent arch of empire on the basis of the Atlantic, which the English settlements penetrated as so many arrows, all pointed towards the west.

Each power had its "friendly Indians." The New Hampshire settlers loosed the Penacooks on the French in Maine, and they, in return, used the Aroostooks against New Hampshire. Small expeditions were continually issuing from the settlements of each race, but no considerable armament was equipped, until the expedition against Louisburg, Cape Breton, in 1744. William Vaughan, of Portsmouth, suggested this expedition; Massachusetts furnished 3000 men; New Hampshire, 500; Rhode Island, 300; New York contributed cannon, and Pennsylvania a quantity of provisions. The place attacked was the Quebec of that day, but it was forced to surrender to the gallantry and skill of the besiegers. This was in June, 1745. The military history of America dates from that remarkable event, — the Trojan war of the future republic.

An Indian frontier war continued in Vermont and New Hampshire for four years. In 1749, there was a truce, but in 1753 the barbarous strife was again renewed. In this year a striking story is told of four hunters from Londonderry, who had "wandered in quest of game" into the territory of the Canadian Aroostooks. Two of them were scalped, and two taken prisoners. They were condemned at St. Francis to run the gauntlet. "This consists in passing through two files of warriors, each of whom is privileged to give the prisoners a blow. The elder of the prisoners passed through first, and suffered little less than death. The younger and remaining one was a lad of sixteen years. When his turn came, he marched forward with a bold air, snatched a club from the nearest Indian, and attacked the warriors as he advanced on the lines, dealing the blows right and left with a merciless and almost deadly force. Nothing in the conduct of a prisoner so charms the savage mind as a haughty demeanor and contempt of death. The old men were amused and delighted; the young warriors were struck with admiration at the gallant bearing of the youthful captive. They next ordered him to hoe corn. He cut it up by the roots, declaring that such work was fit for squaws, but unworthy of warriors. From that period he became their favorite. They adopted him as a son, and gave him the title of "Young Chief." They dressed him in the highest style of Indian splendor, and decorated him with wampum and silver. It was not long after this, that Captain Stevens was despatched on an embassy to Canada to redeem the captives. The first one offered him was their favorite young chief. Captain Stevens received him at their hands with delight. But no one of the rude warriors recognized, in the young chief of their affection, the future American General, JOHN STARK.*

In 1754, Montcalm became Governor of Canada, and made active preparations for war. The Albany Conference for the union of the colonies was held, and though at that time the union miscarried, a greater harmony of

* Barstow's New Hampshire, p. 139. The original name of Stark was Star-kie, or Stark-ey, as it is spelt on the monument of the father of the General, at Stark's Mills, now Manchester, N. H.

action was established. The campaign of 1755 began with three expeditions against the French forts. In that against Crown Point, on Lake George, Captain McGinnes, of New Hampshire, " fell on the French, at the head of 200 men, and completely routed them." After turning the fortunes of the day, he fell, mortally wounded. The other two expeditions utterly failed. It was in covering the retreat of the one against Fort Du Quesne, that George Washington, then very young, first distinguished himself in arms.

The war, at this juncture, brought the " Irish Brigade " in the French armies to the Canadian frontier. They had been brought from the West Indies to the shores of the Saint Lawrence, for their country was with the lilies of France wherever they might grow. In 1756 and 7 they were at Oswego, under Montcalm, and probably participated in the capture of that fort, Fort George, and Fort William Henry.* Some of their number, leaving the service of the Bourbons, settled in the new world, and one, at least, attained to distinguished honors, in after years, under the flag of the Republic.†

In the campaigns of '58 and '59, fortune again returned to the British side. Louisburg was retaken, and Fort Du Quesne carried. Ticonderoga was at first assailed in vain, with terrible loss to the besiegers, but was taken at the second attack, as Niagara, and, finally, Quebec, were also. In 1760, English arms ended the dominion of the French, in Canada, as, twenty years later, French aid ended that of England, at Yorktown. So one nail drove out the other. The treaty of Paris, in 1763, gave America one master less ; the treaty of Paris, 1783, gave her almost complete independence.

Among the officers who commanded under Wolf at the capture of Quebec, was an Irish gentleman, Richard

---

* O'Callaghan Documentary History of New York. It is strange that Forman, in his Memoir of the Brigade, and Mathew O'Connor, in his Military Memoirs, make no mention of their having seen the American "mainland."

† General Hand. In memory of this celebrated legion, a portion of the Pennsylvania line, during the war of the Revolution, styled themselves " The Irish Brigade.'

4*

Montgomery, then in his twenty-first year. He held the
rank of colonel. John Stark, John Sullivan, and others,
served their apprenticeship in the same Canadian war.
Other days, and heavier responsibilities, were reserved
for these brave men.

Each colony had its own Indian wars, which were the
constant schools of the future soldiers of the Revolution.
The formidable Delawares and Hurons kept the settlers
of Pennsylvania and Western New York constantly on
the alert, and trained to hardy enterprise the defenders
of the new clearings.

The power of the Delawares was not thoroughly broken
till after the Revolution, during the progress of which
they were formidable auxiliaries to the Tories and British. Many terrible stories of their cruelties and punishment yet linger in the valley of the Susquehanna. The
escape of Pike, an Irish deserter from the British army,
and three others, from ten Indian sentinels, near Tioga
Point, is one of the best of these anecdotes, and might
have furnished a subject to the author of the Leather-
stocking Tales. Though less abused than Simon Butler,
Pike required equal courage and skill, to overcome his
guard, and tread back his way to Wyoming.

But it was on the southern frontier, adjoining the Spanish settlements, that Indian warfare was most formidable
and implacable. The Spanish authorities in Florida constantly urged forward the fierce Yemasses to the re-con-
quest of the Carolinas. From the commencement of the
century to the war of independence, the settlers on the
Santee and Savannah never knew repose. The names
of Governor Moore, Captains Lynch and Kearns, and of
Marion, frequently appear as defenders of the whites.
In this most trying warfare was trained that dauntless
guerilla host, afterwards famous as " Marion's Men,"
among whom the names of Colonels Horry and McDon-
ald, of Captains Conyers and McCauley, are so conspicuous.

The peace of 1763 had scarcely been promulgated,
when the question of taxing the colonies, in London, was

raised. In the British Parliament, in 1764, it was first nakedly brought forward. Previous to this, they had submitted to many arbitrary prohibitions on their woollen and iron manufactures, and their West Indian imports. In March, 1764, " the Stamp Act" was enacted at London, and Dr. Franklin wrote to Charles Thompson, one of the Irish settlers of Pennsylvania, " The sun of liberty is set; the Americans must light the lamps of industry and economy." To which Thompson replied : " Be assured we shall light torches of quite another sort." In the Virginia Assembly, Patrick Henry, a gentleman of Scottish origin, in the beginning of 1765, exclaimed, " Cæsar had his Brutus, Charles had his Cromwell, and George the Third — (being interrupted with the cry of ' Treason,' he added) — may profit by their example. If that be treason, make the most of it !"

In the preliminary moral contest, which arose universally, the Irish settlers were not unrepresented. John Rutledge, in South Carolina, was the first man whose eloquence roused that state to the lever of resistance. In the east, Langdon and Sullivan seized the guns at Newcastle, which thundered at Bunker Hill. Washington, at Valley Forge, is reported to have said, " Place me in Rockbridge county, and I 'll get men enough to save the Revolution." In Maryland, Charles Carrol of Carrolton, over the signature of " First Citizen," maintained the rights of the people, in a long and spirited controversy with Daniel Dulany, the royalist champion, "who had long stood the leading mind of Maryland." His services were well appreciated, and public meetings at Baltimore, Frederick, and Annapolis, confirmed the title he had assumed, and Maryland proudly owned Charles Carrol for her " First Citizen." Charles Thompson, of Pennsylvania, afterwards Secretary to Congress, was also one of the earliest and most fearless advocates of the principles on which the Revolution proceeded, that the country could reckon ; and, happily, there was no scarcity of such men, of any European race.

* See Appendix No. II.

CHAPTER V.

OPENING OF THE REVOLUTIONARY ERA — IRISH AT BUNKER'S HILL — DEATH OF MA
JOR M'CLARY — GENERAL KNOX — THE CLINTONS — THE PENNSYLVANIA LINE —
MOYLAN'S DRAGOONS.

THE period of that eventful Revolution, in which the
emigrants, who had chastised the savages and expelled
the French, were to turn the firelocks and cannon of
England against herself, now opens before us. From the
period of the Albany Conference, of 1754, the idea of
confederation had filled the minds of the thoughtful, and
from the capture of Louisburgh, the sense of self-protec-
tion animated the bold. It needed only in England a
meddling minister and a perverse prince, to bring forth
the great resistant qualities of the colonies, and these
appeared in perfection in Lord North and George the
Third.

It is not our place to enter into the preliminaries of
this glorious contest, further than to say that the whole
Irish race threw their weight into the colonial scale. The
Irish Commons refused to vote 45,000 for the war. The
Irish in England, headed by Burke, Barre, and Sheridan,
spoke and wrote openly in defence of America; and the
Irish in France, where several of them then held considerable employments, were equally zealous. Counts MacMa-
hon, Dillon, and Roche Fermoy, General Conway, and
other experienced officers, held themselves ready to volunteer into the American service; and afterwards, at the
desire of the American agents in Paris, did so.

The Stamp Act was repealed in 1766, but the Tea
Tax was enacted in 1767. This measure led to the general combination, which had its corresponding committee
in every town and village, and which finally ripened into
the Continental Army and the Continental Congress.

The first overt act was the massacre of some citizens of Boston, in State street, by a party of riotous red-coats. One of these earliest victims was a native of Ireland. The next aggression was on the other side, and of far greater significance. News having reached Portsmouth, N. H., that the export of gunpowder into America was " proclaimed," Major John Sullivan and John Langdon, with a company of the townsmen, surprised the fort at Newcastle, took the captain and five men, carried off one hundred barrels of gunpowder, fifteen light cannon, and the entire of the small arms, all of which afterwards did effectual service at Bunker Hill. For this act, Sullivan and Langdon were elected to the Continental Congress, which met in May, 1775, and the former was, the same year, appointed by that body one of the eight brigadiers general of the first American army.

In April, 1775, open war began at Lexington. When the British forces were beaten back into Boston, Thomas Cargill, of Ballyshannon, settled at Concord, saved the town records from their ravages, and entered heartily in the war. The American companies formed at Cambridge, their chief outwork being on Bunker Hill, behind Charlestown, divided by the Charles River from Boston. They were commanded by General Artemas Ward, who stationed behind the breastwork, on the left of the main body, 800 New Hampshire militia, under Stark and Reid, both of Londonderry.* Here the first

* The contribution of the Irish settlement in New Hampshire, to the revolutionary forces, may be judged from the share of the small town of Bedford : Col. Daniel Moor, Major John Goffe, Capt. Thomas M'Laughlin, Lt. Joh. Patten, Joh. Patten, Jr., Sam. Patten, Jas. Patten, Robert Patten, John Gault, Isaac Riddle, John Riddle, Amos Martin, Jas. Martin, Stephen Goffe, (lost at sea,) Hugh Horton, (died in service,) Burns Chandler, (taken at the Cedars and never after heard of,) Samuel Moor, Samuel Barr, John Collahan, (killed,) James Moor, Robert Cornell, Ira Greer, Jones Cutting, Wm. Parker, John Hiller, John McAllister, Barnet McClair, John Griffer, Luke Gardiner, Robert Victorey, Robert Dalrymple, (killed,) Danl. Larkin, Samuel Patterson, James Patterson, Solomon Hemp, (killed,) John O'Niel, John Dorr, (killed,) George Hogg, Wm. Houston, Whitefield Gilmore, Zachariah Chandler, James Houston, Valentine Sullivan, (taken prisoner in the retreat from Canada, and died,) John Ross, John Steel, Stephen March, Robert Morril, John Tyrril, Patrick O'Murphy, Patrick O'Fling, Calvin Johnson, (died in service,) David Riddle, John Gardiner, and eighteen others, of whom three died in service. —*Hist. Coll. of N. H.*, vol. i., p. 291

act of hostilities befell, and nobly did the conscripts of the colonies hold their own. After a great destruction of the enemy, they slowly retired to an adjacent hill, where they were re-formed, and placed under the command of Brigadier General Sullivan. Major Andrew McClary, whose great size and desperate valor made him peculiarly conspicuous, fell while crossing " the Neck." Eighteen others of Stark and Reid's command were killed, and eighty-nine were wounded in the same eventful field.

The army awaited at Cambridge the arrival of General Washington, appointed commander-in-chief by the Continental Congress, in session at Philadelphia, on the same week the battle of Bunker Hill was fought. It is necessary to inquire what forces the new commander-in-chief had at his disposal, and, for our purpose, what part of those forces were derived from the Irish settlements.

At the first Council of War, held at Cambridge, [July 9th, 1775,] it was found that " the Continental Army," then investing Boston, was nominally 17,000 strong, but actually but 14,000. It was resolved to prosecute the siege, but that 22,000 were necessary. Of the four majors general, [Ward, Lee, Schuyler, and Putnam,] none were Irish ; of the eight brigadiers general, two, Richard Montgomery, of New York, and John Sullivan, of New Hampshire, were Irish. Of the other officers we cannot now say what precise proportion our nation contributed ; but we will find, in the course of the war, that a full third of the active chiefs of the army were of Irish birth or descent. Of the rank and file, New Hampshire's contingent were in great part of Irish origin ; and in other colonies, recruiting prospered most in the Irish townships.

The command of the ordnance department was a post of the greatest importance, and the selection made by Washington, in this case, was most fortunate. Henry Knox, born in Boston, in 1750, was the son of Irish parents. Though early left an orphan, with a widowed mother to support, he had risen against circumstances, from a book-binder's apprentice to be a prosperous publisher, and a persevering student of tactics. He had early joined a local Grenadier Company, and learned with them the manual exercise. Married into the family of a British official, he never swerved from the cause of his country. He succeeded in inspiring his wife with his own patriotism, and in June both escaped from the city, she concealing on her person the sword with which her husband fought at Bunker Hill. Knox now undertook to bring to Cambridge the cannon taken on Lake Champlain by Ethan Allen; and, after incredible exertions against the difficulties of transit in those days, succeeded. These and Sullivan's guns formed the first artillery of the United States army, and Knox became its first master of ordnance.

The Irish in New York early enlisted in the cause of the Revolution, and James Clinton, in 1775, was elected colonel of the third regiment raised in that colony. His brother-in-law, Colonel James McClearey, commanded in the same militia, and is called "one of the bravest officers America can boast."* The elder brother, George Clinton, after the death of Montgomery, was appointed brigadier general for New York; and in 1776, with his two kinsmen, gallantly defended the unfinished forts on the Hudson, and held the Highlands against the repeated assaults of Sir H. Clinton.† By this check, he prevented the junction of that commander with General Burgoyne, which, with General Stark's victory at Bennington, cut

---

* Quoted in Hoosick's Life of De Witt Clinton.

† On one occasion the brothers narrowly escaped capture. The anecdote is related by Dr. Joseph Young, a contemporary, who says, at the taking of the forts, " they both remained until it grew dark, and got mixed up with the enemy. The governor escaped in a boat to the east side of the river, and James slid down the very steep bank of a creek, which ran near the redoubt, and fell into the top of a hemlock tree, and made his escape by going up the bed of the brook, in which there was but little water at the time. When the enemy rushed into the redoubt, Colonel McClearey and a Mr. Humphrey, the cock of whose musket had been shot off, turned back to back, and defended themselves desperately. They were assailed on all sides, and would undoubtedly have been killed; but a British senator, who witnessed their spirit and bravery, cried out that it would be a pity to kill such brave men. They then rushed on and seized them; and when the colonel was brought to the British General Clinton, he asked where his friend George was? The colonel replied, " Thank God, he is safe beyond the reach of your friendship! " — *Washington and his Generals*, vol. ii., p. 206.

him off from either base, and compelled his surrender at
Saratoga, — a victory which completed the French alliance, and saved the revolutionary cause.

In Pennsylvania, where the Irish were more densely
settled, their martial ardor was equally conspicuous.
They inhabited chiefly in Ulster and Chester counties,
and in Philadelphia. In the summer of 1775, Congress
ordered the raising of several regiments in Pennsylvania,
and, among the rest, gave commissions as colonel to Anthony Wayne, William Irving, William Thompson, Walter
Stewart, Stephen Moylan, and Richard Butler, all Irishmen
The regiments of Wayne, Irving, Butler, and Stewart,
formed part of the famous " Pennsylvania Line." Thomp
son's was a rifle regiment. Moylan, a native of Cork, after
being aide-de-camp to Washington and commissary gen
eral, was finally transferred to the command of the Dra
goons ; and in almost every severe action of the war
where cavalry could operate, we meet with the fearless
" Moylan's Dragoons." Dr. Edmund Hand, who came
to Canada with the Irish Brigade, as surgeon, was appointed lieutenant colonel in Thompson's regiment, and
on the first of March, 1776, raised to the full rank of
colonel, from which, on the first of April, 1777, he was
promoted to be " brigadier general." Colonel Butler,
a sound shoot of the Ormond tree, and his five sons, displayed equal zeal, and merited from Lafayette the compliment, that whenever he " wanted anything well done,
he got a Butler to do it." So actively did these gentlemen exert themselves, that, on the 14th of August, 1776,
a great part of the Pennsylvania Line arrived in the
camp at Cambridge, which enabled Washington, by the
beginning of September, to put his plans for the siege of
Boston into execution.

While in camp at Cambridge, the commander-in-chief
planned the expedition against Canada. This was to be
undertaken in two divisions ; that of Arnold to penetrate
by the Kennebec and the forests of Maine ; that of
Montgomery to advance by the Sorel and St. Lawrence.
Both were to unite at Quebec.

CHAPTER VI.

THE CANADIAN EXPEDITION — DEATH OF MONTGOMERY — BURIAL REFUSED TO HIS REMAINS BY THE BRITISH — RETREAT OF THE INVADING CORPS — THOMPSON, SULLIVAN AND GATES IN COMMAND — ADVANCE OF BURGOYNE — STARK'S VICTORY AT BENNINGTON — SURRENDER OF BURGOYNE.

IT was not without deep reflection, that General Washington, at Cambridge, ordered the advance of two invading divisions into Canada. The one was placed under Arnold, a brave soldier assuredly, but one who cast away the jewel of fidelity, and left a figure in the annals of that glorious war, over which his country would long since have drawn a veil, were it not useful to perpetuate the infamy of treason, for the terror of the venal, and the warning of the weak.

The head of the other corps was not a braver, but a much better, man — a soldier without reproach, as well as without fear. Richard Montgomery was then in his 39th year, having been born in Ireland in 1736. He had distinguished himself, at the age of twenty-three, in the second siege of Louisburg, and served as colonel under Wolfe at the capture of Quebec. After spending nine years in Europe, he emigrated to New York, and made his home at Rhinebeck, Duchess county. He had married a lady every way worthy of him, the daughter of Chancellor Livingston, and looked forward to a life of peace spent in the pursuits of agriculture. . In accepting the appointment in June, 1775, he wrote, "The Congress having done me the honor of electing me brigadier general in their service, is an event which must put an end for a while, perhaps forever, to the quiet scheme of life I had prescribed for myself; for though entirely unexpected and undesired by me, the will of an oppressed people, compelled to choose between liberty and slavery,

5

must be obeyed." Major General Schuyler, having fallen
ill at Ticonderoga, the sole command devolved on Montgomery, who certainly conducted it with rare judgment.
Fort Chambly and St. John were successively taken.
Montreal was captured, and, in the midst of a Canadian
winter, he pressed on his men towards Quebec, where
Arnold's party were already arrived. On the 1st of
December, Montgomery took the chief command. An
eye-witness has graphically sketched his first review of
his troops. "It was lowering and cold, but the appearance of the general here gave us warmth and animation.
He was well-limbed, tall, and handsome, though his face
was much pock-marked. His air and manner designated
the real soldier. He made us a short, but energetic and
elegant speech, the burden of which was in applause of
our spirit in crossing the wilderness; a hope our perseverance in that spirit would continue ; and a promise of
warm clothing; the latter was a most comfortable assurance. A few huzzas from our freezing bodies were returned to this address of the gallant hero. New life was
infused into the whole corps."* It was the last day of
that memorable year 1775, before the arrangements for
assaulting Quebec were complete. In two bodies, Arnold's towards the suburb of St. Roque, and Montgomery's
by the river bank, they advanced to the attack. It was
the night of the 31st of December. The Saint Lawrence
was floored with ice; the shore, the pine woods, the
distant fortress, all wore the white livery of winter in the
north. The divisions were to communicate by rockets,
and Arnold was already at the Palace Gate, when a
severe wound obliged him to yield his command to Morgan. Montgomery had reached Point Diamond, by a
road guarded by an outwork of two guns. At daybreak,
perceiving the Americans so near, the Canadian militia,
in whose charge the work was, deserted their post, but a
New England sea-captain, who had slept in the work,
before leaving, applied a match to one of the loaded guns,

* Mass. Hist. Coll. vol. i.

and by this chance shot Montgomery was killed.* The artillery from the main fortress now played in the same direction, and when the winter's day had fairly come, a party of British soldiers, found, lying dead on the frozen ground, with three wounds in his breast, and his sword arm stretched towards Quebec, the remains of the gallant general, surrounded by several of his staff, all lifeless.

Both corps, deprived of their chief officers, fell back from the fatal walls, and retreated along the bank of the river. As to the dead, Sir Guy Carleton at first refused the chief the poor courtesy of a coffin,† and the prayer of a woman at length obtained Christian burial for the remains of those brave gentlemen, who left their homes and friends, and wives, to perish in that pitiless climate, for the cause of their unstipendiary devotion. As yet America had no flag, no Declaration of Independence, and no Articles of Confederation. Montgomery knew that he risked the fate of a rebel; but even that could not deter him from his duty.

Three generals have fallen at Quebec under three different flags. All were brave, all merciful, all young. Montcalm, with blood ardent as the wine of his own France; Wolfe, with a courage as indomitable as the enterprise of his island, which can wring a prize from every rock; Montgomery, the last and best of all, with soul as noble as his cause, and honor bright as his own sword. Three deaths, Quebec, do consecrate thy rock; three glories crown it, like a tiara! Of the three, his death was the saddest, and even so has his glory become brightest of them all.

Tributes of respectful condolence poured in from all distinguished Americans to Montgomery's widow; the nation mourned him as its eldest child, its proto-martyr; and, forty years after his fall, New York gathered together his ashes, and entombed them in the most conspicuous church of its great city. The widow of the hero, deso-

* Hawkins' Hist. of Quebec.
† Mass. Hist. Collection, vol. i., p. 3 — year 1792.

late to death, assisted at these last sad honors to the
memory of "her soldier," for whom she still retained all
the affection of her girlhood.

The retreat from Quebec was at first committed to
Generals Wooster and Arnold, and afterwards to Brigadier General William Thompson. Under the latter, the
remnant of the American army fought, in the spring of
1776, the unsuccessful battle of Three Rivers. General
Sullivan was then despatched to take the command, and
hoped to regain much of what had been lost, when the
forces were placed under General Gates, who slowly
retreated before Burgoyne, into New York.

Burgoyne advanced steadily towards the Hudson,
sending out a large party, under Colonel Baum, to for-
age in Vermont, or, as it was then called, "the New
Hampshire Grants." John Stark was, at the time, in
New Hampshire, having retired from the service, in
consequence of the injustice done him by Congress in
raising junior officers over him. But his native state
now called him to lead a new militia of its own, irre-
spective of the continental army, and with these he fell
on Baum, at Bennington, on the 14th of August, cut up
his division, captured his guns, stores and colors. The
Clintons, somewhat earlier in the month, had prevented
relief reaching Burgoyne through the valley of the Hudson;
and so, in September, that clever play-wright, but ill-
starred soldier, was compelled to lay down his arms, and
surrender to the Americans under General Gates. Thus,
the remnant of the Canadian army, reinforced and rested,
became in turn the conquerors; and John Stark, recently
censured for insubordination, was forthwith raised to the
rank of major general.* Among the American loss at
Bennington was Captain McClary, whose relative fell at
Bunker's Hill.

* The British guns taken by Stark were captured with Hull at Detroit, in
the war of 1812. The old hero was dreadfully annoyed at the intelligence.
"My guns! my guns!" he would exclaim, and even thought of returning to
active service, in order to wipe out that disgraceful event.

CHAPTER VII.

IRISHMEN IN THE UNITED STATES NAVY — COMMODORE BARRY — CAPTAIN MACGEE — CAPTAIN O'BRIEN — MIDSHIPMAN MACDONOUGH — PURSER MEASE — BARRY'S LIEU-TENANTS, MURRAY, DALE, DECATUR, AND STEWART.

THE organization of the infant Navy of the United States was one of the heaviest anxieties of the first Congress. Among a people bred to the use of arms, and annually involved in Indian warfare, it was a much easier matter to raise an army, than, out of the limited shipping of the young seaports, to find vessels and officers to whom the national flag could be intrusted on the other element.

Fortune had thrown in the way of Washington, a man most useful for this department of the public service. This was John Barry, a native of the parish of Tacumshane, Wexford county, Ireland. Barry was born in the year 1745, the son of "a snug farmer," and had but to step out of his own door, to stand beside the sea. He conceived so strong a love for a sailor's life, that, at fourteen or fifteen years of age, he crossed the Atlantic, and began to sail to and from Philadelphia. He rose from one trust to another, teaching himself as he rose, till, at twenty-five years of age, he was captain of "the Black Prince," one of the finest London and Philadelphia packets, afterwards a vessel of war. Mr. Rese Meredith was the owner of this ship, and Washington's host when in Philadelphia. It was in his house the illustrious Virginian met, and marked, the future commodore.

In the latter part of 1775, Congress had purchased a few merchant ships, and hastily fitted them up as vessels of war. Captain Barry was given the command of the principal, the Lexington; and in another, "the Alfred," Paul Jones entered as first lieutenant. These

5*

vessels both lay in the Delaware, and, when the flag of
the Union was agreed on, they were the first to hoist it,
afloat.

From the Lexington, in 1776, Barry was transferred
to the frigate Effingham, and while the Delaware was
frozen that winter, served on land, acting as aide-de-camp
to General Cadwallader, at the battle of Trenton. In
1777, the British fleet destroyed the two or three ships
of Congress, in the Delaware, but Barry conceived and
executed many most successful manœuvres, such as capturing store-ships, and intercepting supplies, in the small
craft and in armed boats. Washington publicly thanked
him and his men for these effective services. In 1778
and 9, he commanded the " Relief," and received the
rank of Commodore, being the first on whom it was conferred. In 1781, he brought the American Agent to
France, in his new ship, " The Alliance," and on his
way home captured the British ship " Atalanta," and
British brig " Trespasa," both in the same battle. Captain Barry was badly wounded in the action, but continued to give orders till the enemy struck. In 1781, he
brought Lafayette and Count Noailles to France ; and in
1782, engaged three British frigates in the West Indian
waters, who retired badly damaged. This was the last
year of the war.

From 1783 till his death, Barry was constantly engaged in superintending the progress of the navy. He
induced the government to adopt the model for ships of
war, which has been found so well suited to its uses.
He was particularly fond of aiding the younger officers
in the service, and we shall see what his " boys " came
to be. He was an exceedingly affable and hospitable
man, and, what is unfortunately not usual in his profession, practically religious. He died in September, 1803,
and his chief legacy was to the Catholic Orphan Asylum.
He has been called, by naval writers, " The Father of the
American Navy." He is buried in St. Philadelphia.

The personal character of Commodore Barry was made

of noble stuff. When Lord Howe tempted him with a vast bribe, and the offer of a British ship of the line, he replied, "he had devoted himself to the cause of his country, and not the value or command of the whole British fleet could seduce him from it." He never was ashamed of his native land, and, after the peace of Paris, paid a visit to the place of his birth, which fact is still remembered with gratitude in his native parish. When hailed by the British frigates, in the West Indies, and asked the usual questions as to the ship and captain, he answered, "The United States ship Alliance, saucy Jack Barry, half Irishman, half Yankee, — who are you?"

In 1778, Captain James McGee, while commanding "in the service of the Commonwealth," was shipwrecked in Massachusetts Bay, and seventy-two of his men lost. The survivors were very kindly treated by the inhabitants of Plymouth, who, also, "decently buried such bodies as were recovered."[*] In 1791, Captain James McGee was admitted a member of the Irish Charitable Society of Boston, and in 1810, was its president. Captain Bernard McGee was admitted the same time. I regret that I have been able to find no further data about either of these officers.

Two of the earliest prizes carried into the United States were captured by five brothers, of Machias, named O'Brien, natives of Cork, two of whom, Jeremiah and John, afterwards held naval commissions.

On board the other ships of the new navy there were several Irish officers, of minor grades, some of whom afterwards rose to independent commands.

In the quarrel between America and France, or rather, the Directory, one of the severest actions fought was that of The Constellation, commanded by Commodore Truxton, with the French frigate L'Insurgente. In this action, Midshipmen Porter and James McDonough distinguished themselves. The former was of Irish descent, the latter of Irish birth. Mr. McDonough had his foot shot off,

---

[*] Holmes' American Annals, vol. ii., p. 293.

and was obliged to retire from the navy, but his younger brother, Thomas, who entered the same year, more than justified the expectations of the friends of that family. Their father, Major McDonough, had settled at Newcastle, Delaware, shortly before the birth of Thomas, who used to say of himself, that " his keel was laid in Ireland, but he was launched in America." Major McDonough died in 1796.

Mr. Mathew Mease, Purser in the *Bon Homme Richard*, with Paul Jones, was a very brave man. In the conflict with the Serapis frigate, he begged to be allowed to direct the quarter deck guns, which he did, very gallantly, till, says Paul Jones, "being dangerously wounded in the head, I was obliged to fill his place." He was most respectably connected in Philadelphia, where he died, in 1787.

Under Commodore Barry some of the most brilliant ornaments of the American Navy were trained, such as Murray, Dale, Decatur, and Stewart, all of whom became conquerors and commodores. Dale, especially, was a favorite of " the Father of the Navy," and his noble conduct through life fully justified the confidence placed in his character, by Barry, from the first day of his entering under his charge.

In the war of 1812, Barry's pupils all rose to eminent distinction, as we shall find when we arrive at that period.

* See Appenix No. III.

CHAPTER VIII.

THE dissatisfactions which invariably arise, when military promotions are arbitrarily made by the civil power, we have seen driving the gallant Stark from the service of the Revolution. He was not the only officer so dis satisfied by the congressional mode of promotion. Schuyler, Sullivan, and others, were several times on the eve of resignation, from being inconsiderately treated. Brig adier Roche Fermoy and Brigadier Armstrong had actually retired for similar reasons. Roche Fermoy was originally an Irish officer in the service of Piedmont. In the New Jersey campaign of 1778, he was at the head of the Corps of Observation, "appointed to receive and communicate" reports of the enemy's movements, to Washington. After resigning his commission to Congress, he returned to France, where an essay on "the Military Resources of Ireland" was published in his name. It is a pamphlet of extraordinary merit, both for style and science. The retirement that Washington most regretted was that of General Andrew Lewis, the son of Irish parents, born in Augusta County, Virginia. They had served together in the Indian wars and at Fort Necessity, and the commander-in-chief was strongly prepossessed in his favor. Poor Lewis died in 1778, on his return from the Ohio, where he had reduced the Indian tribes to submission, for the time being, at least.

After Lafayette, the most constant and conspicuous figure in the campaigns of 1777 and 1778 (chiefly fought upon the Delaware) was Anthony Wayne. In Febru-

ary, 1777, he had been promoted to a brigade, and at the
Brandywine, in September, and on the Schuylkill, in
October, he was the most conspicuous chief. At "the
drawn battle" of Germantown he held the first place,
and during the dismal winter in Valley Forge he kept
the field, foraging right and left. In the battle of Mon-
mouth (June, 1778) he turned the fortune of the day, and
won the special thanks of Washington and Congress.
But his two most brilliant actions followed, — the capture
of Stony Point, and the battle of Bergen Neck.

Stony Point, on the Hudson, commanded the King's
Ferry, the usual route from the eastern to the midland
states. It also formed the key of the Highlands. On
two sides it was washed by the river, on the third
guarded by a deep and wide morass. Art had fortified
what nature had made strong, and six hundred infantry
garrisoned the formidable fortress. Major Stewart, his
countryman and brother-in-law, with Colonels Fleury,
Febiger, and Meigs, commanded under the general.
The force arrived before the fort at eight o'clock of a
July night, and carried it by one of the most dashing
assaults in military history. Universal applause hailed
this brilliant exploit. The action of Bergen Neck was
fought the week following. General Irvine was with
Wayne, and Moylan's dragoons acted a conspicuous part.
The enemy were compelled to cross the Hudson, and seek
for safety under the walls of New York. For his daring
valor in this expedition, Wayne obtained, in the army,
the soubriquet of "Mad Anthony."

Another Pennsylvania Irishman figured in these same
campaigns almost as conspicuously as Wayne. General
Hand's corps, "up to the battle of Trenton," "was distinguished in every action of the war." In October,
1778, he succeeded General Stark in the command at
Albany, and conducted a successful expedition against
the Five Indian Nations, whose conquest was completed
by Sullivan the following year. In 1780, on the formation of the Light Infantry corps, he and General Poor
were appointed to the two brigades. In this campaign,

after chastising the perfidious Delawares, Sullivan and his officers were entertained at a banquet by the citizens of Wyoming. Colonel Butler presided, and one of the regular toasts was, "May the kingdom of Ireland merit a stripe in the American standard." In 1781, General Hand was appointed adjutant general, an office he continued to hold till the army was disbanded. In 1798, when Washington consented to act again as commander-in-chief, he recommended General Hand's re-appointment as adjutant general. He was frequently honored with civil appointments, and, in 1790, was one of the authors of the constitution of Pennsylvania. In the army, he was remarkable for his "noble horsemanship," and his favorite horses have been often mentioned by his comrades as "an active grey," and "a sorrel roan remarkable for lofty action." General Hand died at Lancaster, Pa., in 1803. His life ought to be written in detail.

We have here to record a less grateful fact, connected with a distinguished Irish officer.

It was during the New Jersey campaigns that "the Conway Cabal," as it is called, exploded. This was an attempt, on the part of several officers, traceable mainly to the ambition of General Gates, to deprive Washington of the command-in-chief, and to substitute that general in his stead. Gates, Schuyler, Lee, and others were parties to this movement, which was finally revealed by Lafayette, and broken up. General Conway, who had come from France at the first outbreak, and ranked as brigadier general, after a quarrel and duel with General Cadwallader, returned home, first writing Washington a manly and regretful letter. The cabal has been called by his name, mainly, we believe, for the sake of the alliteration.*

In North Carolina there had been constant operations throughout the war, and the cause of the Revolution had sustained a severe loss at the outset by the death of Brigadier General Moore, (grandson of Governor Moore,)

* General Sullivan, in his letter to Washington, says Conway was "imprudently led into the cabal."

in 1775.   His most active successor in the state seems to
have been James Hogan, also of Irish origin, who entered
the service, as paymaster of the third regiment, in 1776,
and the same month was made major of the Edenton and
Halifax regiment.   Hogan's services were more onerous
than brilliant; in 1799, he was appointed brigadier general in the line, with a view to the required operations
in his neighborhood.

It would be impossible, did we descend from the officers of the first rank, to record all the heroic actions performed by those of lower standing through these two
critical campaigns.   The name of Colonel Fitzgerald,
Washington's favorite aide-de-camp, deserves special
mention.   The most striking event, in his long and honorable career, befell him at Princeton.   We shall let the
heir of his general record it, as he had it from the lips
of the actors themselves.

"Col. Fitzgerald," says Mr. G. Washington Custis,
"was an Irish officer in the old Blue and Bluffs, the first
volunteer company raised in the South, in the dawn of the
Revolution, and commanded by Washington.   In the campaign of 1778, and retreat through the Jerseys, Fitzge-
ald was appointed aide-de-camp to Washington.   At the
battle of Princeton occurred that touching scene, consecrated by history to everlasting remembrance.   The
American troops, worn down by hardships, exhausting
marches, and want of food, on the fall of their leader,
that brave old Scotchman, General Mercer, recoiled before the bayonets of the veteran foe.   Washington
spurred his horse into the interval between the hostile
lines, reining up with the charger's head to the foe, and
calling to his soldiers, ' Will you give up your general to
the enemy?'   The appeal was not made in vain.   The
Americans faced about, and the arms were levelled on
both sides, — Washington between them, — even as
though he had been placed there as a target for both.
It was at this moment that Fitzgerald returned from carrying an order to the rear ; and here let us use the gallant veteran's own words.   He said : ' On my return, I

perceived the general immediately between our line and that of the enemy, both lines levelling for the decisive fire that was to decide the fortune of the day. Instantly there was a roar of musketry, followed by a shout. It was the shout of victory. On raising my eyes, I discovered the enemy broken and flying, while, dimly, amid the glimpses of the smoke, was seen Washington alive and unharmed, waving his hat, and cheering his comrades to the pursuit. I dashed my rowels into my charger's flanks, and flew to his side, exclaiming, "Thank God! your excellency is safe." I wept like a child, for joy.'"

In the eulogy which he bestowed on Fitzgerald, Mr. Custis has not forgotten Moylan, Stewart, Proctor, and other Pennsylvania Irishmen. Of them, we may repeat what Teeling says so well in his Narrative of 1798: — "They may sleep in the silent tomb, but the remembrance of their virtues will be cherished while liberty is dear to the American heart."

We have to leave, for a time, the officers of the army, to look after the condition of its commissariat. In 1777, dreadful distress was suffered at Valley Forge, and the following year did not alleviate the condition of the army. In 1779, the Connecticut militia mutinied, and were only quelled by calling out " the Pennsylvania Line," and arraying it against them. In 1780, even these latter began to murmur, half fed, unpaid, and ill-clothed, that they were. Wayne himself, their idol when in action, was unable to control them ; and, had it not been for an extraordinary effort of patriotism on the part of the merchants of Philadelphia, the army would have utterly fallen to pieces. On the 17th June, 1780, ninety-three Philadelphia merchants signed the following paper : —

" Whereas, in the present situation of public affairs in the United States, the greatest and most vigorous exertions are required for the successful management of the just and necessary war in which they are engaged with Great Britain : We, the subscribers, deeply impressed with the sentiments that on such an occasion should gov-

ern us in the prosecution of a war, on the event of which
our own freedom, and that of our posterity, and the freedom and independence of the United States, are all
involved, hereby severally pledge our property and credit
for the several sums specified and mentioned after our
names, in order to support the credit of a bank to be
established for furnishing a supply of provisions for the
armies of the United States : And do hereby severally
promise and engage to execute to the directors of the
said bank, bonds of the form hereunto annexed.

" Witness our hands this 17th day of June, in the
year of our Lord 1780."*

Twenty of these, of Irish origin, subscribed nearly
half a million of dollars, in the following proportion : —

Blair M'Clenachan,	£10,000	John Patton,	2,000
J. M. Nesbitt & Co.,	5,000	Benjamin Fuller,	2,000
Richard Peters,	5,000	George Meade & Co.,	2,000
Samuel Meredith,	5,000	John Donaldson,	2,000
James Mease,	5,000	Henry Hill,	5,000
Thomas Barclay,	5,000	Kean & Nichols,	4,000
Hugh Shiell,	5,000	James Caldwell,	2,000
John Dunlap,	4,000	Samuel Caldwell,	1,000
John Nixon,	5,000	John Shee,	1,000
George Campbell,	2,000	Sharp Delany,	1,000
John Mease,	4,000	Tench Francis,	5,500
Bunner, Murray & Co.,	6,000		
		Being	$442,500

This bank continued to exist during the war, and then
gave way to the Bank of North America. By this
timely expedient the war was enabled to go forward,
and Washington found himself free to execute his final
plans.

The theatre of the war was now transferred to Virginia, the Carolinas, and Georgia. Beaten at all points in
the North, the British attempted the South, under Cornwallis. Gates, the victor at Saratoga, was defeated, in
turn, at Camden, and superseded by Greene. Wayne,
despatched to the same scene of operations, captured
Yorktown, and shut up the British in Savannah. In

* American Remembrancer, vol. x., p. 229 ; 6 Haz. Reg. of Pennsylvania, p. 28, — 2 do. 259, 261; Hood's Sketch of " The Friendly Sons of St.
Patrick," p. 43.

July, he had the pleasure to beat them out, and, in December following, he took possession of Charleston as they gave it up. Throughout his southern campaign, (the last of the war,) he was accompanied by "the remnant of Moylan's Dragoons." Before the evacuation of Savannah, Cornwallis had got cooped up in Yorktown, cut off by Washington on the land side, and the French fleet by sea. On the 19th of October, 1781, he surrendered himself and 7000 men as prisoners of war ; and the following spring proposals were made for peace by Great Britain, which agreed to acknowledge the independence of "the United States of North America."

The surrender of Cornwallis was the signal for peace. England, baffled by the heroism and perseverance of America, relinquished all her claims to sovereignty over the revolted colonies, and prepared to sign her abdication with the best grace she could assume. In 1782, the Peace of Paris was completed, and at the opening of the next year it was proclaimed. Thus, after a war of seven years, the liberties of America were won, and the field prepared for the plantation of those democratic institutions whose influence already penetrates the world. The soldiers returned to their homes, and the labors of the statesmen commenced where those of the army ended.

* See Appendix No. IV.

CHAPTER IX.

THE important civil services rendered to the American people abroad, by Edmund Burke, Colonel Barre, Richard Brinsley Sheridan, and the then young Henry Grattan, in demonstrating the justice of the colonial cause, and vindicating the character of the early Congress, are but a portion of the part borne by the Irish race in the politics of the Revolution.

So well aware was the first Congress of the importance of separating the sympathies of our nation from George the Third, that one of the first acts of the Congress of 1775 was the adoption of an address to the Irish people, in which they drew a marked distinction between the Irish and English Parliaments. "*Your* Parliament has done us no wrong," said they. "In defence of our persons and properties, under actual invasion, we have taken up arms. When that violence shall be removed, and hostilities cease on the part of the aggressors, they shall cease on our part also." They conclude by hoping that the extremes to which the colonies have been driven may have the effect of deterring the king's ministers from a continuance of a similar policy in Ireland.

This wise distinction between England and Ireland was first made by Franklin, who, in 1771, made a tour of Ireland, and was the guest of Dr. Lucas, at Dublin. In a letter to Thomas Cushing, of Boston, dated London, January, 1772, he gives the following key to his diplomacy in Dublin : —

"Before leaving Ireland, I must mention that, being desirous of seeing the principal patriots there, I stayed till the opening of their Parliament. I found them disposed to be friends of America, in which I endeavored to confirm them, with the expectation that our growing weight might in time be thrown into their scale, and, by joining our interest with theirs, a more equitable treatment from this nation might be obtained for them as well as for us. There are many brave spirits among them. The gentry are a very sensible, polite, and friendly people. Their Parliament makes a most respectable figure, with a number of very good speakers in both parties, and able men of business. And I must not omit acquainting you that, it being a standing rule to admit members of the English Parliament to sit (though they do not vote) in the House among the members, while others are only admitted into the gallery, my fellow-traveller, being an English member, was accordingly admitted as such. But I supposed I must go to the gallery, when the Speaker stood up and acquainted the House that he understood there was in town an American gentleman of (as he was pleased to say) distinguished character and merit, a member or delegate of some of the parliaments of that country, who was desirous of being present at the debates of the House ; that there was a rule of the House for admitting members of English Parliaments, and that he supposed the House would consider the American Assemblies as English Parliaments ; but, as this was the first instance, he had chosen not to give any order in it without receiving their directions. On the question, the House gave a loud, unanimous *aye*, when two members came to me without the bar——"*

After the declaration of war, in 1775, Franklin, then at Paris, issued a letter to " the People of Ireland," embodying in more striking terms these private views formed in 1771, and ably enforcing the policy of their refusing to join in the war against the colonies.

One effect followed from the publication of these addresses, — an effect still operating, and likley to con-

* The remainder of the letter is lost, —*vide* Franklin's Correspondence, vol. i.

tinue long, — namely, the thorough identification of Irish feeling with American success. If Ireland, no longer a power in Europe, was unable to respond to these sentiments, by national alliance or subsidies, the hearts and the arms of her individual sons were freely offered, and as freely used, throughout the contest for independence.

Irish intellect, also, volunteered its services, and was employed. Charles Thompson, born in Maghera, county of Derry, in 1730, had reached Pennsylvania at the age of eleven. His father died while the emigrant ship was entering the Delaware, and his children, by a harsh construction of a bad law, were deprived of the property he left. Two elder brothers labored to supply their father's place; and under Dr. Allison, also of Ireland, (by whom, first at New London and afterwards at Philadelphia, several of the revolutionary chiefs were educated,) young Charles received a thorough education. In his youth he became intimate with Benjamin Franklin, with whom he "agreed on all subjects except religion." In 1758, he was one of the agents to the Indian Treaty at Oswego; and so favorably did he impress the red men, that the Delawares adopted him into their tribe, conferring on him an Indian name, which means "one who speaks the truth." In 1774, he was chosen secretary to the first Congress, and continued to fill that onerous office until 1789, when the formal adoption of the Constitution closed its functions. He wrote out the Declaration of Independence, from Jefferson's draft, and was the medium through which Franklin received his instructions, and Washington was informed of his election as first President of the Union. He lived to a patriarchal age, ten miles from Philadelphia. "He was," says a contemporary, "about six feet high, erect in his gait, dignified in his deportment, and interesting in his conversation." He spent his retirement in translating the Septuagint, a work of great learning, which appeared, in four volumes, in 1808. He continued till his death to take great interest in politics, and, in 1824, in relation to the contest about the United States Bank, exclaimed to a friend,

"Money, money, is the god of this world!" He died on the 16th of August, in that year.

Mr. John Dunlap, a native of Strabane, who, in 1771, issued the "Pennsylvania Packet," (the first daily paper published in America,) was printer to the Convention of 1774, and to the first Congress, and the first who printed the Declaration of Independence. That august document, copied by Charles Thompson, was also first read to the people, from the centre window of the hall in which Congress met, by Colonel John Nixon, an Irishman. In 1815, Alderman John Binns, of Philadelphia, another Irishman, published the document, for the first time, with fac similes of the signers' signatures. This he had proposed to do by subscription, but that mode not succeeding, he issued, at his own expense, the most perfect engraving of a state paper ever given to the American public.*

Mr. Dunlap was captain of the first troop of Philadelphia horse, and when asked, in 1799, when he could be ready to march against the rioters in Northampton County, replied, " When the laws and government of this happy country require defence, the Philadelphia Cavalry need but one hour's notice."

The Declaration of Independence was signed by fifty-six names, of whom nine (including Secretary Thompson) were of Irish origin. Mathew Thornton, born in Ireland in 1714, signed it for New Hampshire. He was afterwards Chief Justice of the Common Pleas, and died June 24th, 1803. James Smith, who signed for Pennsylvania, was born in Ireland in 1713, and died in 1806. George Taylor, a signer from the same state, was born

---

* It is worthy of remark, that before the publication of Mr. Binns, there never had been a correct copy of the Declaration printed — not even on the Journals of Congress. In all preceding copies, the caption ran, " A Declaration by the Representatives of the United States of America in Congress assembled." Whereas, on the original parchment, signed by the members of the Congress which adopted it, it is as follows : — " In Congress, July 4th, 1776 — The Unanimous Declaration of the Thirteen United States of America." This is a remarkable fact, and a strong proof of the necessity of consulting, in such cases, original documents. For this splendid publication, Mr. Binns received at the time the special thanks of General Lafayette, John Quincy Adams, and other eminent friends and citizens of this republic.

in Ireland, in 1716, so poor that his services were sold on his arrival to pay the expense of his passage out. He died at Easton, (Pa.,) February 23, 1781. George Read, of Delaware, was the son of Irish parents, one of the authors of the Constitution of Delaware, and afterwards of the Federal Constitution. It was he who answered the British tempters—"I am a poor man, but, poor as I am, the King of England is not rich enough to purchase me." He died in 1798. Charles Carroll, of Carrollton, was of Irish descent, and very wealthy. He affixed his address after his name, that the pledge of his "fortune" might be beyond doubt. He was the last survivor of the signers, and died Nov. 14, 1832. Thomas Lynch, Jr., of South Carolina, succeeded his father, who died, while at Congress, in 1776, and signed the Declaration. He went abroad soon after for his health, but was lost at sea. Thomas McKean, a signer for Pennsylvania, was also of Irish parentage. He was successively, senator, chief justice, governor of Pennsylvania, and president of Congress. After fifty years of public life, he died, on the 24th of June, 1817. Edward Rutledge, of South Carolina, was also "a signer," fought in the southern campaign, and was for three years kept prisoner in Florida. He became governor of South Carolina in 1799, and died in January, 1800.* Of these illustrious names, destined to live forever on the New Charter of Human Freedom, Ireland should be wisely jealous, for the world's revolutions will never present such another tablet of glory to the children of men.

After the peace of Paris, six years elapsed before the Constitution of the Federal Union could be definitely fixed and adopted. Many thought the old articles of confederation sufficient—many thought a regular Capital and Congress dangerous to liberty—many overstated the value of centrality, and alarmed ardent and ill-balanced minds into the opposite extreme. In this interim, while all the fruits of the hard-fought war of independence were

* " Lives of the Signers."

in danger of being forever lost, the true patriots of the
country had heavy cares and labors to undergo. To
George Washington, Thomas Jefferson and James Madison, of Virginia, to Alexander Hamilton, of New York,
and John Rutledge, of Carolina, the fortunate establishment of the present Constitution is directly attributable.

John Rutledge, elder brother of Edward, was born in
1739, and commenced the practice of the law at Charleston, in his twenty-first year. While yet a youth he was at
the head of his profession. "He burst forth at once the
able lawyer and accomplished orator;" "the client in
whose service he engaged was supposed to be in a fair
way of gaining his cause."* His exertions, mainly,
carried South Carolina into the Revolution. In 1775
and 1776, he sat in Congress; in 1777 and 1778, he
was governor of his native state; and in 1781 and 1782,
he was a commissioner from Congress to induce states south
of Philadelphia to form a Federal Constitution. He was
appointed, under Washington's administration, first asso-
ciate judge of the Supreme Court, and survived his brother
only a few months. His services in the founding of the
Constitution are justly considered the crowning glory of
his life.

In the Convention for ascertaining the Constitution,
some of the Irish race bore part, though they were not so
numerous here as in the field.

Of the thirty-six delegates, by whom the Constitution
of the United States was, in 1787, promulgated, six, at
least, were Irish. Read, McKean, and John Rutledge
are already known. The other Irish delegates at the
adoption of the Constitution, were Pierce Butler, of South
Carolina, another descendant of the Kilkenny clan, Daniel
Carroll, of Maryland, cousin to Charles, "the signer," and
Thomas Fitzsimons, of Pennsylvania. The latter had
commanded a volunteer company during the war, and
represented his adopted city in Congress during several
sessions. He was much consulted on affairs of commerce,

* Ramsay's South Carolina, vol. ii., p. 217

by Washington and Jefferson; he was president of the Insurance Company of North America till his death, which occurred about the year 1820. These venerable men had the pleasure to see their Constitution adopted by all the thirteen original states, almost as soon as it was promulgated. Immediately after, George Washington, as President, and John Adams, as Vice-President, were elected to execute its provisions and administer its powers.

The choice of a Federal Capital being by courtesy left to Washington, he examined with that view the Potomac, then the central river of the republic. A farm held by Daniel Carroll was freely tendered to him, and upon that farm the plan of the Federal City was laid. The original proprietor lived to see ten Presidents inhabiting " the White House," where once the smoke of his chimney ascended in solitude over the waters of the calm Potomac.*

Under the administration of John Adams, at the beginning of the century, Congress finally removed from Philadelphia to the new capital, which, in honor of the illustrious man, then lately deceased, was solemnly baptized WASHINGTON.

The adoption of the Federal Constitution was not the only labor, of the kind, devolving on those who had carried the colonies through the Revolution. Each state had to be legally organized under a republican constitution, and a body of fundamental laws and precedents were to be shaped and established. Then it was that the wise and able of America found how much easier it is to tear down than to build up, to agitate than to organize. During the presidency of Washington and Adams, nearly all the colonial charters were expanded into constitutions, or substituted by more liberal instruments, and in all such changes the Irish race had hand and part.

The state and national offices, for nearly thirty years, were chiefly filled from the revolutionary ranks. Thus

---

* The site of Baltimore was also purchased from the Carroll family, in 1729; Daniel Carroll died at Washington city, in 1849, at an extreme old age.

Henry Knox became Washington's minister of war, and Anthony Wayne, Adams' commander-in-chief of the army. Governorships, embassies, and judgeships, were chiefly (and properly) bestowed on these venerable men.

The first governor of Pennsylvania, after the adoption of the Federal Constitution, was George Bryan, a native of Dublin. In 1789 and 1790, he was mainly instrumental in procuring the passage of a law for the gradual abolition of slavery in his adopted state. He died in January, 1791, at an advanced age.

Among the senators of the first Congress were Charles Carroll, and Thomas Fitzsimmon; and among the representatives John Sullivan and George Read. The latter retired from the Legislature, to be chief justice of his own state, and the other three to enjoy the repose of private life.

In New Hampshire, the Hon. Mathew Patten, born in Ireland, May 19th, 1719, was "the first judge of probate after the Revolution." He was appointed in 1776, and continued to hold that and other judicial offices until his death, August 27th, 1795. The Hon. John Orr, of the same state, who died in 1823, was for many years a state senator, and the oldest magistrate of Hillsborough county. After the war of Independence, General Sullivan was elected senator to Congress, and remained two sessions. From 1786 to 1789, he was president (that is, "governor") of the state, which he resigned, to accept the office of judge of the Federal Court. In this situation he died in 1795, in the 54th year of his age.

Even Massachusetts partially forgot its ancient prejudices against the Irish race, and, in 1788, sent James Sullivan, the second son of the Limerick schoolmaster, as one of its representatives to Congress. In 1790, he was made attorney general of the state, about which time he projected the Middlesex Canal, and aided in forming the State Historical Society; in 1794, the Legislature ordered his "History of the District of Maine" to be published; in 1807, he was elected governor, and re-elected in 1808. He died in the latter year, after having assisted in the

settlement of Maine and written its history; after gov
erning Massachusetts and defining its boundaries; after
having studied under the British officials, and beat them
with their own weapons.   The son of this eminent statesman was the Hon. Willian Sullrvan, for many years a
state senator and United States representative for Boston, whose biography has already fallen into very com-
petent hands.*

Other states, unconscious of minor distinctions, were
equally anxious to reward past services, and employ the
best talents of all classes of men in the public service.

* Public Men of the Revolution, by the Hon. Wm. Sullivan, LL. D.
(Sketch of the author, by John T. S. Sullivan.)   Philadelpha : Carey &
Hart, 1847.

CHAPTER X.

COLONIAL PENAL LAWS — RISE OF CATHOLIC MISSIONS — WASHINGTON'S REPLY TO
THE CATHOLIC ADDRESS — ST. MARY'S COLLEGE.

THE successful assertion of American Independence
drew large numbers of emigrants from Europe. From
Ireland, in the first decade, the increase was not very
visible, as that nation enjoyed comparative freedom
towards the end of the century, and, with freedom, a
larger share of prosperity than had previously fallen to
its lot. But the breaking out of the French War, in
1793, the failure of the rising of 1798, and the degrad-
ing legislative Union of 1800, had deprived many of
bread, and all of liberty at home, and made the mechanical as well as the agricultural class embark in multitudes to cross the Atlantic.

Hitherto the Irish had colonized, sowed, and reaped,
fought, spoke, and legislated in the New World; if not
always in proportion to their numbers, yet always to the
measure of their educational resources. Now, they are
about to plant a new emblem — the Cross, — and a new
institution — the Church, — throughout the American
continent; for the faith of their fathers they do not
leave after them; nay, rather, wheresoever six Irish
roof-trees rise, there will you find the Cross of Christ,
reared over all, and Celtic piety and Celtic enthusiasm,
all tears and sighs, kneeling before it.

Whatever thou art, oh reader! do not despise the
institution, or the emblem, or the agent. If the creed is
not yours, it was Christopher Columbus', Calvert's, and
Charles Carroll's. Nor wonder that we, who regard the
Church Catholic as the pillar and ground of all truth,
should think its plantation in America the greatest labor
of the Irish Hercules. We can sympathize with a Rut-

7

ledge and a Carroll, in council; with Sullivan and Wayne, upon the field; with Barry and McDonough, on the quarter-deck; — but even more, and more proudly, do we sympathize with the laborious layman and the poor priest, coming together in the backwoods, to offer to God the ancient sacrifice, where the interwoven foliage is the rude screen, the rock the altar, the soaring pine the tower of the holy place, and the wayside well the fountain of salvation.

The first Catholic missions had been those of the Jesuits among the red men. Marquette, Joliet, Brebeuf, Lallemand, Rasles, and Marest, all Frenchmen, and all Jesuits, were the first standard bearers of the Cross, over the blue breadth of the great lakes, down the yellow torrent of the Mississippi, among the homes of all the Indian race, from the Algonquins of Quebec to the Cherokees of the Ozark mountains. But these missions and their missionaries had passed away; and, though the Holy Cross still gleamed upon the frontier of population, its shadow fell on no village square, but, rather, its arms, on either side, but pointed to desolation.

The English and Dutch colonies, planted in the very noon-day of "the Reformation," inherited all its virulence against priests and Jesuits. The so-called freemen of New England sought Rasle in his chapel by the Norridgewock, and slew him on its threshold. Penn forbade Mass to be celebrated in his Sylvania, and, in 1741, a Catholic clergyman was hanged in New York for entering that province contrary to law. The French and German emigrants, of the midland and southern states, did sometimes keep a concealed priest among them; but, under God, it was Irish emigration which, overcoming the malice of the bigot and the injustice of the laws, gave freedom to the altar and security to its ministers.

The earliest notices of Irish Catholics in America that we have found, were those of Maryland and Pennsylvania. The Carroll family emigrated before the year 1700, and settled in Prince George's county. As, at the revolution of 1688, Catholics were disfranchised, and their religious rites proscribed, clergymen could only officiate in private houses, and the fathers of the Carrolls had chapels under their own roofs. In such a chapel-house was born John Carroll, the first bishop and archbishop of the United States, on the 8th of January, 1735. The first Catholic church that we find in Pennsylvania, after Penn's suppression of them in 1708, "was connected with the house of a Miss Elizabeth McGawley, an Irish lady, who, with several of her tenantry, settled on land on the road leading from Nicetown to Frankfort." Near the site of this ancient sanctuary stood a tomb inscribed, "John Michael Brown, ob. 15 Dec. A. D. 1750. R. I. P." He had been a priest residing there *incognito.* In 1734, Governor Gordon and council prohibited the erection of a Catholic church in Walnut street; and, in 1736, a private house having been taken at the corner of Second and Chestnut streets, for the same object, it was again prohibited. Saint Joseph's chapel had, however, been opened in a more retired position, in 1733; and, in 1763, Saint Mary's church was erected. About this time, Protestant prejudice began to abate in Pennsylvania, as well it might, when the Catholics could reckon the Moylans, Barrys, Meases, and Fitzsimons, among their congregation.

In 1756, by a special act, the Catholics of Maryland were assessed for tithes to support the pastors of the Protestant denominations; while, in the very same session, an act was introduced to prevent Catholic clergymen holding lands for church purposes. The latter, however, was rejected. In 1770, Saint Peter's church, in Baltimore, was founded, and, in 1774, there were but nineteen clergymen in Maryland, all of whom were Jesuits. In 1784, Father John Carroll, of the same order, was made first Bishop of the United States, (the colonies had been attached to the Apostolic Vicarate of London,) and "administered the sacrament of confirmation for the first time," in free America.[*] In 1785, he estimated the Catholic population of the republic, — "in Maryland

---

[*] Campbell's Life of Archbishop Carroll.

16,000; in Pennsylvania over 7,000; and, as far as information could be obtained in other states, about 1,500." However, the local statistics of the states show this estimate to be quite too low. Instead of 25,000 Catholics in the old thirteen states, in 1785, 100,000 would be nearer the mark. The marvellous increase of the church may be estimated by the fact that, in 1838, Bishop England estimated the Catholic population at 1,200,000, which, in half a century, would be a twelve-fold multiplication of the original number.

Throughout the war of the Revolution the Catholic Irish population continued to bear their full share in its dangers and councils. In 1774, Dr. Carroll and Charles Carroll were sent, with Dr. Franklin and Mr. Chase, on an embassy to Canada, which had the effect of securing the neutrality of the French Canadian population. If the bigotry of the local legislatures were not so fresh in the memory of the brave *habitans*, there is little doubt but they would have espoused the cause of the Revolution. But they remembered the martyrdom of Rasles, and the priest executed at New York in 1741. Even while the commissioners were in Montreal, they received a copy of the address of the Continental Congress to the British people, stigmatizing Lord North for establishing in Canada " a religion which had deluged their island in blood, and diffused impiety, bigotry, persecution, murder, and *rebellion* (!) through every part of the world." This foolish piece of rhetoric rendered it impossible for the ambassadors to secure the native Canadian population to their side, whom, however, they persuaded to stand neutral in the contest.

In 1784, the first Catholic congregation was assembled, in Boston, by the Abbe La Poitre, a French chaplain; and, in 1788, they obtained the old French church, in School street. The present cathedral was dedicated in 1803, by Bishop Carroll, assisted by the venerable Dr. Cheverus, afterwards Cardinal of Bordeaux, in France. This was the beginning of the Church in the east.

The conduct of the Catholic Irish during the war,

drew from GEORGE WASHINGTON, after his election as President, the graceful acknowledgment, in reply to the address given below :

"ADDRESS

"*Of the Roman Catholics to George Washington, President of the United States.*

" SIR, — We have been long impatient to testify our joy and unbounded confidence, on your being called, by an unanimous vote, to the first station of a country, in which that unanimity could not have been obtained without the previous merit of unexampled services, of eminent wisdom, and unblemished virtue.   Our congratulations have not reached you sooner, because our scattered situation prevented the communication, and the collecting of those sentiments which warmed every breast.   But the delay has furnished us with the opportunity, not merely of presaging the happiness to be expected under your administration, but of bearing testimony to that which we experience already.   It is your peculiar talent, in war and in peace, to afford security to those who commit their protection into your hands.   In war, you shield them from the ravages of armed hostility ; in peace, you establish public tranquillity, by the justice and moderation, not less than by the vigor of your government.   By example, as well as by vigilance, you extend the influence of laws on the manners of our fellow-citizens.   You encourage respect for religion, and inculcate, by words and actions, that principle on which the welfare of nations so much depends, that a superintending Providence governs the events of the world, and watches over the conduct of men.   Your exalted maxims, and unwearied attention to the moral and physical improvement of our country, have produced already the happiest effects.   Under your administration, America is animated with zeal for the attainment and encouragement of useful literature ; she improves her agriculture, extends her commerce, and acquires with foreign nations a dignity unknown to her before.   From these happy events, in which none can

7*

feel a warmer interest than ourselves, we derive additional pleasure by recollecting that you, sir, have been the principal instrument to effect so rapid a change in our political situation. This prospect of national prosperity is peculiarly pleasing to us on another account; because, whilst our country preserves her freedom and independence, we shall have a well-founded title to claim from her justice the equal rights of citizenship, as the price of our blood spilt under your eyes, and of our common exertions for her defence, under your auspicious conduct; — rights rendered more dear to us by the remembrance of former hardships. When we pray for the preservation of them, where they have been granted, and expect the full extension of them from the justice of those states which still restrict them; when we solicit the protection of Heaven over our common country, we neither admit, or can omit, recommending your preservation to the singular care of Divine Providence; because we conceive that no human means are so available to promote the welfare of the United States, as the prolongation of your health and life, in which are included the energy of your example, the wisdom of your counsels, and the persua sive eloquence of your virtues.

"In behalf of the Roman Catholic clergy,

"J. CARROLL.

"In behalf of the Roman Catholic laity,

"CHARLES CARROLL, of Carrollton.

"DANIEL CARROLL,

"THOMAS FITZSIMMONS,

"DOMINICK LYNCH."

THE ANSWER.

" *To the Roman Catholics in the United States of America.*

"GENTLEMEN, — While I now receive with much satisfaction your congratulations on my being called, by an unanimous vote, to the first station of my country, — I cannot but duly notice your politeness in offering an apology for the unavoidable delay. As that delay has given you an opportunity of realizing, instead of anticipating, the benefits of the general government, you will do me the justice to believe that your testimony of the increase of the public prosperity enhances the pleasure which I would otherwise have experienced from your affectionate address.

" I feel that my conduct, in war and in peace, has met with more general approbation than could reasonably have been expected ; and I find myself disposed to consider that fortunate circumstance, in a great degree, resulting from the able support and extraordinary candor of my fellow-citizens of all denominations.

" The prospect of national prosperity now before us is truly animating, and ought to excite the exertions of all good men to establish and secure the happiness of their country, in the permanent duration of its freedom and independence. America, under the smiles of a Divine Providence, the protection of a good government, and the cultivation of manners, morals, and piety, cannot fail of attaining an uncommon degree of eminence, in literature, commerce, agriculture, improvements at home, and respectability abroad.

" As mankind become more liberal, they will be more apt to allow that all those who conduct themselves as worthy members of the community, are equally entitled to the protection of civil government. I hope ever to see America among the foremost nations in examples of justice and liberality. And I presume that your fellow-citizens will not forget the patriotic part which you took in the accomplishment of their revolution, and the establishment of their government ; or, the important assistance which they received from a nation in which the Roman Catholic faith is professed.

" I thank you, gentlemen, for your kind concern for me. While my life and my health shall continue, in whatever situation I may be, it shall be my constant endeavor to justify the favorable sentiments which you are pleased to express of my conduct. And may the members of your society in America, animated alone by the pure spirit of Christianity, and still conducting themselves as the faithful subjects of our free government, enjoy every temporal and spiritual felicity.   G. WASHINGTON."

The necessity of a native clergy, especially in the diocese of Baltimore, was early felt.   In 1791, Bishop Carroll founded St. Mary's College, and, in 1804, with some of the laity, obtained a charter for Baltimore College, which was first opened in Mulberry street, in that city. In 1805, St. Mary's was much improved, and a handsome Gothic church was added to the college.   This is the *Alma Mater* of the Church in America.*

* Among the public schools of Baltimore, the " Hibernian Free School," founded by Robert Oliver, a native of Ireland, is, to this day, the most considerable and conspicuous.

CHAPTER XI

IRISH SERVICES TO EDUCATION AND SCIENCE IN AMERICA — ALLISON — CHARLES THOMPSON — DAVID RAMSAY — FULTON — COLLES — ADRIAN — MATTHEW CA REY.

AMONG the first educational institutions of America, after its independence, was Pennsylvania College, over which Dr. Allison was chosen provost. He was a native of the north of Ireland, and had spent the best part of his life as a teacher in New London, New York, and subsequently, Philadelphia. He is frequently mentioned in the Biographies of the Men of the Revolution, as their master; as one who had a singular insight into character, and judgment in the management of pupils.

Charles Thompson's version of the Septuagint is a worthy landmark of colonial learning. He was a pupil of Allison's, and in his old age returned to the studies of his youth with renewed ardor. Every literary project of his times found in him a willing and able auxiliary.

David Ramsay, the son of Irish parents, was born at Lancaster, Pa., April 2, 1749. He settled early in South Carolina, and was one of the first advocates there for the Revolution. In 1782, he was sent to Congress, and presided over that body for a year. In 1796, he published his History of South Carolina; in 1801, his Life of Washington, and, in 1808, his History of the United States. The British government prohibited this last work from being sold in England or Ireland, — a high compliment to its truth and power. On May 8, 1815, Dr. Ramsay, in the discharge of his medical duties, was stabbed by a maniac, and almost instantly expired. He is buried at Charleston.

Governor Sullivan, of Massachusetts, the projector of the Middlesex Canal, and Governor De Witt Clinton, James Logan, and Bishop Berkely, deserve special mention in this place ; but men with such connexions are not likely to have their honors mildew. We prefer to dwell rather upon the merits of men less known to the public memory, but not less influential in affecting the present prosperity of America.

Christopher Colles arrived from Ireland on these shores about the time Fulton was born. In 1772, he delivered a series of lectures " on the subject of Lock Navigation," at Philadelphia. " He was the first person," says De Witt Clinton, " who suggested to the government of the state (New York) the canals and improvements on the Ontario route. Unfortunately for him, and, perhaps, for the public," adds the same authority, " he was generally considered as a visionary projector, and his plans were sometimes treated with ridicule, and frequently viewed with distrust."* In 1784, 1785, 1786, and for several successive years, he petitioned the Legislature of that state, on the importance and practicability of uniting the western lakes to the Atlantic. He was, probably, the author of the letters signed " Hibernicus," on the same subject, which were published at New York about the beginning of this century. In 1774, he proposed to supply New York with water by aqueducts, such as now bring in the Croton, and of which he exhibited models at public lectures. During the war, of 1812 he was " the projector and attendant of the telegraph erected on Castle Clinton." He died in obscurity and poverty, while others were growing famous and wealthy upon the stolen ideas of his failing intellect.

Robert Fulton was born of poor Irish parents, at Little Britain, Lancaster county, Pennsylvania, in 1765. He early displayed artist tastes, and painted portraits for a subsistence, in Philadelphia, before he was quite a man. In 1786, he went to London, lived with Benjamin West, and took out several patents; in 1796, he went to Paris, and resided with the Hon. Joel Barlow till 1808, where, in 1803, after many delays and mishaps, he

* O'Reilly's History of Rochester. Mr. Charles King's Memoir of the Croton Aqueduct.

launched the first boat propelled by steam power, on the Seine. In 1806, he returned to America, and ran a more complete model boat on the Hudson. From this time forth, his fortune needed no patron's aid; but he did not live long to enjoy its sweets. He died February 23, 1815, in his 44th year, too soon for his country, though not too soon for history.

It is not now possible for us to estimate how much of the growth and greatness of America is due to the canals of Colles, and the steamboats of Fulton. In fifty years this nation has increased its territory ten fold, its population seven fold, and its wealth a thousand fold. Too seldom do we remember, when borne triumphantly on the tide of all this prosperous increase, that to these humble, studious men, stout-hearted wrestlers with formidable problems, patient bearers, for truth's sake, of ridicule and reproach, we owe so much of all we most boast of and most enjoy.

Among the most distinguished mathematicians of this continent, Robert Adrain holds a conspicuous place. He was born in Carrickfergus, September 30, 1775, and was, in 1798, a United Irishman. After the failure of that memorable insurrection, he emigrated to America, poor and undistinguished. His success on these shores we transcribe from the record made by another hand : —

"Robert was the eldest of five children, and lost both his parents in his fifteenth year. He was an excellent mathematician and linguist, and taught school at Ballycarry when only in his sixteenth year. Mr. Mortimer, a gentleman of great wealth and influence in Cumber, engaged him as an instructor of his children; but when the Irish people made an effort, in 1798, to shake off their ancient oppressors, Robert Adrain took the command of a company of the United Irish, while Mr. Mortimer, being an officer of the English authorities, was offering a reward of fifty pounds for his capture. At the battle of Saintfield, Mr. Mortimer received a mortal blow. But it so happened that Mr. Adrain, having refused his assent to some measure proposed in his division of the army, received a dangerous wound in the back from one of his own men the day before the battle, and was reported to be dead. This stopped further search after him, and after several narrow escapes from the hands of Ireland's enemies, he found a refuge in New York, then suffering from the yellow fever. He first taught an academy at Princeton, N. J., then became principal of the York County Academy, next took charge of the academy at Reading, and became a valuable contributor to Baron's 'Mathematical Correspondent,' and afterwards editor of the *Analist*, which he continued for several years in Philadelphia.

" In 1810, he was appointed Professor of Mathematics and Natural Philosophy in Queen's (now Rutger's) College, New Brunswick, had the degree of Doctor of Laws conferred on him, and was soon after elected a member of the philosophical societies in Europe and America. He edited the third American edition of Hutton's Course of Mathematics, and made important corrections, adding many valuable notes, and an elementary treatise on Descriptive Geometry.

" On the decease of Dr. Kemp, Dr. Adrain was elected, in 1813, Professor of Mathematics and Natural Philosophy in Columbia College, New York ; soon after which he published a paper on the figure and magnitude of the earth, and gravity, which obtained for him great celebrity in Europe.   He contributed to the periodicals of the day, edited the Mathematical Diary in 1825, and was looked up to as having no superior among the mathematicians of America.   The ease and facility with which he imparted instruction, his fluency in reading the Greek and Latin authors, and extensive acquaintance with general literature, his social disposition, strong understanding, and high conversational powers, caused the students and professors greatly to regret his resignation of his office in 1826.   The senior mathematical class had his portrait taken by the distinguished Irish artist, Ingham ; an admirable likeness.

" After leaving New York, he held for several years a

professorship in the University of Pennsylvania, of which institution he was vice-provost. Towards the close of his life, his memory and other faculties of his mind suffered decay. Through life he was a sincere Christian, and few theologians could better explain the more difficult passages of Scripture. His strong and powerful intellect, and pure and fervent piety, were cited as a refutation of the sentiment that the study of the abstruse sciences tends to infidelity." *

Nor must we omit to mention here the name of Mathew Carey, one of the first American writers on Political Economy. Mr. Carey was born in Ireland, in the year 1761, and removed to Philadelphia, about the period of the Revolution. From 1785 till 1830, he was an unwearied student of questions affecting trade, emigration, banking, wages, public schools, benevolent societies, and the public health. He was, we believe, the first to propose a monument to Robert Fulton. He was also a consistent friend of liberty everywhere, of which his "Vindicæ Hiberniæ," "Olive Branch," and "Case of the Greeks," remain as ample evidence. He died at a good old age, in Philadelphia, having reared up a numerous family, full of hereditary ability, who seem destined still further to dignify the name of Carey.†

* McKenzie's Illustrious Irishmen, Part II. In our own time, we are not wholly unrepresented in Irish science. Henry O'Reilly, a native of Cavan, still in the prime of life, has been the most active and successful perfector of the electric telegraph in North America.

† Henry C. Carey, the distinguished political economist, is the son of Mathew Carey. Many of his essays on wages, trade, &c., have been translated in France, Germany, and Sweden.

* See Appendix No. **V**

8

CHAPTER XII.

On the 30th of April, 1789, Washington opened the
first Congress, by an address, delivered in person, which
was the custom, until President Jefferson adopted the
form of the written " Message," still adhered to.

During the second term of Washington's presidency,
the fact that there were two parties radically opposed to
each other became apparent. John Adams, vice-president, and Alexander Hamilton, secretary of state, headed
the one which was in favor of a national bank, a high
tariff, and strong powers of central control. Thomas Jefferson, James Madison, and their friends, were utterly
opposed to these principles of government. The republicans accused the federalists of British predilections, and
the federalists accused them of " French principles."
Washington was believed to be inclined to the former,
but, with excellent temper and feeling, he maintained in
office an unbiassed and equable tone, preserving, till the
last act of his life, the respectful confidence of all parties.

Jefferson's principles exercised an early and a permanent influence on the Irish citizens. He was strongly
anti-British, so were they ; he favored the largest tolera-
tion, so did they ; he was master of a laconic, powerful
style, which they intuitively admired. He practised in
his own person great republican simplicity, unlike the
official reserve of Washington and Adams. He had a
bold tongue, a warm heart, and a strong head, — qualities
which the children of Ireland have always respected and
confided in.

The great majority of the Irish settlers and their descendants were, therefore, Jeffersonian Democrats. But the chiefs of their communities were by no means unanimous. The Carrolls, Harpers, and Rutledges were Federalists, the Sullivans and Butlers, Democrats. The numbers inclined to the Oracle of Monticello, and, after the administration of John Adams, became the warmest partisans of democracy.

The administration of John Adams began in 1797, and is remarkable to us, in the first place, for the events connected with "the United Irishmen," which happened in his time. Soon after the formation of the society in Ireland, a similar one sprung up in America. Its head quarters were at Philadelphia, where Matthew Carey, and other good men, gave it aid and impulse. The publications of the Irish society were reprinted there so early as 1794, funds were collected, and arms promised. Wolfe Tone, flying in despair from Ireland, returned from his "New Jersey farm" to Paris, to make an effort for French aid. The "French party," as the Democrats were called, and the friends of Ireland, were identical here, and, in 1797, "the American Society of United Irishmen" was a very formidable body.

In 1798, on pretence of danger from this and other sources, President Adams suggested and obtained the famous "Alien Law." By this law, the president could order any alien he deemed "dangerous" to quit the country; others were to be licensed to remain during his pleasure, and the neglect to get licensed was an offence punishable by three years' imprisonment, and perpetual disqualification for citizenship. Fourteen years' residence was also the time fixed as necessary to naturalization. This law having been severely commented on by the press, the President procured the passage of "the Sedition Law," making it a seditious libel to reflect on the conduct or motives of the Congress or President. These measures violently inflamed the country, and, more that any other cause, organized the two antagonist parties. The Federalists adhered to Mr. Adams, the Democrats to Mr. Jefferson. The adopted citizens generally joined the latter, whose principles, indeed, were those most favorable to the new-comer and the settler.

Among the first arrests under the sedition law were Dr. James Smith and Mr. Burk, of New York, the one a citizen, the other " an alien." They were publishers of an opposition paper called " The Time-Piece ;" but so violent was the spirit of proscription, that Burk thought it advisable to escape from the country, after which the prosecution against Smith was dropped.*

Mr. Duane, Dr. Reynolds, and other naturalized citizens of Philadelphia, vigorously agitated a repeal of these ob jectionable laws. The former was frequently in personal danger from his opponents, and the doctor was removed from his situation as physician to the Dispensary. In 1798, " The Alien Riot," or " Federal Riot," occurred at Saint Mary's Church, in Philadelphia. The opponents of the law, having brought a petition to the church doors, soliciting the signatures of the congregation, were attacked and badly beaten by the Federalists, headed by a citizen named Gallagher. A trial of the rioters was had, but the jury disagreed, and the case was dismissed.

At this time Sir Robert Liston, the British minister, was considered to be on more intimate terms with Mr. Adams than was consistent with a sound American policy. The minister's letters, so far as published, cer tainly countenance the charge. He seems to have been less an ambassador to, than an adviser of, the govern ment. In one of his letters to the governor general of Canada, (dated May 23, 1799,) he says, in reference to the Federal riots, "The conduct of some of these gentle men, (the Federalists,) being shamefully calumniated by some of the popular newspapers, they have ventured to take the law into their own hands, and to punish one or two of the printers, (by a smart flogging,) a circum stance which has given rise to much animosity, to threats, and to a commencement of armed associations on the side of the Democrats, (particularly the United

* History of the Adams Administration, p. 225.

Irishmen,) and some apprehend that the affair may lead to civil war."* The wish, perhaps, "was father to the thought" of the British minister.

The Irish democratic feeling was further influenced against Mr. Adams' administration by the following circumstances. The elder Emmet, Dr. McNevin, and several of their companions in the Irish revolt of 1798, having been arrested, by surprise, at Bond's, in Dublin, were consigned close prisoners to Fort George, in Scotland. In 1799 and 1800, the British government agreed to let them go, provided they agreed to quit the British dominions forever. Having, at length, arranged the terms, Thomas Addis Emmet, for himself and his compatriots, applied to Rufus King, our minister at London, for passports, but was inhospitably refused by that personage, who added that "there were republicans enough in America." Emmet and McNevin were forced to spend three years in France ; Sampson was imprisoned in Hamburgh, on British suggestion, and Robert Emmet returned from his brother's side, to make an ineffectual attempt at insurrection, and to perish, at the age of twenty-five, on the scaffold. A few years afterwards, Thomas Addis Emmet, then the leader of the New York Bar, by a striking narration of this circumstance, raised a feeling in America, against Mr. King, (then a candidate for the vice-presidency,) which politically extinguished that able, but aristocratic, statesman.†

* Administration of Adams, p. 382.
† These letters, from the *New York Evening Post*, are reprinted in Madden's "Memoir of T. A. Emmet."

* See Appendix No. VI.

8*

CHAPTER XIII.

In 1801, Jefferson, as President, and Aaron Burr, as Vice-President, were elected to the seats of Adams and Pinckney. In the ensuing session of Congress, a bill for repealing the Alien and Sedition laws was introduced by John Smilie, passed, and approved. Some other evidences of a total change of policy were had. All the New England states, as they are called, voted for Adams; New York, Pennsylvania, and Virginia, held the balance, and decided for Jefferson.

The United Irishmen in British prisons, or in European exile, perceiving this change of parties, applied for passports to the new American ministers abroad, and received them. Thomas Addis Emmet and Dr. McNevin came to New York, where they were soon after joined by William Sampson. The son of Wolfe Tone entered the topographical service of the United States. John Caldwell settled on a farm beside the Hudson. Dr. Sweetman made his home in Georgia; and the brothers Binns located at Philadelphia. The influence of these men upon the policy of America, and the fortunes of their poorer countrymen, was, during their time, most salutary.

William Sampson was a barrister of fine attainments, great humor, and unconquerable buoyancy of mind. He was a native of Londonderry, and had reached his fortieth year, when, in 1807, he settled in New York. Here he renewed his professional practice, and soon became distinguished at the Bar. In 1808, he published a collection of his miscellaneous writings, chiefly culled from

"The Press" and "Star," the United Irish organs. To these he added, in subsequent editions, some sketches of American society, admirable for their wit and pathos. The book, though a mere collection of *disjecta membra*, became a great favorite with the public, as did the author, in person, with all those whose acquaintance he made.

M'Nevin, a native of Galway and a Roman Catholic, had represented Gort in the first Catholic Board. He also was in the prime of life, an accomplished chemist and physician. After becoming a citizen, he joined with the Federal, or Whig, party, and continued for nearly half a century to exercise much social influence in New York. He was " President of the Friends of Ireland," which coöperated with the Irish Catholic Association, and, in 1834, he revived the society, to coöperate with the Repeal agitation. He did not live to see the failure of his hopes, in this last respect. His " Pieces of Irish History," is his sole memorial to his race, on this continent ; as yet, he has no other monument.*

The most distinguished of the refugees was Thomas Addis Emmet, born in 1764, in the city of Cork. Educated at Edinburgh, he had for class-fellows Sir James Mackintosh, afterwards Lord Advocate of Scotland, and Benjamin Constant, who became a tribune under the French Republic. He spent three years in Edinburgh, and his popularity may be imagined from the fact that he was president of no less than five college societies at the same time. Leaving college, he visited the continent, spending two years on his tour. He observed institutions with the eye of a philosopher, and analyzed their conditions with the keenness of a politician.

On his return to Ireland, Mr. Emmet passed through London, where he met his old school-fellow, Mackintosh. In their conversation, that eminent man advised him strongly to choose law as his profession, assuring him that

---

* Some funds were collected in New York, several years ago, for the purpose of erecting a monument to his memory, and placed in the hands of Mr Robert Emmet. Probably they were insufficient.

if he did so he was destined to rise. On his return to Dublin, he found his eldest brother, Temple, dead, and soon after entered himself as a law student, and, in 1790, was duly admitted. The succeeding year he prosecuted, on behalf of James Napper Tandy, the lord-lieutenant and council, for issuing an illegal proclamation! This bold step reminds one of the old adage, of warring with the devil, and holding the court in his own dominions. Nothing resulted from it favorable to the national cause, except the evidence of Emmet's legal ability. The government were astonished at the boldness, the research and acuteness, of the young advocate ; and a proposition was immediately made to him of judicial preferment ;— but this he, as immediately, declined.

In 1804, he reached New York, with the *prestige* of defeat heavy upon him. But he soon made his powers felt at the American bar. Story, Sullivan, Kent, and Jones, his contemporaries, have spoken enthusiastically of his virtues and abilities.

His style of pleading is well described by Charles Gliddon Haines, of New Hampshire — himself an eminent lawyer — in his biographical sketch of Mr. Emmet : —

" Helvetius remarks," says Haines, " that the sun of glory only shines upon the tomb of greatness. His observation is too often true, but facts and living proofs sometimes contradict it. Mr. Emmet walks on in life, amid the eulogiums, the admiration, and the enthusiastic regard of a great and enlightened community. Without the glare and influence of public office, without titles and dignities, who fills a wider space, who commands more respect, than Thomas Addis Emmet? Like a noble and simple column, he stands among us proudly preëminent, — destitute of pretensions, destitute of vanity, and destitute of envy. In a letter which I recently received from a friend who resides in the western part of the Union, a lawyer of eminence, he speaks of the New York bar. ' Thomas Addis Emmet,' says he, ' is the great luminary, whose light even crosses the western mountains.

His name rings down the valley of the Mississippi, and we hail his efforts with a kind of local pride.'

" If to draw the character of Homer needs the genius of the immortal bard himself; if to portray the powers of Demosthenes requires the gigantic intellect of the great Athenian orator, Mr. Emmet has nothing to expect from me. In presenting the features of his mind, I shall describe them from the impressions they make on me. I paint from the original. I catch the lineaments of the subject as living nature presents them.

" The mind of Thomas Addis Emmet is of the highest order. His penetration is deep, his views comprehensive, his distinctions remarkably nice. His powers of investigation are vigorous and irresistible. If there be anything in a subject, he will go to the bottom. He probes boldly, reaches the lowest depths by his researches, analyzes everything, and embraces the whole ground. He may be said to have a mind well adapted to profound and powerful investigation. In the next place, he has great comprehension. He sees a subject in all its bearings and relations. He traces out all its various operations. He begins at the centre, and diverges until it becomes necessary again to return to the centre. As a reasoner, — a bare, strict reasoner, — Mr. Emmet would always be placed in an elevated rank. No matter how dry, how difficult, how repulsive, the topic ; no matter what may be its intricacies and perplexities, if any man can unfold and amplify it, he is equal to the task.

* * * * * *

" I have spoken of his talent for deep and rigid investigation. I will now again recur to another feature of his mind, — his talent for reasoning on whatever data or premises he relies on. All the illustrations, and all the analogies, which can well occur to the mind, are readily and adroitly arranged in his arguments. He makes the most of his cause, and often makes too much, — giving a front that is so palpably over-formidable, that men of the plainest sense perceive the fruits of a powerful mind, without being at all convinced."

Thus spoke an American of his mind. Hear now an Irishman, on the qualities of his heart : —

"In men who are 'fit for treason, stratagem, and spoils,' the passions and mental qualities we expect to find are ambition, vanity, malignity, restlessness, or recklessness of mind. Were these the characteristics of T. A. Emmet ? The question, with perfect safety to the memory of Emmet, might be put to any surviving political opponent of his, of common honesty, who was acquainted with those times, and the men who were prominent actors in them. Emmet's ambition was to see his country well governed, and its people treated like human beings, destined and capacitated for the enjoyment of civil and religious freedom. For himself he sought no preëminence, no popular applause ; he shrunk from observation where his merits, in spite of his retiring habits, forced them into notice. No man could say that Emmet was ambitious.

"Emmet's vanity was of a peculiar kind. He was vain of nothing but his name ; it was associated with the brightest of the by-gone hopes of Irish genius, and with the fairest promises of the revival of the latter in the dawning powers of a singularly gifted brother. No man could say, with truth, that vanity or selfishness was the mental infirmity of Emmet.

"No malignant act was ever imputed to him. The natural kindness of his disposition was manifested in his looks, in his tone of voice. Those who came in contact with him felt that his benignity of disposition, his purity of heart and mind were such, 'and the elements so mixed in him, that nature might stand up and say to all the world, this was a man.' Malignity and Emmet were as dissimilar in nature as in name."*

He died of paralysis, which seized him in court, in 1826, and, amid the universal respect of all his fellow-citizens, he was interred in Saint Paul's churchyard, New York. Montgomery's ashes repose in the same ground.

---

* Haines' Sketch of Thomas Addis Emmet. Madden's United Irishmen,

The brothers, John and Benjamin Binns, settled at Philadelphia. They were natives of Dublin, of the Moravian Church. Both were educated men, and early devoted their talents to the cause of human liberty. In 1798, John was tried at Maidstone, with Arthur O'Connor and Father Coigley, for treason. The evidence against all but Coigley being deemed insufficient, he was executed, and the rest escaped. Soon after, John Binns was rearrested for treasonable practices, and confined to Gloucester jail. Here he remained for nearly three years, and, in 1801, was permitted to come to this country. In March, 1802, we find him publishing the "Republican Argus," at Northumberland, Pa., and, in 1807, he issued, in Philadelphia, "The Democratic Press," for several years the most influential party organ in the Union. For twenty years he has filled the office of alderman of that city, where he survives at a patriarchal age, in the enjoyment of all his fine mental powers.*

Aaron Burr, failing of a reëlection in 1805, engaged in the conspiracy to separate the Southern States from the Union, which has made his name so peculiarly memorable. In this attempt, he deeply compromised Mr. Herman Blennerhassett, a native of Kerry, Ireland, who had purchased an island in the Ohio, and there retired with an elegant and lovely lady, led the life of an uxorious philosopher. Burr, gifted beyond most men with the fascinating powers of persuasion, not only seduced the citizen from his duty, but the wife from her continence. In the memorable state trial of 1807, Blennerhassett, though true bills were found against him, was acquitted; but he returned to a desolate and dishonored home. She, who had given the enchantment to his island, was fled; fled with the very "friend" for whom he had risked life and forfeited fortune.

    "The trail of the serpent was over it all."

The experience of Herman Blennerhassett should be for-

* For details of the eventful and interesting life of Mr. Binns, see American Celt, vol. ii., No. 12. (Boston, 1851.)

ever a warning to those who are tempted by plausible speculators, to violate the laws of their country or the duties of their citizenship.*

Under Jefferson's second presidency, George Clinton, of New York, was Vice-President. The Tripoli War ended in a satisfactory peace, Ohio was admitted as a state, and Louisiana, lately purchased from the French, taken into the Union. Towards the close of Jefferson's second term, " the right of search," in a few instances exercised by French, and in many by English, ships, became the great foreign question ; but it was reserved for his predecessor to settle that dispute.

In 1808, Madison succeeded to the presidency, and for three years exhausted negotiation in attempts at a peaceable solution. Between 1803 and 1810 nine hundred American ships had been seized, searched, or detained. In 1811, Madison sent his "war message" to Congress, the army was raised to 35,000 men, the navy equipped for active service, and a loan of $11,000,000 raised for the purposes of the war. In February, 1812, John Henry communicated to the President that, in 1809, he had been employed, by the governor of Canada, in a secret intrigue to separate New England from the Union. The documents connected with Henry's disclosure stimulated the war spirit, and in February, 1812, hostilities actually commenced. General Dearborn, of Massachusetts, was appointed commander-in-chief ; Pinckney, major general ; and Wilkinson, Hull, Hampton, and Bloomfield, the first brigadiers.

The chairman of the Senate committee on foreign affairs, at this time, was John Smilie, a native of Ireland. He was born in Newtownards, County Down, and had fought in the Revolutionary War. From that time, " he had never been out of the public service," until the hour of his death. In 1802, he had brought in the bill repealing the Adams Alien Law, and, in 1812, he re

---

* Burr was discharged on the ground that the evidence was insufficient Mrs. Blennerhassett, his victim, died some short time since, in New York, in great poverty, and was buried by the charity of some former Irish friends

ported a bill empowering the President to raise a temporary army for the war with Great Britain. On the last day of that year, at the age of seventy-four, he died at Washington, leaving a character, second to none of his contemporaries, for fidelity and usefulness in the public service.

The successor of John Smilie was John Caldwell Calhoun, whose province it was to vindicate the report of his venerable predecessor. Mr. Calhoun was the son of Patrick Calhoun, an emigrant from Donegal, in Ireland, to South Carolina, born March 18th, 1782. At that time Mr. Calhoun was in the meridian of his fame, and of his whole powers of mind. His defence of the war, in reply to John Randolph, placed him among the first men of his generation, a position which he justly held till the close of his long public life.

The war now declared should necessarily be a naval, as well as a military, struggle, and a natural anxiety for the result thrilled the hearts of all Americans, on receiving the "war message" of Madison.

* National Intelligencer, Dec. 31st, 1812.

9

CHAPTER XIV.

THE war had its origin in aggressions which had become intolerable. American seamen were pressed and American ships searched in British waters and on the high seas, at least a thousand times, before President Madison sent his " war message " to Congress, and when at last war was proclaimed, the favorite motto of many a ship was " Free Trade and Sailors' Rights."

The West Indian waters, being the confine of the two fleets, was the scene of some of the first and fiercest of the sea-fights of this war. One of the most memorable of these was the action fought between Captain Boyle's ship, the Comet, (twelve guns and one hundred and twenty men,) and three British vessels, convoyed by a Portuguese ship-of-war. The Portuguese ship carried twenty thirty-two pounders ; the British, twenty guns between them. By superior sailing and manœuvring, the Comet cut off the British ships, and disabled them one by one. Two of them he carried as prizes into Pernambuco, the third foundered, and the Portuguese retreated under cover of the night. On the same cruise, Captain Boyle captured the British ship Aberdeen, of eight guns, and two others of ten guns each. He then returned to the United States, escaped the British squadron in the Chesapeake, and reached Baltimore in safety. Captain Boyle was of Irish birth, but his after career is unknown to us.*

An Irishman, Captain Leavins, of the trading schooner Santee, of Charleston, being captured at sea, in August, was sent in his own vessel, under charge of a British

---

* " Sketches of the Late War," (Rutland, Vt.,) 1815, p. 330.

crew, to Bermuda. Rising singly on them at night, he wounded two badly, and compelled the other three to work the vessel back to Charleston, where he arrived amid universal acclamations.*

Captain Johnston Blakely was born in Seaford, County Down, Ireland, in October, 1781. His father soon after emigrated to this country; but in South Carolina, the family died, one by one, leaving young Blakely alone in the world. While at school, in 1799, the orphan had the additional misfortune to lose the remnant of property left him, and, in 1800, a friend of his family procured him a midshipman's warrant. In 1813, he served in the Enterprise, and, in the beginning of 1814, was promoted to the command of the Wasp. Soon after, he fell in with the British ship Reindeer, in latitude 48° 36′ north, and, after an action of nineteen minutes, captured her. The American loss was twenty-one killed and wounded, the British, sixty-seven. In August, 1814, he captured a British merchant-ship under convoy, and, on the first of September, the Avon also struck her flag to him. Before he could take possession of the Avon, a fresh British ship arrived, and Blakely, whose ship was somewhat damaged, was obliged to sheer off. This is the last authentic account of him. His ship was spoken off the Azores, and was supposed to have foundered at sea. All else is only conceit and conjecture.   " But whatever may have been the fate of Blakely," says Dr. Frost, " this much is certain, that he will, to use his own expression, ' be classed among those names that stand so high.' The lustre of his exploits, not less than the interest excited by those who remember how, in his very boyhood, he was left, without a single being around him with whom he could claim kindred blood, — how, by his merit, he obtained friends, and conferred honor on that country which was not only his parent, but has become the parent of his only child, — and how, last of all, he perished, — God only knows where and how, — has all given to

* "Sketches of the Late War," p. 441.

his character, his history, his achievements, and his fate, a romantic interest, marking the name of Blakely for lasting and affectionate remembrance."*

One more fact (and it is a great one) we have to connect with his name. The Legislature of North Carolina, in December, 1816, "Resolved unanimously, That Captain Blakely's child be educated at the expense of this state ; and that Mrs. Blakely be requested to draw on the treasurer of this state, from time to time, for such sums of money as shall be required for the education of the said child."

John Shaw, a native of Mountmellick, emigrated in 1790 to Philadelphia, being then seventeen years of age. In 1798, in the *quasi* French war, he was appointed to command the armed schooner Enterprise, with a crew of seventy-six men. In six months, his schooner captured eight French privateers, or letters of marque. In 1801, peace was concluded with the French Directory, and Mr. Shaw retired with the grade and half-pay of lieutenant. In 1806, when Burr was fitting out his secret expedition in the Ohio valley, he got command of the United States flotilla before Natchez, and, when that conspiracy exploded, was appointed by Jefferson to the command of the navy yard at Norfolk, Virginia, with the rank of post-captain. In the war of 1812, he ranked as commodore, and commanded, for a year, the United States squadron in the Mediterranean. After the war, he had charge of the navy yard at Charlestown, and died in September, 1823, at Philadelphia. Mr. Fenimore Cooper speaks of him as "second to none on the list of gallant seamen with which the present navy of the Republic commenced its brilliant career," — as personally, "a man of fine presence, beloved by those who served under him."

Thomas McDonough, brother to James, mentioned in the war of Independence, was distinguished in 1805, in the attack on Tripoli. He was the second man to board

---

* Frost's Lives of the Commodores, p. 272.

the Turkish frigate with Stephen Decatur, who was, by his mother, half Irish. He was promoted to the rank of first lieutenant of the Siren, and, in 1806, displayed great spirit at Gibraltar in retaking, out of the British boats, some impressed American seamen. In 1812, he was ordered to Lake Champlain, and in 1814, the British ships built on the Canadian side being ready for a descent on New York, he prepared to meet them. McDonough had under him the Saratoga, twenty-six guns; the Eagle, twenty; Ticonderoga, seventeen; the Preble, seven; and ten galleys with sixteen guns, — in all, eighty-six. The British force mounted ninety-five guns, headed by the frigate Confiance, a powerful ship. On the eleventh of September, the two fleets met at eight in the morning, and at noon McDonough was completely victorious, having taken the frigate, and captured or sunk all the remaining vessels, with the exception of some small galleys which escaped. New York and Vermont voted to the victor large tracts of land, and Congress caused a gold medal to be struck in honor of the event. He married and settled in Middletown, Connecticut, where he died of consumption, in 1825. His grave is in the little cemetery of that quiet town, and the river of " steady habits " flows soothingly before the resting-place of the commodore.

Commodore Charles Stewart was born of Irish parents in Philadelphia, July 28th, 1718, and was the fourth commodore that Ireland gave to America. In 1798, he entered the service as lieutenant to Commodore Barry, and distinguished himself, in 1800, in the *quasi* French war. In the West Indian waters, Stewart captured several French craft, and in 1802, was made commander of the Siren. Like Decatur and McDonough, he won his first laurels at Tripoli, and his chief reputation in the war of 1812–15; having got charge of the Constitution in 1813, and the same year destroyed the British brig Pictou, and schooners Catherine and Phœnix, in the West Indies. In 1814, his ship being refitted, he captured, off the Bermudas, the Lord Nelson; off Lisbon, the Susan; and in

February, 1815, in the West Indies, took, in the same engagement, the British Ship Cyane of thirty-four, and Levant of twenty-one guns. Honors were showered upon him, on his return home, and the various states vied with each other in their presentations. From that period he has been employed, as Barry was before him, in superintending the construction of new ships, at Philadelphia, Norfolk and elsewhere. The love of Ireland, which he has so often manifested, seems likely to be hereditary in his family.*

Among the officers of the second rank, in this war, Decatur bestowed especial praise on Lieutenant Gallagher, and Perry, on Purser McGrath, who commanded the armed Brig "Caledonia," in the memorable battle of Lake Erie. In the same engagement Lieutenant Conklin gave satisfaction, as commander of the schooner "Tigress."

The total number of British vessels captured during this war was 1551 — an unanswerable proof of the bravery, skill, and activity, of the American naval commanders.

* His daughter, married in Ireland, is the author of some fine Irish poetry

CHAPTER XV.

THE campaigns of 1812 and 1813 were chiefly fought on the Canadian frontier. Among the militia which appeared on the American border, many sons of Ireland gained distinction. The names of Brady, Mullany McKeon, Croghan, rank after those of Scott, Brown, and Wool, for services performed on that theatre of war, where, however, the greatest achievement effected was the successful defence of American territory from invasion. The defeat of Hull, and surrender of Detroit, were more than compensated by the brilliant victories of Chippewa, Bridgewater, and Plattsburg ; and the work of security was completed by the utter defeat of Tecumseh and his Anglo-Indian forces, at the battle of the Thames, in the territory of Michigan.

This action, fought in October, 1813, was the last and most complete defeat of the savages of the north-western lakes. Tecumseh was supposed to have fallen by the hands of Colonel Johnson, of Kentucky ; but that veteran soldier has himself said, that all he could say was, when attacked by the chief, he fired, and when the smoke cleared away, the Indian lay dead before him. The popular account attributes the deadly aim and wound to one Mason, a native of the county of Wexford, Ireland, who, though a grandfather, aged four-score, volunteered his services in that expedition. He had been an old revolutionary soldier, and fought in the ranks with his own sons, themselves men of middle age.*

---

* In a cotemporaneous view of the battle, he is represented as firing at Tecumseh, over Colonel Johnson's shoulder, with a rifle, while Johnson is discharging a pistol.

The British "naval operations," on the northern coast, having signally failed, some of the invading force were directed to attempt the shore of the Chesapeake, and to penetrate to Washington. In May, 1813, four hundred men were despatched from Warren's fleet to burn the town of Havre de Grace, Maryland. The few militia in the place abandoned it; but John O'Neale and two others worked a small battery with deadly effect. The enemy having effected a landing, these humble Horatii retreated to the nail factory, and continued a destructive musketry fire on those who approached. A party of marines finally captured O'Neale, who was carried prisoner on board the Maidstone frigate. He would have been instantly executed but for the vigorous interference of General Miller, who threatened to execute two British prisoners, in retaliation, if his life were taken.

During this war such threats alone could have saved the naturalized citizens, formerly British subjects, when taken in arms. A proclamation, dated October 26th, 1812, and signed by the Prince Regent, (George IV.,) distinctly announced that all such prisoners would be treated as "rebels" in arms against their sovereign. In February, 1813, the naturalized citizens of Philadelphia, through Alderman John Binns, chairman of their meeting, drew the attention of President Madison to this declaration. This memorial was answered by the President, as follows : —

"WASHINGTON, Feb. 11, 1813.

"GENTLEMEN,—I have received your communication in behalf of the naturalized citizens in and near Philadelphia, who were born within the British dominions; occasioned by the proclamation of the Prince Regent of Great Britain, dated the 26th of October last, and by other indications of a purpose of subjecting to the penalties of British law, such of that description of citizens as shall have been taken in arms against Great Britain.

"As the British laws and practice confer all the rights and immunities of natural-born subjects on aliens serving even a short period on board British vessels, it might have been concluded that an intention would have been neither formed nor proclaimed, by the head of that nation, which is as inconsistent with its own example as it is repugnant to reason and humanity.

" The rights of naturalized citizens being under the same guaranty of the national faith and honor with the rights of other citizens, the former may be assured that it is the determination, as it will be the duty, of the executive department of the government, to employ whatever just means may be within its competency, for enforcing the respect which is due from the enemy to the rights and persons of those who combat under the banners, and in defence and maintenance of the rights and safety, of their adopted country.

" Accept my friendly respects.

"JAMES MADISON.*

" To JOHN BINNS,
WILLIAM SMILEY,
JOHN W. THOMPSON,
FRANCIS MITCHELL,
JOHN MAITLAND,
GEORGE PALMER,
} Esq'rs."

The decided tone of Mr. Madison's letter tended, in a great measure, to save the lives of many Irish-born officers and men, then in the British prisons at Quebec and Halifax.

The most painful part of the campaign of 1814 was the success of General Ross, who, in August, landed at Benedict, marched on, and burned Washington, and finally fell, by the hand of a patriotic boy, near Baltimore, after having taken and sacked that city.

But the theatre of the closing campaign was now shifted to the Mississippi. On the first of December, 1814, Andrew Jackson, commander-in-chief of the seventh military division of the United States, arrived at New Orleans. This distinguished man was then in the forty-seventh year of his age, and had already acquired a bril-

* Printed from the autograph, presented to the author by Mr. Binns.

liant reputation.   Born in the Waxhaw settlement, of
Irish parents, at thirteen he had fought and been wounded
in the Revolutionary contest.   His mother, an extraordinary woman, had died, a victim to her charity, in attending the prisoners of war, in the prison-ship at Charleston;
his father died when he was a child, and both his brothers
had fallen bravely in battle.   At man's age he removed
to Tennessee, with Judge McCay, and had filled successively the offices of representative, senator, judge of the
Supreme Court, and major general of militia.

His military reputation was founded on a succession
of meritorious actions.   He had subdued the Creek
nation, chased their British and Spanish allies into
Florida, captured Pensacola, and given his eagles air
from the towers of Saint Augustine and Saint Mark.
With jealousy at Washington, and even at home, without
a commissariat, or treasure, he had carried his brave
westerns through swamps, wildernesses, and prairies, had
headed them in assaulting the savage warrior's ambush,
and the civilized soldier's cannon-guarded fortress.
Hitherto, glory had been his shadow, as danger had been
his attraction, and patriotism almost his sole resource.

In his Indian wars, Jackson had bred up Carroll, Coffee,
Higgins, Armstrong, Donaldson, and other officers, some
of whom were connected with him by family ties, and all
by affection.*   The greater part of these brave men were
with him at New Orleans.

He found that important city almost naked of defences.
The state militia, the regulars withdrawn from Florida,
the volunteers from Tennessee, Mississippi, and Kentucky, gave him the command of some 6,000 men, while
Packenham (having effected a landing on the 22nd of
December) had halted within seven miles of the city, at
the head of 14,000, the flower of the old Peninsular army.

The following is a description of the battle of the 23rd

* In his despatch to Major General Pinckney, containing the account of the
battle of Emuckfaw, 27th March, 1814, Jackson alludes to an Irish pioneer.
"The militia of the venerable General Doherty's brigade, (acted) in the
charge, with a vivacity and firmness which would have done honor to regulars."—Eaton's Life of Jackson, p. 85.

December, as detailed to President Monroe by General Jackson himself.

"The loss of our gun-boats near the pass of the Rigolets having given the enemy command of Lake Borgne, he was enabled to choose his point of attack. It became, therefore, an object of importance to obstruct the numerous bayous and canals leading from that lake to the highlands on the Mississippi. This important service was committed, in the first instance, to a detachment of the seventh regiment; afterwards to Col. De Laronde, of the Louisiana militia, and, lastly, to make all sure to Major General Villere, commanding the district between the river and the lakes, and who, being a native of the country, was presumed to be best acquainted with all those passes. Unfortunately, however, a picquet which the general had established at the mouth of the Bayou Bienvenue, and which, notwithstanding my orders, had been left unobstructed, was completely surprised, and the enemy penetrated through a canal leading to a farm, about two leagues below the city, and succeeded in cutting off a company of militia stationed there. This intelligence was communicated to me about twelve o'clock of the twenty-third. My force, at this time, consisted of parts of the seventh and forty-fourth regiments, not exceeding six hundred together, the city militia, a part of General Coffee's brigade of mounted gunmen, and the detached militia from the western division of Tennessee, under the command of Major General Carroll. These two last corps were stationed four miles above the city. Apprehending a double attack by the way of Chief-Menteur, I left General Carroll's force and the militia of the city posted on the Gentilly road; and at five o'clock, P. M., marched to meet the enemy, whom I was resolved to attack in his first position, with Major Hinds' dragoons, General Coffee's brigade, parts of the seventh and forty-fourth regiments, the uniformed companies of militia, under the command of Major Planche, two hundred men of color, chiefly from St. Domingo, raised by Colonel Savary, and under the command of Major Dagwin, and a detachment of artillery under the direction of Colonel M'Rhea, with two six-pounders, under the command of Lieutenant Spotts ; not exceeding, in all, fifteen hundred. I arrived near the enemy's encampment about seven, and immediately made my dispositions for the attack. His forces, amounting at that time on land to about three thousand, extended half a mile on that river, and in the rear nearly to the wood. General Coffee was ordered to turn their right, while with the residue of the force I attacked his strongest position on the left, near the river. Commodore Patterson, having dropped down the river in the schooner Caroline, was directed to open a fire upon their camp, which he executed at about half past seven. This being a signal of attack, General Coffee's men, with their usual impetuosity, rushed on the enemy's right, and entered their camp, while our right advanced with equal ardor. There can be but little doubt that we should have succeeded on that occasion, with our inferior force, in destroying or capturing the enemy, had not a thick fog, which arose about eight o'clock, occasioned some confusion among the different corps. Fearing the consequence, under this circumstance, of the further prosecution of a night attack, with troops then acting together for the first time, I contented myself with lying on the field that night ; and at four in the morning assumed a stronger position, about two miles nearer the city. At this position I remained encamped, waiting the arrival of the Kentucky militia and other reinforcements. As the safety of the city will depend on the fate of this army, it must not be incautiously exposed.

"In this affair the whole corps under my command deserve the greatest credit. The best compliment I can pay to General Coffee and his brigade, is to say, they have behaved as they have always done while under my command. The seventh, led by Major Pierre, and forty-fourth, commanded by Colonel Ross, distinguished themselves. The battalion of city militia, commanded by Major Planche, realized my anticipations, and behaved like veterans. Savary's volunteers manifested great

bravery; and the company of city riflemen, having
penetrated into the midst of the enemy's camp, were
surrounded, and fought their way out with the greatest
heroism, bringing with them a number of prisoners. The
two field-pieces were well served by the officers commanding them.

"All my officers in the line did their duty, and I have
every reason to be satisfied with the whole of my field
and staff. Colonels Butler and Platt, and Major Chotard,
by their intrepidity, saved the artillery. Colonel Haynes
was everywhere that duty or danger called. I was deprived of the services of one of my aids, Captain Butler,
whom I was obliged to station, to his great regret, in
town. Captain Reid, my other aid, and Messrs. Livingston, Duplissis, and Davezac, who had volunteered their
services, faced danger wherever it was to be met, and
carried my orders with the utmost promptitude.

"We made one major, two subalterns, and sixty-three
privates, prisoners; and the enemy's loss, in killed and
wounded, must have been at least ———. My own loss I
have not as yet been able to ascertain with exactness, but
suppose it to amount to one hundred in killed, wounded,
and missing. Among the former, I have to lament the
loss of Colonel Lauderdale, of General Coffee's brigade,
who fell while bravely fighting. Cols. Dyer and Gibson,
of the same corps, were wounded, and Major Kavenaugh
taken prisoner.

"Col. De Laronde, Major Villere, of the Louisiana
militia, Major Latour of Engineers, having no command,
volunteered their services, as did Drs. Kerr and Hood,
and were of great assistance to me."

On the 28th December, and 1st of January, the enemy
again stormed his cotton breast-works, and were again
repulsed. On the 8th the memorable battle was fought,
which established a second time, American Independence.

" On the seventh, a general movement and bustle in the
British camp indicated that the contemplated attack was
about to be made. Everything in the American encampment was ready for action, when, at day-break, on the

10

morning of the memorable eighth, a shower of rockets
from the enemy gave the signal of battle. A detachment
of the enemy, under Colonel Thornton, proceeded to attack the works on the right bank of the river, while
General Pakenham with his whole force, exceeding
twelve thousand men, moved in two divisions under
Generals Gibbs and Kean, and a reserve under General
Lambert. Both divisions were supplied with scaling-
ladders and fascines, and General Gibbs had directions to
make the principal attack. Nothing could exceed the
imposing grandeur of the scene. The whole British
force advanced with much deliberation, in solid columns,
over the even surface of the plain in front of the American intrenchments, bearing with them, in addition to their
arms, their fascines and ladders for storming the American
works. All was hushed in awful stillness throughout the
American lines; each soldier grasped his arms with a
fixedness of purpose, which told his firm resolve to ' do
or die;' till the enemy approached within reach of the
batteries, which opened upon them an incessant and
destructive tide of death. They continued, however, to
advance with the greatest firmness, closing up their lines
as they were opened by the fire of the Americans, till
they approached within reach of the musketry and rifles;
these, in addition to the artillery, produced the most
terrible havoc in their ranks, and threw them into the
greatest confusion. Twice were they driven back with
immense slaughter, and twice they formed again and renewed the assault. But the fire of the Americans was
tremendous; it was unparalleled in the annals of deadly
doing; it was one continued blaze of destruction, before
which men could not stand and live. Every discharge
swept away the British columns like an inundation—they
could not withstand it, but fled in consternation and dis-
may. Vigorous were the attempts of their officers to
rally them; General Pakenham, in the attempt, received
a shot, and fell upon the field. Generals Gibbs and Kean
succeeded, and attempted again to push on their columns
to the attack, but a still more dreadful fatality met them

from the thunders of the American batteries.   A third unavailing attempt was made to rally their troops by their officers, but the same destruction met them.   The gallantry of the British officers, on this desperate day, was deserving of a worthier cause, and better fate.   General Gibbs fell mortally, and General Kean desperately wounded, and were borne from the field of action.   The discomfiture of the enemy was now complete; a few only of the platoons reached the ditch, there to meet more certain death.   The remainder fled from the field with the greatest precipitancy, and no further efforts were made to rally them.   The intervening plain between the American and British fortifications was covered with the dead; taking into view the length of time and the numbers engaged, the annals of bloody strife, it is believed, furnish no parallel to the dreadful carnage of this battle.   Two thousand, at the lowest estimate, fell, besides a considerable number wounded.   The loss of the Americans did not exceed seven killed and six wounded. General Lambert was the only superior officer left on the field; being unable to check the flight of the British columns, he retreated to his encampment.

" The entire destruction of the enemy's army would have been now inevitable, had it not been for an unfortunate occurrence, which at this moment took place on the other side of the river.   General Pakenham had thrown over in his boats, upon that side of the stream, a considerable force, under the command of Colonel Thornton, simultaneously with his advance upon the main body of the American works.   They succeeded in landing at the point of their destination, and advanced to assault the intrenchment defended by General Morgan.   Their reception was not such as might have been expected, from the known courage and firmness of the troops under his command; at a moment, when the same fate that met their fellows on the opposite side of the river was looked for, with a confidence approaching to a certainty, the American right, believing itself to be outflanked, or for some other reason never satisfactorily explained, relin quished its position, while the left, with the batteries of Commodore Patterson, maintained their ground for some time with much gallantry and spirit, till at length, finding themselves deserted by their friends on the right, and greatly outnumbered by the enemy, they were compelled to spike their guns and retreat.

"This unfortunate result totally changed the aspect of affairs. The enemy were now in occupation of a position from which they might annoy the Americans with little hazard to themselves, and by means of which they might have been enabled to defeat, in a very considerable degree, the effects of the success of our arms on the other side of the river. It therefore became an object of the first consequence with General Jackson, to dislodge him as soon as possible. For this object, all the means in his power, which he could use with any safety, were put into immediate requisition."

But, under cover of the night, the enemy, totally disheartened, retreated silently to his ships, and sailed sorrowfully from the place of his punishment, the much-coveted Mississippi. The British loss, in officers and men, was about 5,000, including their general-in-chief; the American loss less than 300.

Well might William Cobbett read a lesson to the British oligarchy from the battle of New Orleans! Well might he exult over the punishment which had fallen upon them, from this " son of poor Irish emigrant parents."*

While at New Orleans, Jackson received news of the ratification of the Treaty of Ghent, and the new-made peace consequent thereon.

* Cobbett's Life of Andrew Jackson. This biting pamphlet was intended to be a vehicle of Cobbett's radicalism, on the questions of the day in Great Britain. It is conceived in a very angry spirit, but executed with great ability. See the Dedication to " The People of Ireland."

CHAPTER XVI.

JACKSON, PRESIDENT — UNITED STATES BANK — "THE IRISH VOTE" — EDWARD KAVANAGH, MINISTER TO PORTUGAL — SENATOR PORTER — JACKSON'S PARTIALITY TO IRISH EMIGRANTS — HIS INFLUENCE ON HIS PARTY — HIS CHARACTER.

By the victory of New Orleans, Jackson had saved the valley of the Mississippi; by the Seminole war of 1817 and 1818, he added the Floridas to "the area of liberty." His native state, as a proof of its confidence, sent him to the Senate, and, in 1824, a great portion of the Democratic party voted for him as President. Two hundred and seventy-one electoral votes were divided between four candidates, thus: — Jackson had ninety-nine; John Quincy Adams eighty-four; W. H. Crawford forty-one, and Henry Clay thirty-seven. The decision, therefore, went to the House of Representatives, who, through some motive, passed over the popular candidate, and elected Mr. Adams President.

In 1825, the Legislature of Tennessee, on motion of Mr. Kennedy, nominated Jackson again for the presidency, and, in 1828, he was chosen by a large majority.

With the eight years' administration of this eminent President, we have in this work little to do. The great action of his civil life was the abolition of the United States Bank, — an institution which threatened to become to our government the *imperium in imperio,* which the Bank of England is in the government of England. All men, at this day, seem to bear testimony to the wisdom of Jackson, in that perilous encounter with the incorporated capital of the Union, — an encounter in which he was assailed with defamation, treachery, faction, and even by the assassin's hand. But Providence preserved him through all; and those who hated him unsparingly in

10*

life, have, of late, been offering repentant prayers upon his grave.

In both presidential contests, the general was enthusiastically sustained by "the Irish vote." Apart from his kindred origin, his military characteristics and thorough democracy secured their suffrages. His surviving friends often repeat that he considered that vote ar essential element of American democracy.

Of the various men, of Irish origin, who found important employments under Jackson's administration, Edward Kavanagh, of Maine, was the most noted. He was of that Leinster house which has given so many distinguished public men to continental Europe.* He had been a state senator and acting governor of Maine. A man of strong Irish and Catholic tendencies, and, at the same time, an ardent Jacksonian. Him, the President sent minister to Portugal, where he gave unbroken satisfaction to his own and the native government. He was a man of refined tastes, and, on his return from Lisbon, brought over an excellent collection of Spanish and Portuguese literature, with which he enriched various institutions and libraries.† He died at his residence at Damariscotta, in 1842, at an advanced age.

During the greater part of Jackson's presidency, Mr. Clay was the leader of the Whig opposition. The unrivalled parliamentary powers of that famous leader would have shaken almost any other man ; but Jackson was incorporated into the very being of the American people, and could not be separated from them. Still, a numerous and formidable party obeyed the banner of Clay, and among these, Senator Porter, of Louisiana, was one of the most devoted and most able, during Jackson's

---

* Within a century it could count, in Europe, an Aulic Councillor, a Governor of Prague, and a Field Marshal Kavanagh, at Vienna ; a Field Marshal in Poland ; a Grand Chamberlain in Saxony ; a Count of the Holy Roman Empire ; a French Conventionist of 1793, Godefroi Cavaignac, co-editor with Armand Carrell, and Eugene Cavaignac, some time Dictator, in France.

† A portion of his collection enriches the library of the Jesuit College, at Worcester, Mass.

second presidency. This gentleman was the son of the Rev. Wm. Porter, pastor of Grey Abbey, Newtownards, county Down, who was executed at the door of his own church, for treason, in 1798. His orphan son came with an uncle to the United States; but we shall let the friends who mourned his death, record his life.

On the second of February, 1841, his death was announced, by Messrs. Barrow and Benton, in the United States Senate. They furnished this account of his useful and interesting career.

Mr. Benton, of Missouri, said : —

" I am the oldest personal friend whom the illustrious deceased can have upon this floor, and amongst the oldest whom he can have in the United States. It is now, sir, more than the period of a generation, — more than the third of a century, — since the then emigrant Irish boy, Alexander Porter, and myself met on the banks of the Cumberland River, at Nashville, in the state of Tennessee, when commenced a friendship which death only dissolved on his part. We belonged to a circle of young lawyers and students at law, who had the world before them, and nothing but their exertions to depend upon. First a clerk in his uncle's store, then a student at law, and always a lover of books, the young Porter was one of that circle, and it was the custom of all that belonged to it to spend their leisure hours in the delightful occupation of reading. History, poetry, elocution, biography, the ennobling speeches of the living and the dead, were our social recreation ; and the youngest member of our circle was one of our favorite readers. He read well, because he comprehended clearly, felt strongly, remarked beautifully upon striking passages, and gave a new charm to the whole with his rich, mellifluous Irish accent. It was then that I became acquainted with Ireland and her children, read the ample story of her wrongs, learnt the long list of her martyred patriots' names, sympathized in their fate, and imbibed the feelings for a noble and oppressed people, which the extinction of my own life can alone extinguish.

"Time and events dispersed that circle. The young Porter, his law license signed, went to the Lower Mississippi; I to the Upper. And, years afterwards, we met on this floor, senators from different parts of that vast Louisiana, which was not even a part of the American Union at the time that he and I were born. We met here in the session of 1833, '34, — high party times, and on opposite sides of the great party line; but we met as we had parted years before. We met as friends, and though often our part to reply to each other in the ardent debate, yet never did we do it with other feelings than those with which we were wont to discuss our subjects of recreation on the banks of the Cumberland.

"Alexander Porter, — a lad of tender age, — an orphan, with a widowed mother and young children, — the father martyred in the cause of freedom, — an exile before he was ten years old, — an ocean to be crossed, and a strange land to be seen, and a wilderness of a thousand miles to be penetrated, before he could find a resting-place for the sole of his foot. Then, education to be acquired, support to be earned, and even citizenship to be gained, before he could make his own talents available to his support: conquering all these difficulties by his own exertions, and the aid of an affectionate uncle, Mr. Alexander Porter, sen., merchant of Nashville, he soon attained every earthly object, either brilliant or substantial, for which we live and struggle in this life. Honors, fortune, friends; the highest professional and political distinction; long a supreme judge in his adopted state; twice a senator in the Congress of the United States; wearing all his honors fresh and growing to the last moment of his life, — and the announcement of his death followed by the adjournment of the two Houses of the American Congress! What a noble and crowning conclusion to a beginning so humble, and so apparently hopeless!

"Our deceased brother was not an American citizen by the accident of birth; he became so by the choice of his own will and by the operation of our laws. The

events of his life, and the business of this day, show this
title to citizenship to be as valid in our America as it was
in the great republic of antiquity. I borrow the thought
of Cicero, in his pleading for the poet Archias, when I
place the citizen who becomes so by law and choice, on
an equal footing with the citizen who becomes so by
chance. And, in the instance now before us, we may say
that our adopted citizen has repaid us for the liberality of
our laws, that he has added to the stock of our national
character by the contributions which he has brought to it,
in the purity of his private life, the eminence of his public services, the ardor of his patriotism, and the elegant
productions of his mind.

"A few years ago, and after he had obtained great
honor and fortune in this country, he returned on a visit
to his native land, and to the continent of Europe. It
was an occasion of honest exultation for the orphan im-
migrant boy to return to the land of his fathers, rich in
the goods of this life, and clothed with the honors of the
American Senate. But the visit was a melancholy one
to him. His soul sickened at the state of his fellow-
men in the old world, (I had it from his own lips,) and
he returned from that visit with stronger feelings than
ever in favor of his adopted country."

Senator Barrow thus described his deceased colleague:

"Judge Porter was born in the land of Curran, and
his father was a contemporary and friend of that brilliant
orator and incorruptible patriot. The father of Judge
Porter was a man of piety and classical education, and
was by profession a minister of the gospel; but the fire
of patriotism and the love of liberty glowed so warmly
in his bosom, that he threw aside the sacerdotal robe and
put on the burnished armor of a soldier, and resolved to
conquer or die in defence of his country's freedom. History informs us what was the result of the patriotic
attempt, made in 1798, by some of the purest and most
gifted sons of Ireland, to emancipate her from the thral-
dom of England; and, from the pages of the same history, we learn that the father of Judge Porter fell a

martyr in the cause of freedom, and was executed as a
rebel. Judge Porter thus became in early life fatherless
and without a home, and he was forced to abandon his
own, his native land, and seek refuge in a land of stran-
gers. To this country, the asylum of the oppressed of
all nations, Judge Porter, in company with his widowed
mother and a younger brother, emigrated and settled in
Nashville, Tennessee, amongst whose generous citizens
he found many ready to comfort the widow and protect
the fatherless.

"In a few years, while thus laboring for his own and a
widowed mother's support, he not only extended the
sphere of his general knowledge, but he laid the
broad and deep foundation of that legal learning which
was the pride and ornament of his matured age, and which
will transmit his name to the latest posterity, as one of
the brightest judicial lights of this age. At this period
of his life we find Judge Porter once more seeking a
new home; and about the year 1809 he removed from
Nashville to the Territory of Orleans, and settled in the
parish of Attakapas, where he lived and died, loved and
admired for his many private virtues, and honored for his
talents and public services.

"The first high station of trust in which we find him
placed by the confidence of the people among whom he
had settled, is in the convention of 1812, to form a constitution for the Territory of Orleans. In that body,
which numbered the ablest men of the territory, Judge
Porter soon acquired a reputation for integrity, learning,
and statesmanship, which placed him at once most conspicuously before the people; and he was, not long after
that period, elevated to the Supreme Court Bench of the
State of Louisiana, which station he occupied for about
fifteen years.

"It was in that office that Judge Porter rendered services to the people of Louisiana above all appreciation,
and acquired for himself a reputation as imperishable as
the civil law itself. The opinions which he delivered dis-
play a depth of learning, a power of analysis, a force of

reasoning, and a comprehensiveness and accuracy of judgment, which justly entitle him to a niche in the temple of Fame, in juxtaposition with even the great, the pure, the immortal Marshall."

This is the language of eulogy, but it contains the evidence of being founded in truth.

Jackson had a natural, but not a blind, partiality for his race. His personal attendants were nearly all natives of Ireland, and he would condescend to reason, advise, and exhort them, as if they were his own family. Many instances of his thoughtfulness, in this regard, have been related to us, by living witnesses of the facts.*

In 1836, Andrew Jackson retired to his "Hermitage," where nine years of peaceful repose, broken only by the pains incident to age, were granted him. He had bequeathed his party influence to Van Buren; and though for a time the Democratic succession was disturbed, he saw it restored before his death, in the elevation of Mr. Polk to the presidency in 1844. He had the gratification to see a vote of Congress, censuring his military conduct in Florida, and the fine imposed in New Orleans, for declaring martial law in 1815, rescinded and refunded. His principles and policy were everywhere spread, and successful; and it would have been no illusion of self-love for him to believe that, next to Thomas Jefferson, he had done most to form a national policy for the Union, acceptable, in the main, to every American.

* We have perused a most kind and characteristic letter from the General to Mr. Maher, the public gardener at Washington, on the death of his children. It is conceived in the most fraternal and cordial spirit of sympathy.

Jackson's man-servant, Jemmy O'Neil, alas! no more, was once in the circle of our acquaintance. Before the days of Father Mathew, poor Jemmy was given to sacrifice too freely to Bacchus, and on those occasions assumed rather a troublesome control over all visitors and dwellers in the "White House." After many complaints, Jackson decided to dismiss him, and sent for him accordingly.

Jackson. Jemmy, you and I must part.

Jemmy. Why so, General?

Jackson. Every one complains of you.

Jemmy. And do you believe them, General?

Jackson. Of course, — what every one says must be true.

Jemmy. Well, now, General, I've heard twice as much said against you and I never would believe a word of it! (*Exit Jackson.*)

The character of Jackson will be an historical study
for a thousand years. His is one of those angular out-
lines which almost defy time to make them commonplace. Like Sixtus Quintus, Columbus, and Cromwell,
much reflection upon him does not beget the sense of
dimness, but of substantiality. We have blood and bone
in every incident of his life and every word he has uttered. Truly has it been said, " he was one of the sin-
cerest of men." Philosophers might be puzzled at the
rigid sequence of his life and language, did they not know
that there are some natures which, founded upon certain
radical principles, can only live a life of unity, or of
madness. Jackson could never have been inconsistent,
unless he had gone insane.

American national character has, since his day, par-
taken equally of Jackson and of Franklin. The Quaker
thrift, the proverbial calculation remains, but with it is
mingled a strange and potent elemental ardor, a desire
of territory, a sense of power, and a Spartan audacity,
unknown to the revolutionary generation. The Virginian presidents had the manners of courts and the discipline of English Benchers. The man of the west, tough
as the hickory trees through which he so often marched,
was as natural in his style, habits, and wants, as any
hunter of the prairies. When the " White House" was
threatened with a mob, he dismissed the naval and military officers, who volunteered their guard, loaded his own
and his nephew's rifle, and, so prepared, the President of
the United States awaited his foes in the executive man-
sion. He would not use a sheet of the public paper; he
allowed no lackeys to attend on his person. In small
things, and in great, he was singular among great men;
but all his singularities, when compiled, will be found to
constitute a grand, original, and compact soldier-states-
man.

CHAPTER XVII.

SPREAD OF CATHOLICISM — ORGANIZATION INTO DIOCESES — WESTERN MISSIONS — SOUTHERN MISSIONS — BISHOP ENGLAND — CHARLESTOWN CONVENT BURNED, A. D. 1834 — THE GREAT CONTROVERSY.

THE United States constitution had swept away all dis abilities on conscience, and, though prejudice remained, open persecution was seen in the land no more. New missions were formed, seminaries were opened, and many additional churches were begun. From the year 1790 onwards, the chief supply of the American mission was from France and Ireland. In 1796, Catholicism in the east gained a treasure, in the person of Mr. Cheverus, afterwards Cardinal in France. The first Catholic congregation in Boston had been collected by the Abbe la Poitre, a French chaplain, during the revolutionary war, who procured a temporary church in School street. Dr. Cheverus, not confining himself to the city, traversed New England, from the Housatonic to the Penobscot. He learned English, and even the Indian dialects, to make his mission understood. He travelled from house to house, in Boston, personally visiting his flock. Prejudice had no fortress against him, labor no terrors ; the plague itself saw him harmless from its worst haunts. He is justly revered as one of the fathers of the American Church ; and, truly, those who knew him, — even those deaf to his doctrine, — admit that he led the life of an apostle, worthy of the Cross.

In April, 1808, Pope Pius VII. issued his Bull, erecting Baltimore into an Archbishopric,* and fixing four Sees at Bardstown, Philadelphia, New York, and Boston.

* On the 31st of May, 1821, the Cathedral of Baltimore, the building of which had been begun in 1806, suspended during the war, and re-commenced in 1817, was consecrated. The form is that of a cross ; its length, 166 feet ; breadth, 77 feet ; and across the transept, 115 feet. It yet wants

11

The Rev. Messrs. Flaget, Concanen, Egan, and Cheverus, were consecrated to the several Sees. Thus, of the original *five* who made the Hierarchy of the Union, France contributed two and Ireland three.

About the year 1800, the Catholic missions began to be formed beyond the Ohio, and in a few years became both numerous and important. The accession of Louisiana to the Union, in Jefferson's presidency, extended the field of Catholic missions, and still further strengthened the church in the south-west. The diocese of Arkansas, and arch-diocese of St. Louis, are recent creations.

In 1791, the mission of Charleston was founded. " In that year, a number of individuals of that communion, chiefly natives of Ireland, associated together for public worship, chose a vestry, and put themselves under the care of Bishop Carroll, of Baltimore. The Rev. Dr. Keating officiated as their minister. The troubles in France and the West Indies soon brought a large accession to their number. Under the auspices of the learned and eloquent Dr. Gallagher, they have built, organized, and obtained incorporation for a respectable church in Charleston."*

To the government of that southern mission was ordained, in the year 1820, the most powerful intellect which had yet ministered at the altar in America. The generation of apostles had passed, — the confessors had now come ; and Dr. England stands, unquestionably, the foremost of the band, whether we look for natural parts, solid learning, rigid self-denial, or unmitigated labor.

Bishop John England was born in Cork city, on the 23d of September, 1786. Educated and ordained at Carlow College, he returned to his native city in 1808. For twelve years he labored there without ceasing. He

the portico on the western front; but through the exertions of an association formed for the purpose, it has been surrounded by a handsome iron railing, and a sexton's lodge has been erected.

* Ramsay's South Carolina, vol. ii., p. 37. This passage was probably written about the year 1796 or 7, and consequently shows that Dr. Gallagher was the precursor of Dr. England.

originated a circulating library, started and edited the "Religious Repository," a monthly magazine, contributed to the "Cork Chronicle," the patriotic organ, lectured three or four times a week at the Cathedral, and yet attended to all the daily personal duties of the mission. One need not wonder if, after twelve years of such labors, his departure from Cork was lamented, by all denominations, as a calamity to the city. On the last day of 1820, he arrived at Charleston, having been consecrated at Cork, the previous September, by the Rt. Rev. Dr. Murphy, assisted by the Bishops of Ossory and Richmond.

The states of North and South Carolina and Georgia, as subsequently the Vicariate of Hayti, were placed under his episcopal jurisdiction. Surveying the ground he was to govern, the indomitable spirit of the great bishop found difficulties enough for the most heroic to face. The variety and extent of his first labors are indicated by a congenial biographer in the following passages : —

"But the herald of the Cross had been 'anointed' to the holy mission 'with the oil of gladness above his fellows!' The enlightened and accomplished citizens of the south were seen crowding around his pulpit, delighted by his eloquence, abashed by his learning, astonished by his logic, — ready to exclaim with him of old, 'Almost thou persuadest!' Churches, temporary in material, and slight in structure, it is true, but suitable for the exigency, rose around him like exhalations. A constitution was formed, and the diocese incorporated by legal charter, which, while it reserved to the bishop all powers essential to discipline, and repressive to schism, guaranteed ecclesiastic property to its legitimate destination, against the possible lapse of himself or his successors ; and, by introducing the principle of public and strict accountability into the management of ecclesiastical revenues, assured to him the confidence of a people proverbially jealous on all subjects connected with the purse.

"His first and greatest want was that of a popular clergy. His diocese, like most poor and thinly-peopled ones, had been a city of refuge to outcasts from others. Men of talent and merit were of eager request, where not only greater temporal advantages, but ampler opportunities to do good, invited them. His sad experience, too, with some valuable co-laborers, whom zeal of martyrdom, or attachment to his person, attracted to that insidious climate, convinced him of the necessity of educating a native clergy, or at least one composed of such as long and early acclimation might seem to ensure against being cut off in the midst of their usefulness. He attached, also, the utmost importance to what might be called the 'naturalization' of Catholicity. He desired that it should no longer be regarded as the religion of the stranger ; but that its ministers should be American, in principle, feeling, and habit, — familiarized, by long experience, with all the practical workings of our political system.

"With these views he founded a seminary. But how, in the destitution of pecuniary means, was it to be supported ? His rapid observation detected the languishing state of rudimentary education. He incorporated a classical and scientific academy with his diocesan seminary, united in his own person the schoolmaster and doctor of divinity, and his embryo theologians were subsisted by the very means that consigned his father to a jail. He was emphatically the restorer of classical learning in Charleston.* His appeals excited direct interest in the subject among the most influential citizens. Sectarian jealousy was awakened, rival institutions were built up to preserve ingenuous youth from ' the snares of Popery ;' and thus, whether ' out of envy and contention,' or ' for good will,' a great public want was supplied. It remains to be felt by the wealthy planters, who subscribed their thousands with unsparing hand to subvert the seminary, that would long ere now have supplied their country with priests, whether they did wisely in retarding the progress of a religion which some of them are now beginning to appreciate, as the only one to which they can entrust the fidelity and happiness of their slaves.

* Southern Review, No. 1.

"But the bishop's comprehensive forecast was not limited to projects connected exclusively with his own immediate objects. He infused new life, by his energy, into the Philosophical and Literary Association, of which he continued till death an honored and useful member; applying his unrivalled powers to instruct and please, as happily to the subjects of scientific or critical contemplation, as to the more accustomed topics of his sacred calling; but ever aiming to hallow his intellectual offering, and direct the attention of his delighted auditory, from the wonders of nature or the beautiful creations of mind, to the 'Author of every good and perfect gift.'

"He witnessed with grief and horror the Moloch ravages of that misnamed spirit of honor that so often carries desolation to the bosom of southern society; quenching in the blood of its victim the hopes of an admiring country or of domestic affection. He rallied about him the chivalry of Carolina, in an Anti-Duelling Society, of which General Thomas Pinckney, of revolutionary fame, was the venerated president; and, through his own personal activity, backed by the moral influence of that association, many hostile meetings were prevented, and valuable lives most probably preserved. I have listened to him, as with merry triumph, and unsparing but playful ridicule, he has talked over, with a gallant officer, their counter manœuvres, on one most interesting occasion, and rejoiced over his opponent's baffled love of mischief.

"He found the Catholic body in America defenceless. The secular press was in the hands of persons so utterly enslaved by the delusion of that great conspiracy against truth, the history and literature of England for the last three centuries, that writers were often unconscious of giving offence, while promulgating the most injurious misstatements or senseless absurdities. Of the journals professedly religious it is unnecessary to speak. He established the " United States Catholic Miscellany," and found time, amidst his immense and various occupations, to supply its columns with a vast amount of original matter, not always, perhaps, as perfect in literary polish, as

11*

if he had read over the blotted manuscript before it was hurried to the printer ; but always resistless in reasoning, charming by its fervid eloquence, overwhelming with its accumulated erudition.　Many of those essays, which the importance of the subjects discussed induced him to extend through a series of numbers, have been collected in such guise as poverty compelled them to wear, — like the hero of the Odyssey in rags at the palace-gate, — but a wider circulation will yet be given them, and future generations look with gratitude and delight on the fulfilment of the modest pledge that announced them to the world :" —

The *Miscellany* was announced to contain —

" ' The simple explanation and temperate maintenance of the doctrine of the Roman Catholic Church ; in exhibiting which, its conductors are led to hope that many sensible persons will be astonished at finding they have imputed to Catholics, doctrines which the Catholic Church has formally condemned, and imagining they were contradicting Catholics, when they held Catholic doctrine themselves.' "*

For two and twenty years, Dr. England was spared to the church in the south.　In all these years he was the prime legislator of his order.　He was "the author of the Provincial Councils," which assemble annually at Baltimore.†　He was almost the first to give to Catholicity a literature and a *status* in the United States.　His various writings on the doctrines of the church, on the institution of slavery, on historical and philosophical subjects, fill five large volumes, which must ever remain among the most precious legacies of the American Church.

On the 11th of April, 1842, the bishop expired, at Charleston.　The chief journals and statesmen of the south rendered spontaneous homage to his memory.　All admitted that " the mighty man, who had served the people," was fallen.　Far and wide as the church has extended since his death, — distinguished as are many

---

* Reid's Memoir, in Dr. England's Works, vol. i., pp. 12, 13. † Ibid., p. 17

of its prelates at the time we write, — there has not
arisen his equal. Such men are not often given to earth,
and the earth should therefore be doubly careful of them,
while she has them.

During the life-time of Bishop England, the most
painful circumstance occurred, of the burning of the Convent, founded in 1820, by Bishop Fenwick, at Charlestown,
Mass. New England, an uncongenial land for convents,
had been shocked by the founding of a house of Ursu-
lines in the near neighborhood of Bunker's Hill. On
Sunday, August 10th, 1834, Rev. Dr. Beecher delivered
three philippics, in three different churches, against the
institution, — a course in which he had many imitators.
Rumors were also artfully circulated of a young lady
being immured in a dungeon of the convent. On Monday night, August 11th, tar barrels were lighted near the
house, by a group of incendiaries, who were soon joined
by a tumultuous crowd from Charlestown and Boston.
The details of this burglary and sacrilege are set forth
by a sub-committee of citizens of Boston, (who gave
several weeks to the investigation,) in the following
report : —

"At the time of this attack upon the convent, there
were within its walls about sixty female children, and ten
adults, one of whom was in the last stages of pulmonary
consumption, another suffering under convulsion fits, and
the unhappy female who had been the immediate cause
of the excitement was, by the agitation of the night, in
raving delirium.

"No warning was giving of the intended assault, nor
could the miscreants by whom it was made have known
whether their missiles might not kill or wound the help-
less inmates of this devoted dwelling. Fortunately for
them, cowardice prompted what mercy and manhood
denied. After the first attack, the assailants paused
awhile, from the fear that some secret force was concealed in the convent, or in ambush to surprise them;
and in this interval the governess was enabled to secure
the retreat of her little flock and terrified sisters into the

garden. But before this was fully effected, the rioters, finding they had nothing but women and children to contend against, regained their courage, and, ere all the inmates could escape, entered the building.

"It appears that, during these proceedings, the magistrate above referred to, with another of the selectmen, had arrived, and entered the convent with the rioters, for the purpose, as they state, of assisting its inmates. The mob had now full possession of the house, and loud cries were heard for torches or lights. One of the magistrates in question availed himself of this cry to deter the rioters from firing the building, by stating that if lights were brought they might be detected.

"Three or four torches, which were, or precisely resembled, engine torches, were then brought up from the road ; and immediately upon their arrival, the rioters proceeded into every room in the building, rifling every drawer, desk, and trunk, which they found, and breaking up and destroying all the furniture, and casting much of it from the windows ; sacrificing, in their brutal fury, costly piano-fortes, and harps, and other valuable instruments, the little treasures of the children, abandoned in their hasty flight, and even the vessels and symbols of Christian worship.

"After having thus ransacked every room in the building, they proceeded, with great deliberation, about one o'clock, to make preparations for setting fire to it. For this purpose, broken furniture, books, curtains, and other combustible materials, were placed in the centre of several of the rooms ; and, as if in mockery of God as well as of man, the Bible was cast, with shouts of exultation, upon the pile first kindled ; and as upon this were subsequently thrown the vestments used in religious service, and the ornaments of the altar, these shouts and yells were repeated. Nor did they cease until the cross was wrenched from its place and cast into the flames, as the final triumph of this fiendlike enterprise.

"But the work of destruction did not end here. Soon after the convent was in flames, the rioters passed on to the library, or bishop's lodge, which stood near, and, after throwing the books and pictures from the windows, a prey to those without, fired that also.

"Some time afterwards, they proceeded to the farm-house, formerly occupied as the convent, and first making a similar assault with stones and clubs upon the doors and windows, in order to ascertain whether they had anything to fear from persons within, the torches were deliberately applied to that building; and, unwilling to have one object connected with the establishment to escape their fury, although the day had broken, and three buildings were then in flames, or reduced to ashes, the extensive barn, with its contents, was in like manner devoted to destruction. And, not content with all this, they burst open the tomb of the establishment, rifled it of the sacred vessels there deposited, wrested the plates from the coffins, and exposed to view the mouldering remains of their tenants."

This report is signed by Charles G. Loring, chairman, and by a committee of thirty-seven persons, including several eminent legal and political characters.

But it was not alone with the torch and the fagot that Bishop England's contemporaries were assailed. The pulpit and the press, for several successive years, were chiefly occupied with what, for brevity, we may call the great Catholic Controversy. Drs. O'Flaherty and Beecher, at Boston; Drs. Levins and Powers against Messrs. Brownlow and others, at New York; Messrs. Hughes and Breckenridge, in Philadelphia; Messrs. Purcel and Campbell, in Cincinnati, debated very fully the great points in dispute between the Church and Protestantism. Much theological and historical learning was manifested on each side, but the defenders of Catholicity could afford to publish the arguments of their opponents and their own, — a declaration of confidence in their own success, which was not assumed on the other side.

In Philadelphia the controversy was perpetuated longest, and with least result of good. Some minor controvertists, indulging in sarcasm and calumny on the one

side, called down retorts and philippics on the other.
The imprudence, also, of certain naturalized citizens,
and the proneness to faction in great cities, produced the
scandalous riots of the year 1844, in that city, — a
subject which requires a separate chapter.*

* See Appendix, No. VII.

CHAPTER XVIII.

A NATURAL consequence of the large emigration from Ireland to America was, that a deep interest continued to be felt in Irish affairs by the emigrants themselves, and all whom they could influence in this Republic. We have seen Benjamin Franklin, the Father of American Diplomacy, sanctioning such an intimacy so early as 1771, maintaining, even then, that America and Ireland had a common interest in resisting the centralization of such vast political power in London.

"The United Irishmen" were the first organized American sympathizers in Irish political movements. They were strong enough to excite the attention of the then British minister, Sir Robert Liston, and their system was pleaded as a justification (after the fact) for the enactment of the Alien Law. No doubt, the discourtesy shown by Rufus King to the imprisoned United Irishmen in England and Scotland, when they applied for passports, was inspired, in the first place, by the recollection that their American colleagues had been rather troublesome to the Adams administration.

When the Catholic emancipation movement began to assume national proportions, — between the years 1820 and 1830, — various societies were formed in our large cities, under the title of "Friends of Ireland." In New York, Emmet, McNevin, Sampson, and the O'Connors, lent great importance to such an organization; in Philadelphia, the Binns and others; in Boston, John W. James; in Charleston, Bishop England; in Savannah and Mobile it had active promoters; in New Orleans, St.

Louis, Cincinnati, and Detroit, associations existed auxiliary to the Dublin association.

This sympathetic movement, as well as the peculiar
wants of an increasing class, brought a number of Irish-
American journals into existence. In 1822, Dr. England issued his "Catholic Miscellany" at Charleston;
in the same year, Mr. Denman issued his "Truth Tel-
ler" at New York; soon after, George Pepper, a native
of Ardee, County Louth, started his "Irish Shield" at
Philadelphia, which gave place to his "Literary and
Catholic Sentinel," published at Boston.

In Boston, Mr. Pepper died. He was the first, I believe, to attempt any literary project exclusively for his
emigrant countrymen. His "History of Ireland," though
a poor performance, was useful in its day; his papers
were always stored with anecdote and biography. He
was often scurrilous and sometimes fulsome, but it was
the time of the tomahawk, in literature as in war. He
died poor, and sleeps in the side of Bunker's Hill. The
gratitude of an after time placed a slab above his ashes,
and the only shamrock in the churchyard, some years
ago, was found growing on his grave.

In 1828, 1829, and 1830, when the Catholic spirit
everywhere rose with the tidings of O'Connell's victory,
the "Catholic Telegraph," in Cincinnati, the "Catholic
Diary," in New York, and the "Jesuit," in Boston,
were added to the journals intended for the Irish in America. The "Jesuit" became the "Pilot," and the "Diary," the "Freeman's Journal," under other proprietors.

The chief writers for this class of newspapers, besides
occasional pieces by the clergy, were, in New York,
Patrick Sarsfield Casserley, Rev. Dr. Leavins, and John
Augustus Shea; in Boston, Rev. Dr. O'Flaherty, Walter
James Walsh, and others. In the other cities the jour-
nals were chiefly in clerical hands.

The standing topic of these journals being the state
and hopes of Ireland, it was a consequence that any
cheering organization in Ireland should produce a corresponding one here. Thus, in 1834, and still more in 1840,

when Mr. O'Connell attempted the repeal of the legislative union with England, auxiliary societies sprung up in every considerable city of the United States. In 1842, Mr. Robert Tyler, son of the president, joined the movement in Philadelphia, and in September, 1843, he presided over a Repeal Convention in New York. Delegates from thirteen states and one territory sat in that convention, which deliberated for three days on its own relations to the cause of Irish liberty. It adjourned, resolving to organize each state of the Union, and intending to come together again, whenever the exigencies of the cause required it.

Large contributions of money were in this and the successive years forwarded to Ireland. Boston alone, in the first six months of 1844, remitted $10,000 to the funds of the Irish society. Undivided confidence in the wisdom and power of Mr. O'Connell everywhere existed, and all the emigrant children of Ireland fondly believed they were soon to see their native island possessed of a senate, flag, and militia of her own. The total disappointment of their hopes, in this instance, would have driven any other people, for a generation at least, into despair.

In 1847, they ceased their contributions to the Repeal movement, but gave most generously to the support of the famishing. In 1848, the French and European revolutions seemed to offer a prospect of a speedy cure for Ireland's woes. Up to this time, " the Young Ireland party" (so called) had not attracted American sympathy, but no sooner did they move with the revolutionary momentum, than they found new and powerful friends in America.

This they had themselves expected. In the spring of that year they had arranged to send Thomas Francis Meagher as their agent to America, but his premature arrest unfortunately defeated that purpose. Mr. William Mitchell was made their " bearer of despatches," and another gentleman, as a substitute for Mr. Meagher, was soon after sent over.

The interest in America was intensely excited. Skil
ful officers and engineers volunteered their services; the
rich and the poor, the stranger and the Celt, all contributed. Thousands of dollars were placed in the hands of
the several local "Directories," and, in many cases, the
donors did not wait to have their names recorded. Every
European mail was watched for with intense anxiety, and
the very streets were too small to contain the crowds that
flocked from all quarters in quest of news. Grave dignitaries in church and state were infected with the prevail
ing enthusiasm, and contributed freely to the patriotic
project. The New York Directory received, in a few
weeks, over $40,000 in cash, and the other states and
cities of the Union would no doubt have done equally
well.

It was evident enough, if Ireland had taken and kept
revolutionary ground for three months, American officers
and American gold would not be wanting.

It ended otherwise; and dense snow-clouds of despair
covered all the horizon of the Irish in America!

CHAPTER XIX.

THE most affecting event, in the connexion of Ireland with America, is the conduct of the latter towards the victims of the Irish famine, which began in the winter of 1846 and 1847, and endured, in its worst forms, till the close of 1848.

The famine is to be thus accounted for : The act of union, in 1800, deprived Ireland of a native legislature. Her aristocracy emigrated to London. Her tariff expired in 1826, and, of course, was not renewed. Her merchants and manufacturers withdrew their capital from trade and invested it in land.* The land! the land! was the object of universal, illimitable competition. In the first twenty years of the century, the farmers, if rack-rented, had still the war prices. After the peace, they had the monopoly of the English provision and produce markets. But in 1846, Sir Robert Peel successfully struck at the old laws, imposing duties on foreign corn, and let in Baltic wheat, and American provisions of every kind, to compete with and undersell the Irish rack-rented farmers.

High rents had produced hardness of heart in "the middleman," extravagance in the land-owner, and extreme poverty in the peasant. The poor law commission of 1839 reported that 2,300,000 of the agricultural laborers of Ireland were "paupers ;" that those immediately above the lowest rank were "the worst clad, worst fed, and worst lodged" peasantry in Europe. True,

---

* Between 1820 and 1830, two thirds of all the manufactories in Ireland were closed, and abandoned, as ruinous investments.

indeed! They were lodged in styes, clothed in rags, and fed on the poorest quality of potato.

Partial failures of this crop had taken place for a succession of seasons. So regularly did these failures occur, that William Cobbett and other skilful agriculturalists had foretold their final destruction, years before. Still the crops of the summer of 1846 looked fair and sound to the eye. The dark green crispy leaves and yellow and purple blossoms of the potato fields were a cheerful feature in every landscape. By July, however, the terrible fact became but too certain. From every townland within the four seas tidings came to the capital that the people's food was blasted—utterly, hopelessly blasted. Incredulity gave way to panic, panic to demands on the imperial government to stop the export of grain, to establish public granaries, and to give the peasantry such reproductive employment as would enable them to purchase food enough to keep soul and body together. By a report of the ordnance captain, Larcom, it appeared there were grain crops more than sufficient to support the whole population — a cereal harvest estimated at four hundred millions of dollars, as prices were. But to all remonstrances, petitions, and proposals, the imperial economists had but one answer, " they could not interfere with the ordinary currents of trade." O'Connell's proposal, Lord George Bentinck's, O'Brien's, the proposals of the society called "The Irish Council," all received the same answer. Fortunes were made and lost in gambling over this sudden trade in human subsistence, and ships laden to the gunwales sailed out of Irish ports, while the charities of the world were coming in.

In August authentic cases of death by famine, with the verdict " starvation," were reported. The first authentic case thrilled the country, like an ill-wind. From twos and threes they rose to tens, and in September, such inquests were held, and the same sad verdict repeated twenty times in the day. Then Ireland, the hospitable among the nations, smitten with famine, deserted by her imperial masters, lifted up her voice, and uttered that cry of awful anguish, which shook the ends of the earth.

The Czar, the Sultan, and the Pope, sent their roubles and their Pauls. The Pasha of Egypt, the Shah of Persia, the Emperor of China, the Rajahs of India, conspired to do for Ireland, what her so-styled rulers refused to do, — to keep her young and old people living in the land.

America did more in this work of mercy than all the rest of the world. On the 9th of November, 1846, a number of gentlemen assembled at the Globe Hotel, South Sixth street, Philadelphia, convened by the following circular, issued by the venerable Alderman Binns :

" In Ireland, the men, women and children at this time are, everywhere, from the north to the south, and from the east to the west, falling victims to hunger and the diseases consequent upon hunger. The heart sickens in the knowledge that thousands of people, among the most hospitable on the earth, are perishing from famine ! We are in a land abounding with food of all sorts, good and wholesome, for man and every creature that lives.

" It is thought to be the duty of this city, which has so often been among the foremost in works of mercy and charity, to do something for the famishing people of Ireland. What that something shall be, we do not undertake to say. To consider what is best to be done, and the best way of doing it, a meeting will be held in South Sixth street, between Chestnut and Walnut streets, at the Globe Hotel, on Thursday evening, at seven o'clock ; at that time and place, you are requested to attend. As this meeting is intended to be select, and that business shall be entered upon at the hour proposed, you are requested to be punctual in your attendance."

" This is believed to have been the first meeting of a public character, held in America, on the subject of Irish relief."* An important public meeting followed, which was addressed by the most distinguished citizens includ-

* Report of the Gen. Ex. Committee of Philadelphia, p. 5.

ing Mayor Swift and Hon. Horace Binney, in favor of a general contribution throughout Pennsylvania.

Alderman Binns concluded a few apposite remarks with the following preamble and resolution, which were adopted unanimously : —

"In 1775, before these United States had existence, — before her stars had lighted her to glory, or her stripes had been felt by her foes, — before the voice of independence had been heard on her mountains, or the shouts of victory had echoed through her valleys, — her statesmen and patriots assembled at their seat of government, in their future Hall of Independence, and, by a public address, made known to the world her grateful and affectionate sympathy and respect for the Parliament and people of Ireland, kindly inviting her people to come and inhabit ' the fertile regions of America.' Many thousands accepted the invitation, and by their toil and their sufferings, their sweat and their blood, assisted to make ' Great, Glorious, and Free,' the country which had adopted them.

"Since that invitation, threescore and ten years have passed, and the United States have become a great nation ; her stars and stripes float freely over every sea ; she is a sure refuge, yea, a tower of strength for the oppressed of every clime, and her voice is respected among the mightiest powers of the earth ; but dark, deep, and general distress, with the gloom of night, overshadows unhappy Ireland ; her people perish under the pangs of hunger, and are swept by pestilence ; they exist in shelterless cabins, with scant garments to cover them, and fall by thousands into unwept, too often uncovered, graves. A knowledge of their miseries has crossed the Atlantic, and touched the hearts of the statesmen and patriots of the United States, and again they have assembled at their seat of government, and invited their fellow-citizens to meet in their cities, towns, and villages, to consider, compassionate, and relieve the heartbroken, the famishing, the dying men, women, and children of Ireland ; therefore be it, and it hereby is,

"*Resolved*, That the statesmen and patriots of ' the

low and humble and of the high and mighty' states of America have, in the conduct stated, given illustrious examples to those of all nations of the earth, deserved the thanks of the people whom they have faithfully represented, and reïnsured to them and to their country the heart-warm gratitude and renewed attachment of the people of Ireland."

An influential city committee was organized. By May, 1847, they had received above $48,000 in cash, and $20,000 in articles suited for shipping. They loaded three barks and four brigs, for various Irish ports, all which safely arrived. Munster and Connaught received the greater part. In their closing report, at the end of 1847, the committee, among other resolutions, passed the following : —

"While we gratefully acknowledge the services cordially rendered to us and to the cause of humanity, by individuals in various parts of Pennsylvania and Ohio in particular, we feel ourselves called upon in an especial manner to make known our high sense of the very important assistance given to us by our esteemed friend and fellow-citizen, Allen Cuthbert. Not only have we had the free use of his warehouses for the deposit of breadstuffs, but the benefit of his constant and anxious services and experience in receiving them from every quarter, and in shipping them to Ireland. Conduct such as this confers honor not only on himself, but on the community of which he is a worthy member."

New York and Boston were not behind Philadelphia, nor the Grinnells, Lawrences, and Everetts, behind the Cuthberts and Binneys.* In the spring of 1847, a national

---

* In his address on the subject, in Boston, Mr. Everett recalled a reminiscence of Colonial times, which must have told powerfully on his audience.

In the prosecution of the Narraganset war, with King Philip, the Cape towns, in which were already some Irish families, contracted a heavy debt. The city of Dublin, being made aware of the condition of the settlers, remitted £124 10s. "for the relief of such as were impoverished, distressed, and in necessity, from the war." — *Pratt's Hist. of Eastham, Wellfleet, and Orleans. Yarmouth*, 1844.

Another writer adds : "The donation from Ireland, is a gratifying proof of the generous influence of Christian sympathies, and is supposed to have

meeting was held at Washington, at which Mr. Dallas, Vice-President of the United States, took the chair. Mr. Webster, Mr. Cass, and other eminent senators, spoke. The government placed two vessels of war, " The Macedonian " and " The Jamestown," at the disposal of the committee sitting in Boston and New York. Boston and New England, it is calculated, contributed nearly a quarter of a million of dollars, and New York city and state an equal amount. The Protestant as well as the Catholic pulpit resounded with appeals for " aid to Ireland." Sect and party were forgotten, and all-embracing Charity ruled the New World, unopposed. America was even more blessed in the giving, than Ireland was in receiving, such assistance.

It was the noblest sight of the century, those ships of war, laden with life and manned by mercy, entering the Irish waters. England's flag drooped above the spoil she was stealing away from the famishing, as the American frigates passed hers, inward bound, deep with charitable freights. Here were the ships of a state but seventy years old, — a state without a consolidated treasury, — a state, but the other day, a group of unconnected struggling colonies. And here, in the fulness of her heart and her harvest, she had come to feed the enslaved and enervated vassals of Victoria, in the very presence of·her throne. If public shame or sensibility could localize itself on any individual of so vile and vast a despotism, what must not that individual have felt!

Those who know what it requires to feed an army, may imagine that, abundant as was America's gift, it was not effectual to banish famine. Oh, no! tens of thousands, hundreds of thousands, perished miserably. But it preserved many thousands of precious lives, and gave an undying feeling of redemption to come, to all who lived at that day, in Ireland. The Central Relief Committees of Dublin and Cork accounted for the trusts committed to them. The " Irish Confederation " made national acknowl-

been procured through the exertions of the Rev. Nathaniel Mather, at that time a minister of the congregational denomination in Dublin." — *Ibid.*

edgment of Ireland's indebtedness to Mr. Dallas, and to Captain Forbes of " The Jamestown." * Many an Irish soldier, on the battle-fields of Mexico, did the like, in deeds, instead of words.

* It is a source of sincere satisfaction to the present writer, that both addresses were prepared by him, and adopted by a committee, of which Duffy, O'Brien, Meagher, and Mitchel, were members.

CHAPTER XX.

AN epoch in this history, which it would be culpable to pass over in parenthesis, is formed by "the Native American" organization of the year 1844. In all our great seaports there has existed, more or less, from the beginning of the Federal government, a feeling opposed to foreign emigration, — opposed, especially, to Irish Catholic emigration. This feeling has been manifested from time to time, by fanatics of extreme Protestant opinions : by merchants and professional men of a pro-British bias, and by native workmen who have been brought into competition with, and frequently underbid by, emigrant workmen. But the two latter sections, though much the more reasonable in their prejudice, have never been able to affect public sentiment with anything like the influence created by the ultra Protestant agitators.

Philadelphia city and its Liberties had long been the home of a theological controversy, which reached its acme at the beginning of the year 1844. The Boston riots of 1834, the New York "school question," (as to whether the Protestant Scriptures should be used as a public school-book,) the increase of emigration, had all been artfully seized upon by the local speculators in excitement, who hoped to fish up civic honors from the troubled waters of discord. During the first three months of the year the most inflammatory appeals were made to the passions of the Protestants of Philadelphia. A paper called *The Sun* became the daily organ of disturbance, and "an English Jew," named Levins, and others, the heads of the new association. The firemen, and many of the military, were ardent disciples of this school, whose avowed principles were, — 1. That no foreigner should be naturalized under a residence of twenty-one years; 2. That the Catholic religion was dangerous to the country; 3. That the Protestant Scriptures should be the foundation of all common school education.

On the 6th and 7th of May, Kensington and Southwark were the scenes of the first demonstrations against the Catholic churches and convent. Upon the former day, a party of Nativists had fired from an engine-house upon some Irish residents of Kensington, killing one and wounding others; whereupon, the friends of the attacked, in large numbers, issued out to capture the assailants.* These being reinforced, the riot became general, and amid the din the cry was raised, " To the Nunnery ! " That building was soon dismantled, the nuns and orphans expelled with blows and curses, its sacred vessels shamefully defiled, and its many graves violated. Saint Augustine's church was next attacked, and burned to the ground. In its tower, the old clock of Independence Hall, which had struck the hour of independence, was consumed ; and all its sacred furniture was destroyed. One fragment of the wall alone remained, where, above the marks of the smoke and flame, might be seen, for months, the picture of an eye, with the words, " The Lord seeth." This was all that had been left of Saint Augustine's. Saint Michael's church shared the same fate, and for nearly a week the city was in the hands of the mob.

The military companies, the municipal officers, and the press, (with one honorable exception,†) connived at outrage after outrage, until the indignant expressions of opinion from other cities seem to have roused the guardians of the law to a consciousness of their neglected

---

* Testimony of Clarke, Hague, Wood, Mathews, Fougeray, &c., native citizens of Philadelphia, before the city Grand Jury, 1844.

† J. S. Du Solle, editor of the Philadelphia *Spirit of the Times*, displayed, throughout the entire riot, a courage and ability as admirable as they are rare, in times of trial like these.

duties. Sheriffs and generals apologized to the rioters for interfering with their projects, and induced them to postpone their riot and arson for a short interval.

The scene of the July riot was Southwark, on the other side of the city, but men were now in command of the military, who resolved not to temporize. A contemporaneous account runs thus : —

" On Friday, the 5th inst., information was communicated by letter to the pastor of the church of Saint Philip Neri, Southwark, that it would be attacked on that evening. Having already taken some measures of precaution, with the approbation of Major General Patterson, and authority having been received from his Excellency the Governor, to form a company for the protection of the church, some fire-arms were procured, and introduced into the basement in the afternoon. This was an occasion of a gathering of persons in front of the church, who industriously reported that a design on the lives of citizens was entertained. The sheriff was soon on the ground, and, to remove all apprehension, took from the church the arms. A committee from the mob was allowed to search it thoroughly, and clear it of all fire-arms. The church, however, continued to be besieged by the mob, but no attack was made. On Saturday evening, General Cadwallader attempted to disperse the mob, and, on their refusal, ordered the military to aim ; but Charles Naylor, the late Whig member of Congress from the third district, cried out, *Don't fire !* and the military did not fire. Mr. Naylor was put under arrest, and detained in the basement of the church until Sunday, at eleven o'clock, A. M., when the mob, having obtained from a vessel lying at the wharf, two pieces of ordnance, brought one piece to the front of the church, and with a battering-ram beat down one of its doors, and carried away Mr. Naylor in triumph. The captain of the Montgomery Hibernia Greens, with a very small force, had been left in charge of the church and of the prisoners, about thirteen having been put under arrest, who were, however, discharged by the magistrates. A small body of the Markle and Mechanic Rifle companies were sent to his aid. The mob clamored for the dismissal of the Montgomery Hibernia Greens, and promised to let them pass unmolested, threatening destruction if they continued to defend the church. Seeing themselves entirely unsupported, they consented to leave it, and came forth, not with reversed arms, as some papers have misstated. They had not proceeded far, when the mob assailed them, and they defended themselves by firing as they retreated ; but, overpowered by numbers, they at length broke, each one seeking to save his own life. Robert Gallagher, a private, sought refuge in a house in Small street, and was pursued and inhumanly beaten almost to death. The mob, with a battering-ram, broke down the wall lately erected near the church, and forced an entrance into the church itself, which they desecrated, and attempted several times to fire.

"In the evening, about eight o'clock, General Cadwallader, with a part of the first division, arrived on the ground, and got possession of the church. The mob soon got into collision with the military, some of them attempting to wrest the arms from them. By command of their officer they fired, and six or seven persons were killed. The mob rallied with desperate resolution, and used effectually their fire-arms, the military maintaining their position bravely. Cannon were employed on both sides, and a number killed and wounded ; how many, it is not known. Colonel Pleasenton was slightly wounded; and Captain R. K. Scott, commander of the Cadwallader Grays, dangerously, but, it is now hoped, not mortally. Sergeant Guier, of the Germantown Blues, was killed. Corporal Henry G. Troutman received a wound, of which he has since died. The military took one or two pieces of ordnance from the rioters, and made a few arrests. On Monday, the mob increased in number, and force, and violence, threatening to exterminate the military. The civil authorities of Southwark, fearing a desperate and bloody collision, requested the troops to be withdrawn, and expressed their confidence that peace would be restored.   Some acts of violence were, however, committed on some Irishmen, after the withdrawal of the troops. The governor arrived in the city, and issued a proclamation requiring all to be disarmed, unless those who report themselves, and are authorized to preserve the peace."

The decided conduct of the authorities at Southwark put an end to the Philadelphia riots, and every attempt to "get up" similar demonstrations in New York and Boston signally failed.   In the former city, the life of the Catholic bishop was threatened, and, in the latter, the office of *The Pilot*, (then edited by the present writer,) was placed under the formal protection of the city authorities.   This was a very necessary step, since that journal was then the only one, in the state which contains Mount Benedict, which dared to defend the church, or to stigmatize, as they deserved, the church-burglars and women-assaulters of Philadelphia.*

A political party, animated by the principles, but rejecting the tactics, of Kensington and Southwark, enjoyed a short success.   In New York, they elected Mr. James Harper, mayor; in Boston, Mr. Davis; and in Philadelphia, Mr. Levins to Congress.   Several public men, hitherto much respected, deceived by this hectic flush of victory, permitted them to use their names, among whom the adopted citizens saw, with deep pain, the names of Major General Scott and Daniel Webster.

In 1845, they again succeeded in electing some civic officers in the same cities; but, in 1846, they utterly failed in their political designs, and since then the party has dwindled down into a secret trades' combination.

A national party never could have been organized on that "platform."   The west, that counts its growth by the shipful of emigrants crossing the Atlantic, the labor-market, which would otherwise have no regulating me-

* The familiar phrase, "cowards and sons of cowards," was applied, at the time of the second series of Philadelphia riots, to the nativist faction, by the present writer.   It occurs in a lengthy article, in which he labored to show that, instead of representing the Washingtons and Jeffersons of the past, as they claimed, that party represented the Arnolds, Deanes, and Hulls, if they had any American parentage, — which was disputed.

dium, the youth of the continent, the justice of the constitution, all protest against excluding emigration. To admit emigration, but prohibit naturalization, is to admit the danger, and cast away the protection. Whosoever wants to disarm foreign emigration of its anti-American tendencies, let him naturalize the emigrant. That is the only way in which he can effect his object.

The truth of this argument soon began to be felt, and, for several years past, no public man has been elected on "Nativist" ground. The former candidates of that faction have paid for their fatal success, by utter extinction, and even Mr. Levins no longer enjoys a seat in Congress, or any other public position.

CHAPTER XXI.

DURING the generation, of whose good and evil actions we have been discoursing, a series of events transpired in South America, which exercised a material influence over the Irish settlers at the north, and deserves to be mentioned in detail, in this place:

The revolution in South America dates from the year 1808, and its independence from the year 1823, when the last of the Spanish forces evacuated Caraccas. That struggle of fifteen years was marked by events worthy of the pen of the greatest of historians.

The contest might be said to have three divisions, — Bolivar's in Columbia, O'Higgins' in Chili, and that of the Argentine Republic on the Rio de la Plata.

Of the life and actions of Simon Bolivar, this is not the place to speak. We introduce his name here, as bringing with it that of many distinguished Irish soldiers, who were constantly by his side. Ireland felt a deep interest in his cause, and, in 1817, sent out her Irish brigade, under the command of General Devereux, a native of Wexford.* Bolivar seems to have reciprocated the partiality of that nation, his staff being in great part composed of Irish officers.

"The doctor who constantly attended him," says the English General Miller, "was Dr. Moore, an Irishman, who had followed the Liberator from Venezuela to Peru. He is a man of great skill in his profession, and devotedly attached to the person of the Liberator. Bolivar's first aide-de-camp, Colonel O'Leary, is a nephew of the

---

* See Charles Phillips' Speech at the Farewell Dinner given to Devereux; —Phillips' Speeches, passim. General Devereux, we believe, recently died, old and blind, near Nashville, Tenessee.

celebrated Father O'Leary.   In 1818, he embarked, at
the age of seventeen, in the cause of South American
independence, in which he has served with high distinction, having been present at almost every general action
fought in Colombia, and has received several wounds.
He has been often employed on diplomatic missions, and
in charges of great responsibility, in which he has always
acquitted himself with great ability.

"Lieutenant Colonel Ferguson, already mentioned as
a distinguished officer of rifles, was also an aide-de-camp.
He too was an Irishman by birth.   When a mere youth,
he quitted a counting-house at Demerara, and joined the
patriot standard.   During the war of extermination, he
was taken by the Spaniards.   He was led, with several
others, from a dungeon at La Guayra, for the purpose
of being shot on the sea-shore.   Having only a pair of
trousers on, his fair skin was conspicuous amongst his
unfortunate swarthy companions, and attracted the attention of the boat's crew of an English man-of-war, casu-
ally on the strand.   One of the sailors ran up to him, and
asked if he was an Englishman.   Ferguson was too much
absorbed by the horror of his situation to give an answer;
but, on the question being repeated, he replied, 'I am
an Irishman.'   'I too am an Irishman,' said the sailor,
'and, by Jesus, no Spanish rascals shall murder a countryman of mine in daylight if I can help it!'   Upon
which, he ran off to his officer, who interceded with the
Spanish governor, and the life of Ferguson was saved.
He related this incident to Miller, who has forgotten the
name of the English man-of-war, and also that of the
generous preserver of the gallant Ferguson.   This unfortunate officer fell a sacrifice in the defence of Bolivar, on
the night of the conspiracy at Bogota, in September,
1828.   It is a matter of regret that we do not possess
sufficient data to give that full biographical account of
the above-named officers to which their merits and services so fully entitle them."*

* Memoirs of Gen. Miller, vol. ii., pp. 233—234.

In Chili, the Irish had been still more distinguished. Don Ambrosio O'Higgins, the last captain-general, had planted new trades and towns, opened canals, deepened rivers and harbors, and, in a thousand other ways, promoted the interest of that province.   His son, Don Bernardo, a native of Chili, inherited all his enterprise, and more than his patriotism, and, under him as supreme director, Chili successfully struggled for its independence of Spain.   The first four years of his command, assailed by force without and faction within, were the years of his trial and his glory.   A fellow-soldier has recorded them in the vivid language of a witness:

" Colonel Don Bernardo O'Higgins, who, on the 24th of November, 1813, succeeded Carrera in the command of the army, had distinguished himself for personal courage and rectitude of conduct; whilst the prudence and talents of Mackenna made up in some measure for the deficiency of discipline and want of organization in 'the patriot forces.

" The independents were formed into two brigades; one under O'Higgins, in Concepcion, the other under Mackenna, at Membrillar, near Chillan.

" About this time the royalist cause was strengthened by a reinforcement from Lima, under the command of General Gainza, whose personal and professional qualities rendered him a formidable enemy; but, in spite of these changes, almost a year passed without producing any important occurrence.

" On the 19th of March, 1814, Mackenna repulsed, at Membrillar, a sharp attack of General Gainza, who, on the following day, was again worsted by the corps of O'Higgins, hastening from Concepcion to the support of Mackenna.*   Discouraged by these rencontres, Gainza left the patriot brigades behind him, and marched towards the capital, an open city without a garrison.   The movement was made under the supposition that O'Higgins would be unable to follow for want of horses. —

* This officer, a native of Ireland, was killed by one of the Carreras, in a duel fought at Buenos Ayres, in 1814.

Gainza crossed the river Maule eighty leagues south of Santiago, and took the city of Talca, but not without an heroic, though unavailing, opposition from a party of the inhabitants, who, unprovided with means of defence, perished in the vain attempt to preserve the town.

" The people of Santiago ascribed the loss of Talca to the negligence of the executive. It was therefore considered opportune to dissolve the governing junta of three persons, and to nominate a supreme director. Don Francisco Lastra was the first invested with that dignity. He hastily collected a small division, and sent it, under Don Manuel Blanco Ciceron, against the enemy; but that officer was totally defeated at Cancharayada by the vanguard of the royalists.

" In the mean while, O'Higgins prepared to follow Gainza; and, by forced marches, made under great difficulties, arrived on the left bank of the river. He immediately bivouacked, as if it had been his intention to remain there for the purpose of watching the enemy's motions; but as soon as it became dark, he crossed the rapid Maule at several points, a few miles above the Spanish posts, and, when morning broke, the astonished enemy beheld the patriot army in a strong position, which commanded the road to Santiago, as well as that to Chillan, the centre of the royalist resources. The masterly passage of the Maule may be considered as equivalent to a victory. General Gainza, cut off from retreating either way, was compelled to shut himself up in Talca.

" Don José Miguel and Don Luis Carrera had been set at liberty by the royalists, in virtue of the treaty of Talca. Don Juan José had been banished across the Andes, but had returned. In May, 1814, a court martial was ordered to assemble, for the purpose of exhibiting (as was stated to the public) the bad conduct of the three brothers. Don Luis was arrested, but Don José Miguel and Don Juan José succeeded in concealing themselves. The present juncture was considered by them to be favorable to a new usurpation of the reins of government. They secretly organized in the capital a party with which they had never ceased to correspond, and which now assisted in carrying into execution their criminal designs. A part of the garrison having been gained over, the Carreras showed themselves on the 23d of August, 1814, and deposed the supreme director, Lastra.

" A junta was formed, and the elder Carrera placed himself at the head of it, as in the first usurpation. The indignant citizens, although much dissatisfied with Lastra, immediately assembled, and signified their extreme displeasure to the Carreras; but finding the latter deaf to remonstrances, unsupported by the bayonet, they appealed for protection to O'Higgins, who lost no time in obeying the call. He marched from Talca, and a partial rencontre took place in the vicinity of Santiago. The rival parties were on the eve of a general action, when a messenger appeared from the royalist general, and a suspension of arms was agreed upon, to receive his despatches.

" The messenger was the bearer of an official letter, intimating that the viceroy had refused to ratify the treaty of Talca; that the only measure left for the insurgent authorities to secure the royal clemency was by surrendering at discretion. The despatch concluded by the assurance that the sword was unsheathed, in order not to leave one stone upon another in case of resistance.

" It also appeared that Gainza had been recalled to Peru, although he had some claims upon the consideration of a viceroy remarkable for his disregard of public faith towards the patriots, but who in other respects bore an honorable character. Gainza had violated the treaty by remaining, under various pretexts, in Concepcion, until General Osorio arrived with fresh troops, and a supply of military stores of every kind; and events ultimately proved that he had signed the treaty for no other purpose than that time might be gained for these reinforcements to arrive. The plan of the Spaniards was so well formed, that 4000 troops were already within fifty leagues of the capital when the summons for unconditional submission was received.

"Agitated by conflicting feelings, O'Higgins magnanimously sacrificed his just resentments, to save his country. He acceded to the demands of his rival, and nobly turned his arms against the common enemy. Carrera followed O'Higgins with a strong division; but discipline no longer gave efficiency to soldiers who had often fought gloriously: desertion to an alarming extent prevailed. To consolidate his ill-acquired power, Carrera had weakened the army by removing some deserving officers, and had banished from the capital many distinguished citizens, for no other reason than their discountenance of his arbitrary proceedings.

"O'Higgins encountered the royalist force on the bank of the river Cachapoal; but, having only 900 men, was defeated, and he took shelter in the town of Rancagua, twenty-three leagues from Santiago. He caused the entrances of the streets to be blocked up, and made the place as difficult of access as his very slender means permitted.

"On the 1st of October, 1814, the royalists commenced an attack, which lasted for thirty-six hours, during which time the fire on both sides was kept up with unremitting vigor. Each party hoisted the black flag, and no quarter was given. In the hottest of the action, the magazine of the patriots exploded, and produced the most destructive effects; but, undismayed by the heavy misfortune, their efforts seemed to redouble, and the Spanish general determined to abandon the enterprise. He had actually given orders to retreat, under the impression that Carrera, who had remained an unmoved spectator, would cut off his retreat, and that his exhausted royalists would be attacked in a disadvantageous position by that chief with fresh troops. But General Ordonez, the second in command, perceiving the inaction of Carrera, who evidently exhibited no intention to effect a diversion, or to send to O'Higgins the smallest succor, determined upon making another grand effort. By means of the hatchet and the flames, the royalist penetrated through the walls of the houses, and at length fought their way, inch by inch, to the square in the centre of the town Here O'Higgins made his last stand with two hundred survivors, worn out with fatigue, tormented with raging thirst, and surrounded by heaps of slain; till observing all was lost, he, although wounded in the leg, headed the brave relics of his party, and gallantly cut his way through the royalists. Such was the impression produced by this desperate act of valor, that none ventured to pursue the patriots, who continued their retreat without further molestation to the capital. The royalists remained in Rancagua to despatch the wounded, to butcher the few remaining inhabitants, and to destroy what had escaped the flames.

"The Carreras had still under their command one thousand five hundred men; but they abandoned the capital without a struggle. The depredations committed by the troops of the Carreras irritated the citizens to such a degree, that a deputation was sent to Osorio, to request him to enter Santiago and reëstablish order. Six hundred troops crossed the Andes with Carrera. General O'Higgins emigrated with about one thousand four hundred persons, many of whom were ladies of rank, who passed the snowy ridges of the Andes on foot. All were received at Mendoza with generous hospitality by General San Martin, and few returned home until after the battle of Chacabuco, in 1817."*

Colonel O'Connor, son of Roger, and nephew of Arthur O'Connor, chief of the staff to San Martin, had raised a fine regiment at Panama, and embarked in the first attempt at Peruvian independence. He fought throughout the war, until the final battle of Ayachuco ended the struggle, by establishing the liberties of the colony. In that engagement he acted as adjutant general, and contributed materially to the "crowning victory."

Colonel O'Carroll, another officer in the same service, after a distinguished career, perished at the hands of the

* Memoirs of Gen. Miller, vol. i., pp. 117—119, 120—124.

guerilla, Benavides, who cut out the tongue of his cap
tive before putting him to death.

Captain Esmonde, a native of Wexford, and an early
adherent of the South American cause, captured and
imprisoned in 1811, by the royalists, underwent various
singular adventures.

" One of the authorities at Pisco, to whose charge the
patriot prisoners had been consigned, was Don Francisco
Algorte, who, in addition to the brutal tyranny which he
exercised over the unfortunate prisoners, descended fre
quently to the cowardly violence of striking Esmonde
upon the head with a cane. From this situation, more
horrible than death to the mind of a gentlemanly and
high-spirited officer, Esmonde was removed to the case-
mates of Callao, whence he was liberated by the kind
interposition of Captain Shirreff, with whom, in compliance with the terms of his release, he returned to England.

" On the capture of Pisco, in 1821, by the patriots,
under the command of Miller, an estate of Algorte was,
as belonging to a violent and uncompromising Spaniard,
taken possession of, and subsequently confiscated.

" Algorte repaired to Lima, and, in the course of a
few months, by well-directed presents, secured the support of some powerful friends, whose influence had nearly
obtained from the protector the restoration of his estate.
Nothing was wanting to complete his success but the
report of Miller, upon a reference made to him, and
which was necessary to legalize the restoration. To
ensure his acquiescence, Algorte had recourse to a mutual
friend, a rich Spanish merchant of the highest character.
This gentleman, without venturing to enter into particulars, intimated that he was authorized to subscribe to *any*
terms. An intimate friend of Miller's, an English merchant, was also employed, and who, in a jocose manner,
hinted that, in the event of a favorable report, five or six
thousand dollars might be accidentally found at the door
of the colonel's apartments.

" Esmonde, who had fulfilled the conditions of his

release, and returned to Peru, happened at this moment to be in Lima. To him, therefore, Miller, who had heard some reports of Algorte's treatment of the prisoners, referred for their correctness, without mentioning, either then or afterwards, the motive for his inquiries. Esmonde simply recounted the conduct of Algorte towards himself and his fellow-prisoners. The result may be anticipated. Miller's report was immediately forwarded, and Algorte's estate irrecoverably lost.

" Captain Esmonde was afterwards employed by the Peruvian government to examine and report upon the possibility of making canals near Tarapacá. The vessel, on board of which he embarked, having never been heard of, is supposed to have foundered at sea."*

On the royalist side, the only Irishman of note was General O'Reilly, taken prisoner by Saurey, on his march from Canta to Pisco, in 1820. He was allowed to return to Spain, but so afflicted by his defeat, that he is " supposed to have thrown himself overboard, as he was drowned at sea."

In the service of Buenos Ayres, beside Colonel Mackenna already mentioned, Captain O'Brien, of the first Argentine ship-of-war, and Colonel, now General, O'-Brien, of the army, were early distinguished. The former lost his life early in the contest, but the latter survived to prove himself worthy of almost every civil and military trust, in the gift of his adopted country. After rising from rank to rank, during the war, he was successively minister of Venezuela at London, and chief of the Venezuelan republic. He still survives.

Such were some of the services to liberty which made the Irish name illustrious in South America, and revived the passion for military glory in the hearts of the Irish settlers of the northern confederation.

* Memoirs of General Miller, vol. i., pp. 224, 225.

CHAPTER XXII.

WHILE Irish soldiers were so actively engaged in the
South American revolutions, men of the same origin were
about to introduce the mixed northern race into the possessions of Mexico, and to take the first steps in that
onward aggressive march, which has placed the flag of
"The Union" on the headlands of the Pacific.

Under its first presidents, the republic of Mexico,
anxious to encourage emigration, had given a large tract
of country between the rivers Neuces and Rio Grande to
an Irish colony. In 1820, a considerable Irish population
had settled there, and their grant was known as " The
County of San Patricio." This county became afterwards
a party in asserting and maintaining Texian independence of Mexico.*

In 1812, when the early attempts at revolutionizing
the Spanish colonies bordering the Gulf, were made; when
Fray Hidalgo, the last Mexican chief of his generation, had
been publicly executed, " a young man, named McGee,
who had been a lieutenant in the United States service,
after resigning for the purpose," raised the standard of
independence on the Sabine and Trinity rivers. With
about four hundred United States recruits, chiefly riflemen, and an equal force of Spanish under one Bernardo,
he crossed the Sabine. He "took Nacodoches, then
marched to and took La Bahia, where, with his four hun-

---

* It was represented in the " Texian Consultation" of 1835, by Messrs.
McMullen and Powell. It continued a Texian county until it was depopu-
lated, in the late Americo-Mexican war, being the theatre of some of its
severest battles. That part of the original tract now included in the state of
Texas is called " Neuces County."—*Debate on the Texian Boundary.in Congress, August 8th*, 1850.

14

dred, he withstood a siege of three months, the American riflemen making such havoc among the Spanish soldiers, in their occasional sorties, that their commander was compelled to raise the siege and retire to San Antonio. McGee, in the mean time, died, not more than twenty-two years of age."* For his time, he had something to show!

The American and friendly Texian force continued in arms for over twelve months, in the heart of the country; they took San Antonio, defeated General Elisondo, at the head of 1600 men, and were in turn defeated by the recreancy of Manchaco, one of their native allies, and an overwhelming force, under Arredondo.

The proximity of Texas to the United States of course attracted to it the adventurous spirits of the Mississippi Valley. This attraction did not cease with Mexican independence, established, in 1821, through the patriotism of Iturbide, and the moderating influence of O'Donoju, the last captain-general of Mexico.

While Mexico was forming her new boundaries, the United States had frequently proposed, through her ministers, to obtain the Rio Bravo del Norte as the boundary between the two republics. Mr. Poinsett, in 1825, and Mr. Butler, in 1827, proposed to purchase up to this definitive frontier, in vain.

Under the presidency of Santa Anna, in 1832, Texas declared against the then administration, and for the Federal constitution of 1824. An armed force was sent to seize the local authorities and disarm the inhabitants. The settlers, a majority of whom were from the Valley of the Mississippi, resisted; conflicts ensued; and finally Texas raised its separate flag, and, in 1836, by the victory of San Jacinto, established its separate sovereignty.† In 1837, its independence was acknowledged by the United States, France, and England; and, even in that year, General Jackson, in his message, suggested the probability

---

* "Mexican Letters," by Judge Brenckenridge, (written in 1846–7.)
† General Houston, the hero of the Texian revolution, has personally mentioned to me his Irish descent, paternally, and Scotch, maternally. His life will be the most American of books, whenever it is worthily written.

of its future admission into the Union. The Mexican and American ministers respectively demanded their passports, and left the capitals to which they were accredited; and so the seeds of quarrel were deposited in two willing soils.

In 1840, a commission to settle the disputes of the two republics was agreed on; but, in 1842, it terminated, leaving untouched the Mexican claim of sovereignty over Texas. In 1843, Mr. Tyler being President, the annexation of Texas was much discussed, and finally looked on as an administration measure. Mr. Webster and Mr. Upshur, successively secretaries of state, prepared the way for it; and, notwithstanding the protest of Mexico, Mr. Calhoun, their successor, in April, 1844, signed the treaty of annexation, with the Texian commissioners, at Washington.

Mexico, never having acknowledged the separate sov ereignty of Texas, could not see her pass bodily over to the republic of the north, without resistance. She had repeatedly protested, in the most impressive accents of diplomacy; and when the act of annexation was known to be under consideration at Washington, she avowed that she would look on its completion "as a declaration of war."* Both countries, pending the treaty, were increasing their military forces, and it was evident, a collision, or a total retrogression in policy, would take place. On the 3d of March, 1845, Congress confirmed Mr. Calhoun's negotiation, and Texas became a state of the Union ; on the 10th, the Mexican minister obtained his passports ; in July, Texas formally accepted her admission with the conditions; on the 25th of July, eight companies of United States troops moved towards the Texian (now become the United States) boundary, while soon after, General Taylor made his head quarters at Corpus Christi. In March of 1846, after wasting the winter in Slidell's negotiation, Taylor was ordered to take up his march to the Rio Grande, with about 3,000 men

* Executive doc.: No. 2. House of Representatives — twenty-ninth Con gress.

of all arms; and Arista, by his government, to cross the Rio Bravo, with thrice the number, and drive the Americans back.   In April, the first blood was shed, Colonel Cross being assassinated, and Lieutenant Porter's party, in quest of him, cut to pieces; and now the war, in reality, begins.

In this, "the third great war" of the Union, Texas, as being immediately involved, and the southern states, were likely to play the earliest part; but the quarrel was a national one, and we shall soon find that nearly every state in the Union supplied its contingent to the roll of the dead, and the list of the successful.   We shall find, too, many striking instances of the usefulness of the Irish race in an era of action such as this was.

Scott, Taylor, Worth, Wool, and Perry, are purely American reputations; but though they are the most brilliant of the war, there are others, also, worthy of honorable remembrance.

In the early battles, (Taylor's,) we find the Rangers under Gillespie, Hays, Conner and McCulloch, playing an ubiquitous part.   As scouting and foraging parties, as covering movements of artillery and infantry, in regular engagements and in street fighting, mounted or dismounted, there is no battle without them.   The names of the several officers indicate their paternity.

When General Taylor's force was sufficiently augmented, by arrivals of volunteers, and some additional regulars, to take the offensive, (after the victories of the 8th and 9th of May, 1846,) we begin to find the officers of other corps distinguishing themselves.   The capture of Matamoras and Monterey, and the battle of Buena Vista, have associated the names of Butler and O'Brien, of the regular army, and Gorman,* (Indiana,) and McKee, (Kentucky,) with some of the most memorable passages at arms, in the annals of America.

William O. Butler, of Kentucky, the grandson of an Irish emigrant, was trained in the Florida war, in the camp of Jackson.   As major general, he served with

---

* At present, we believe, a member of Congress from Indiana.

Taylor, superseded Scott, and, on the conclusion of peace, conducted the American forces back to their country.   In 1848, he was the candidate of the Democratic party, for Vice-President, with Lewis Cass for President.

O'Brien, whom death has removed in the midst of peace, is mentioned by Taylor, for his efficient direction of his battery at Buena Vista.   He was brevetted major for his conduct upon that field.   He was born in Philadephia, of Irish parents, and educated at West Point. Besides his military services, he is entitled to remembrance, for his compilation, "O'Brien's Military Law of the United States," the standard work of its class, and one likely to remain so.   He was a practically pious man, and none the worse soldier for that.   He died of cholera, in Texas, on the 30th of March, 1850, being but little beyond thirty years of age.

Colonel McKee, of the Kentucky Volunteers, did not survive the deadly conflict of Buena Vista.   Descended of one of the early pioneers of that state, he gallantly upheld its character for daring courage.   With his fellow-statesman, Clay, he fell before the hour of the victory, but not until he had done his share to secure it to his own side.

We must now trace quickly over the campaigns of Scott, and see what men, of marked distinction, were there, of Irish origin or birth.

14*

CHAPTER XXIII.

IN November, 1846, Major General Scott, commander-in-chief of the United States army, was despatched to Mexico, with orders to besiege Vera Cruz, and endeavor to penetrate from that city, by a direct route, to the Mexican capital.

In this brilliant expedition, of which the successive steps were Vera Cruz, Cerro Gordo, Puebla, Contreras, Churubusco, Chepultepec, and Mexico, many noble deeds of arms, and fine combinations of skill, were exhibited.

One of Scott's most efficient officers was Colonel, since General, Riley, a native of Baltimore, of Irish parentage, and an old volunteer in the war of 1812. In every action of the war he was distinguished, and no promotion was considered, by the soldiers of the war, more justly deserved. Under General Riley, the territory of California was organized and prepared for admission into the Union in 1850.

Among the other officers of Scott's army were many of Irish origin, as Brigadier Patterson, of Pennsylvania; Captains Lee, of the engineers, Casey, of the regular infantry, and Magruder, of the artillery; Lieutenant Neal, and many others.

Major McReynolds, of the dragoons, a lawyer, long settled in Michigan, was distinguished wherever cavalry had ground to operate on. A cotemporary biographer writes of him : —

" Mr. McReynolds, a native of Dungannon, county Tyrone, came to this country when a youth of eighteen, and has, we believe, since then, resided in Detroit, Michigan. To the Legislature of that state he has been several

times elected, and in it he has occupied a highly honora
ble position. He was a member of the Michigan Senate
when the war with Mexico broke out, and immediately
tendered his services to the government. The President
promptly gave him a captain's commission in the dragoons, and the gallant discharge of his duties in that
position has won for him enduring honors. The assault
of Kearney's and McReynolds' dragoons, on the bloody
field of Churubusco, was one of the most daring and brilliant deeds of heroism among the many proud instances
of valor which have shed such undying lustre on the
American arms, in the history of the Mexican war."

The commanding general of the division thus speaks
of this charge, in his official report : —

. " Captain McReynold's 3d dragoons nobly sustained
the daring movements of his squadron commander, and
was wounded in his left arm. Both of these fine companies sustained severe losses in their rank and file also.
We are informed that the enemy numbered, by their own
report, five thousand infantry and one thousand cavalry,
while our dragoons did not exceed one hundred. This
small force drove the Mexicans upwards of two miles,
and ceased not until they were within the battery that
covered the gate of the city. In this charge, the dragoons cut down more than their entire number of the
enemy. When we consider the extraordinary disparity
in point of numbers, and the raking position of the enemy's battery, into the very mouth of which our brave
dragoons fearlessly threw themselves, we think we may
safely say it has no parallel in modern warfare."

The same village in which Major McReynolds was
born, also gave birth to James Shields. Both families
are Milesian Irish, old as the hills, in Ulster. Under the
Celtic Pentarchy, the O'Shields were the standard-bear-
ers of the north, — an office of special honor and trust,
in those military ages.

While a mere boy, James Shields emigrated to this
country, and, while still in his teens, served as second
lieutenant of volunteers in the Florida war. In the long

years of peace which succeeded, he did not abandon military studies, and, though he held an important civil employment in the department for Indian Affairs, he at once volunteered into the war with Mexico. On the 1st of July, 1846, he was appointed brigadier general, and joined the division under General Wool. With that officer he shared the famous march through Chihuahua and New Mexico to Monterey, from whence he was detached to the army under Scott, then before Vera Cruz.

" But the military talents of General Shields were first fully developed at Cerro Gordo. In the general orders of April 17th, he was entrusted with the care of the Jalapa road, in order to keep the enemy in that quarter engaged during the main attack, and to cut off retreat. In both these objects he was successful. By his activity he contributed largely to the victory of that memorable day, and elicited the admiration of both General Scott and his brother officers. In the pursuit, he received a musket ball through the lungs, by which he was immediately prostrated, the command devolving on Colonel Baker. His life was for a while despaired of, but eventually, to the astonishment of all, he recovered.

" During the long stay of the army at Puebla we hear little of General Shields ; but he again appears amid the toils and dangers of the march towards the capital. Late on the 19th of August, while the storming of Contreras was in progress, he was sent to a village near that fort, in order to afford assistance to General Smith. A deep, rugged ravine, along whose bed rolled a rapid stream, was passed with great difficulty, in consequence of the increasing darkness ; after which, the general ordered his weary troops to lie upon their arms until midnight, in order to prepare for further duty. In the mean while he threw out two strong pickets, who, perceiving a body of Mexican infantry moving through the fields toward the city, opened a sharp fire, and succeeded in driving them back. At midnight, Shield's troops resumed their march, and soon joined Smith's brigade, at the place appointed.

"At this time, General Shields performed an action so delicate and magnanimous as to deserve record with the more dazzling ones which were soon to follow. Previous to his arrival, Smith had completed those judicious arrangements, for turning and surprising the Mexican position, which were afterwards so brilliantly successful. As Shields was the senior officer, he could have assumed the command, as well as the execution, of General Smith's plans, thus debarring that officer from the fruit of his labor. But this he nobly refused to do, and withdrew his men to the position formerly occupied by his brother veteran. About daybreak, the Mexicans opened a brisk fire of grape and round shot upon the church and village where the general was stationed, as also upon a part of the troops displayed to divert him on his right and front. This continued until Colonel Riley's brigade opened its fire from the rear, which was delivered with such terrible effect, that the whole Mexican force was thrown into consternation.

"At this juncture, Shields ordered the two regiments of his command to throw themselves on the main road by which the enemy must retire, so as to intercept and cut off their retreat. Although officers and men had suffered severely during the night's march, as well as from exposure, without shelter or cover, to the incessant rain until daybreak, this movement was executed in good order and with rapidity. Crossing a deep ravine, the Palmetto regiment deployed on both sides of the road, and opened a most destructive fire upon the mingled masses of infantry and cavalry ; and the New York regiment, brought into line lower down, and on the road-side, delivered its fire with a like effect. At this point many of the enemy were killed and wounded, some three hundred and sixty-five captured, including twenty-five officers.

"Meanwhile the enemy's cavalry, about three thousand strong, which had been threatening the village during the morning, moved down toward it in good order, as if to attack. General Shields immediately recalled the infantry, so as to place them in a position for meeting the threatened movement; but the cavalry soon changed its position, and retreated toward the capital. Orders now arrived from General Twiggs for the troops to advance by the main road toward Mexico; and accordingly, having posted Captain Marshall's company of South Carolina volunteers and Captain Taylor's New York volunteers in charge of the wounded and prisoners, Shields moved off with the remainder of his force, and reached the position of those divisions already moving on the main road.

" After turning the village of Coyoacan, Shields moved with his command toward the right, through a heavy cornfield, and gained an open and swampy plain, in which is situated the hacienda de los Partales. On arriving there, he established his right upon a point recommended by Captain Lee, an engineer officer of great skill and judgment, at the same time commencing a movement to the left, so as to flank the enemy's right, and throw his troops between them and the city. Finding, however, their right supported by a body of cavalry, three thousand strong, and perceiving that the enemy answered to his own movements by a corresponding one toward the American right flank, and owing to the advantages of the ground, gaining rapidly upon him, he withdrew his men to the hacienda, for the purpose of attacking the enemy in front. The conflict was close and stubborn, until General Shields, taking advantage of a slight wavering in the Mexican ranks, ordered a charge. This was obeyed with alacrity and success, the enemy breaking and flying on all sides. Shields continued to press upon the fugitives, until passed by Colonel Harney with his cavalry, who followed the routed foe into the very gates of the city.

" On the 10th of September, General Shields, with the New York and South Carolina regiments, was ordered first to Piedad, and subsequently to Tacubaya, preparatory to the assault upon Chapultepec. Here he continued a heavy cannonade upon the enemy's lines until early on the morning of the 13th, when his command moved to the assault. While directing the advance, Shields was severely wounded in the arm, yet no persuasion could induce him to leave his command or quit the field. In company with the remainder of Quitman's division, he pushed rapidly forward along the Belen road, exposed to the most tremendous fires, overthrowing one after another of the Mexican strongholds, until finally his victorious banners were planted over the principal gateway. When night fell, he was carried from the field sick, exhausted, and writhing with pain. His wound, although severe, was, happily, not mortal; and rest, together with careful attention, united with a strong constitution, speedily restored him to health."

On his return to the United States, the general was everywhere welcomed with enthusiasm. Alabama came out with all her dignitaries to meet him; South Carolina presented him with a magnificent sword; and Illinois, proud of her adopted son, elected him to the Senate of the United States.

In the short session of 1850, '51, General Shields, from the committee on military affairs, reported in favor of conferring the rank of lieutenant general on Scott, — which was adopted. Strange chance of fortune! that he whom Scott mourned dead on the field of battle, should live to present him the title, hitherto worn in war only by Washington.*

---

* A recent visitor at Washington thus describes Shield's personal appearance : —

"I found the general seated among his papers, — a spare man, of middle size, and apparently about forty years of age, with the amber tinge of health on his cheeks, an eye like a live coal, large brows, and a fine head. I felt an electrical thrill pass through me, as I took the hand of the first soldier of our race, not excepting Cavaignac or Guyon. I believe I stared at him rather rudely, for I was anxious to detect whether his constitution had recovered from the terrible results of his Mexican wounds. I was satisfied by the scrutiny, and it will give joy to many an Irish heart to know that in all probability the general has as many years, as any man of his age, yet to come.

"I shall not here commit the indecency of printing private conversations, but I may say that the more I heard of General Shield's opinions, the more he rose in my estimation. He is a very thoroughly read man, with a very reflective turn of mind. He has thought much on all subjects and countries. He speaks French as fluently as English, and during my first call held a long Spanish conversation with a Mexican general, Herrera, who, he observed, had been ' in the same war with him, but not on the same side.' "

Of the conduct of the non-commissioned officers and men of Irish birth, during the war, both Taylor and Scott have spoken in the highest terms of praise. Their eulogiums are too recent to need repeating.

"Although the attempts to conclude a treaty of peace immediately after the battle of Churubusco had not been successful, yet, in concert with the commander-in-chief, Mr. Polk lost no opportunity to repeat his overtures for so desirable an object. It was not, however, until the beginning of the following year, that the Mexicans would listen to such proposals. Their army was then reduced to a few insignificant parties, scattered here and there, more for safety than any hope of opposition to the invaders. Even the guerillas manifested symptoms of weariness. Accordingly, when, in January, 1848, General Scott laid before the Mexican Congress articles of a treaty, based upon those formerly rejected, that body immediately appointed Luis G. Cuevas, Bernardo Conto, and Miguel Atristain, as commissioners. These gentlemen, with Mr. Trist, acting on behalf of the United States, assembled at Guadalupe Hidalgo, and concluded a treaty of 'peace, friendship, limits, and settlement' between the two republics.

" The only thing still necessary to the conclusion of the war, was the ratification of the new treaty by the legislature of each country. In February, the attested copy was received at Washington by President Polk, and transmitted to the United States Senate. After being slightly amended, it was passed in that body, on the 10th of March, by a large majority. Mr. Sevier was appointed envoy extraordinary and minister plenipotentiary to present it for ratification to the Mexican Congress. In company with Mr. Clifford, he soon arrived at Queretaro, where the national legislature was sitting, and laid before that body the corrected copy for their final action. It passed through both houses by a large majority, and was received with marked satisfaction by the Mexican people.

" By this instrument, the boundary line between the

two republics was made to begin at the mouth of the Rio
Grande, ascending the middle of that river to the southern
boundary of New Mexico, thence westwardly, along the
whole southern boundary of New Mexico, to its western
termination ; thence northward, along the western line of
New Mexico, to the first branch of the river Gila ; thence
down the middle of this branch and river to its junction
with the Colorado ; thence between Upper and Lower
California to the Pacific.   It secured to the United States
the vast territories of New Mexico, California, Western
Texas, and the Pacific coast, together with the fine harbor of San Francisco, and the internal navigation of the
Colorado, Gila, and other rivers.   Fifteen millions of dollars were to be paid to Mexico by the United States, as
compensation for part of this grant.

 "By an article of the treaty, arrangements had been
made for withdrawing all the United States troops from
the Mexican territory within three months after the final
ratifications, provided it could be effected before the commencement of the sickly season.   In furtherance of this
provision, the most active preparations immediately commenced for marching different portions of the army from
the capital and interior towns to Vera Cruz, whither they
were to embark for New Orleans.   Previous to this, General Scott had left Mexico to attend a court of inquiry
appointed by government to investigate reciprocal charges
between himself and Generals Worth and Pillow.   The
duty of superintending the evacuation of the capital, and
subsequent embarkation from Vera Cruz, devolved upon
the temporary general-in-chief, Major General Butler.
In the early part of June, the greater part of the soldiers
in the city of Mexico marched for Vera Cruz, under the
supervision of Mr. Sevier.   They left the latter city by
detachments, reached New Orleans about the middle of
June, and thence proceeded, by steamboat or railway,
towards their respective homes.   Nothing can exceed
the enthusiasm with which these toil-worn veterans were
hailed, as they entered, regiment by regiment, into the
cities, from which, two years before, they had marched
15

to the scene of strife.   Business was suspended, the population rushed to meet them, military and civic processions attended their march, banquets were spread,
addresses delivered, and presents bestowed on them
throughout their route.   Thus closed, after a duration of
two years, the Mexican War."

CHAPTER XXIV.

NEW STATES OF THE SOUTH-WEST — HON. W. R. KING — JUDGE PHELAN — THE SHARKEYS — IRISH MILLIONAIRES — BEIRNE OF VIRGINIA, MULLANPHY OF MISSOURI, M'DONOGH OF NEW ORLEANS, DANIEL CLARKE — ARKANSAS.

WITHIN the memory of the present generation, seven states have been admitted into the confederacy, from what was at the south, Indian, or foreign territory. These states, from their tropical situation and their earliest origin, being cultivated chiefly by slave-labor, have not attracted a very numerous Irish emigration. The white race, however humbled by oppression at home, will not compete with the born slave, for work or wages, in the tobacco and cotton fields of that productive region. Hence, south of the Potomac, the history of the Irish settlers is rather a series of family anecdotes, than the various record of a widely diffused population. These families, however, are neither few nor undistinguished.

For the most part, such families removed into the southern from the old midland states. This was the case with the Butlers, of both branches, and also with the Kings, of Alabama. The emigrant founder of this family first lived near Fayetteville, North Carolina, where he came from the North of Ireland. William Duffy, a lawyer of some celebrity, also a native of Ireland, was his neighbor and friend. In Fayetteville, April 7th, 1786, was born William R. King, who, after studying law with Duffy, removed to Alabama. For that state he sat as senator of the United Sates, from 1823 to 1844, without intermission. In the latter year he was sent as minister to France, from which he returned in 1846, and in 1848 was reëlected to the Senate. In 1850, upon the death of President Taylor, and the consequent advancement of Vice-President Fillmore to the chief magistracy, Mr. King was unanimously chosen President of the Senate, in which position he acts as Vice-President of the United States. During the stormy debates of 1850, known in congressional annals as "the Compromise Session," Mr. King's excellent qualities of mind and temperament were of most essential service to his country. The number of his years and honors will probably be even yet increased.

Alabama has another distinguished family, at the head of which is John Dennis Phelan, one of the judges of its Supreme Court. John Phelan, father of the judge, was a native of Queen's County, in Ireland, who settled at New Brunswick, New Jersey, where the Costigans and other families of his old neighbors had preceded him. During the war of 1812–15, he was cashier of the Bank of New Brunswick. He afterwards removed, first to Richmond, Virginia, and, in 1817, to what was then the Alabama territory. His son graduated with honor, at Nashville, in 1828; became the editor of a Democratic newspaper, in Huntsville; was elected in 1833 and the six succeeding years to the State Legislature; in 1841 was appointed circuit judge, and in 1852, at the age of forty-two, a judge of the Supreme Court.*

---

* A characteristic anecdote of his entry into public life has been related to us, by one who had it from the Judge himself, and who tells it in his own words : "The first gathering I went to," he would say, when speaking of that canvass, "was at Cloudtown, and I found that all the old candidates were for ground-talking, but did not care about making speeches   I knew a speech was my only chance, so I said, modestly, to one or two about the grocery, where they were all drinking and talking, that if I could get the attention of the people, I would like to speak. Nobody noticed me. Thinks I, this will never do. There was a tall fellow, named Bill Sartain, who had the end of his nose bit off, then in the grocery, ' half slewed,' making great fuss, and bantering any one to dance with him for a treat.   I stepped in : says I, ' Sartain, I am a candidate here, as little as you may think of it, and I want to make a talk to these people ; now, if you 'll engage that, should I beat you, by the judgment of this crowd, at a jig, you 'll fix me a box at the door, and make them give me their attention while I speak to them, I 'll go in with you, and treat to boot.'   ' Good,' says he ; ' spread out, men, and make room for me and the little squire.'   They made a good large circle, and several fell to patting ' Reuben Reed, the cedar breed,' and Bill Sartain and I went at it.   I don't know whether I did outdo him or not, although, as most of my friends understand, I am not bad at double ' troulle.' However, the crowd gave it in my favor, and, after a laugh and a treat, Bill Sartain was as good as his word.   He got me a box, and I got an attentive hearing, and made a pretty good speech about the ' Union,' and ' Nullification,' and the ' Monster,' which were the themes of that day.   In a word, I got a breeze in my sail by my jig with Bill Sartain, that finally carried me safe into harbor."

Among the first settlers in Tennessee was Patrick Sharkey, a native of the West of Ireland, some of whose descendants still remain in Tennessee, while a more distinguished branch descend from Patrick Sharkey, junior, a soldier of the Revolution, who, about the beginning of this century, removed into the State of Mississippi, then belonging to Spain. William Louis Sharkey, one of the sons of this emigrant, was born August 12th, 1798, and, at the age of fifteen, lost both his parents. He spent the first years of his orphanage picking cotton in the fields in the busy season, and obtaining instruction with the proceeds in the intervals. In 1821, he was enabled to enter a law-office at Natchez, and in 1825, we find him established as a lawyer at Vicksburg. In 1827, he was elected to the State Legislature, and in the two following years was its speaker.

In 1831, Gerard C. Brandon, born in Ireland, was governor of the state. He was a man of fine attainments and most upright character. By him the foundations of Mr. Sharkey's legal fortune were laid, in appointing him to fill the place of a circuit judge who had resigned. A well-informed periodical gives the following account of his honorable career as a judge, during twenty years of office :

"Judge Sharkey presided as Circuit Court judge only one term in each county of his district. His appointment only qualified him till the Legislature should elect a successor, and, greatly to the disappointment of the people of the district and the bar, the Legislature, which soon afterwards assembled, elected over him Alexander Montgomery, Esq., then comparatively obscure, but who, during his judicial term, acquired the respect of the bar and community, and, after his retirement, reaped a plentiful harvest in the practice of law.

" The evidences which Judge Sharkey had given of his capacity and learning induced the people of the First Judicial District to elect him, under the constitution of 1833, one of the judges of the High Court of Errors and

15*

Appeals. In 1833, he took his seat with Daniel W.
Wright (since deceased) and Cotesworth Pinckney
Smith, the two judges elect from the other judicial
districts. Judge Sharkey was appointed chief justice
by his associates. He drew the short term of two years,
it being required by the constitution that a new judge
shall be elected every two years.

"In 1835, Judge Sharkey was reëlected without opposition, and again appointed by his colleagues chief
justice. Six years afterwards, his term having expired,
he was reëlected over E. C. Wilkinson, Esq., by an
overwhelming majority, after an arduous canvass, during
which he visited and addressed the people of every
county in his district, embracing an area of two hundred
miles in length by one hundred in width. It will,
doubtless, appear strange to those not accustomed to a
constitution which makes the judiciary elective by the
people, and not acquainted with the circumstances existing in 1841, which rendered it necessary for Judge
Sharkey to 'take the stump,' that such means should
have been resorted to by candidates for a high judicial
station, one of whom wore the ermine at the time. But
the exigency demanded it; and it is only an additional
evidence of his intrinsic worth and dignity, that, by so
doing, Judge Sharkey lost none of the veneration and
regard which he had previously acquired. The people
found the man as worthy of their homage as the chief
justice had been.

"A question vitally affecting the fortunes of numerous
families, growing out of their indebtedness, either as
principals or sureties, to the banks, agitated the public
mind, and, it was supposed, would materially bias
popular suffrage. It was known that Judge Sharkey
was in favor of enforcing payment by the debtors, notwithstanding the disfranchisement of the banks; it was,
on the other hand, supposed that Judge Wilkinson
entertained different views, and to the election of the
latter, the debtors of the banks, their friends and
relatives, looked forward with intense solicitude. Men

acting under such an influence would not be over-scrupulous in their choice of the means of accomplishing their end. Combinations were secretly formed, money was liberally subscribed, pamphlets and newspapers teeming with misrepresentation were profusely disseminated where their poisonous influence could not be counteracted, and to that end runners were dispatched into quarters inaccessible by the usual avenues of communication. All this was done without the consent of Judge Wilkinson, who would have spurned any other than the most honorable warfare; but, nevertheless, it became necessary for Judge Sharkey to take the field in person, and disabuse the minds of the people of the false and injurious impressions which his enemies had produced. Everywhere he drew vast assemblies, and, in all his addresses, exhibited a style of lofty and persuasive eloquence, which, united with his venerable appearance and benignant manners, rendered him irresistible. He well merited the compliment paid him by his generous opponent, who said that 'he considered it a high honor to have been pitted against such an adversary.'

"This victory virtually extinguished the hopes of the debtors of the banks, to whose want of punctuality the failure of those institutions was mainly attributable, and who, as was wittily observed by S. S. Prentiss, Esq., 'not content with having sucked all the eggs, were now anxious to break up the nests.'

"Judge Sharkey was again elected chief justice, and resumed the arduous duties of his station with the same fidelity that had always characterized him, and with a moral influence greatly augmented by his recent triumph.

"On another and more trying occasion, in the exercise of his judicial functions, Judge Sharkey had violated the wishes of a majority of the people of the state, by deciding that the supplemental charter of the Union Bank, under which the bonds of the state had been issued by A. G. McNutt, and known as the 'Union Bank Bonds,' was constitutional. The effect of this decision was to establish, in theory at least, the validity of these bonds ; but as, without an appropriation by the Legislature of sufficient funds out of the public treasury, they could not be paid, the decision was of little use to the bondholders. The recollection of this obnoxious opinion might, nevertheless, have defeated his reëlection, but that he was elected by the people of a district, and not by the whole state, and in that district the repudiating class was not as numerous as in others. It was fortunate for the state, that this circumstance prevented the election to the Supreme Bench, in lieu of Judge Sharkey, of an individual of opposite sentiments, and thus excluded from the fountain of justice the contaminating doctrine ‘that the debtor shall be the judge of his own liability to the creditor.’ Those desirous of learning the reason of the Supreme Court on this long-mooted and agitating question, may be gratified by referring to the case of Campbell *vs.* Mississippi Union Bank, 6 *Howard, Miss. Rep.* 625.”

In 1850, the excitement in the South, and in Mississippi especially, in relation to “ the Compromise Measures ” and “ the Wilmot Proviso,” was such as to fill our wisest statesmen with alarm. Governor Quitman, whose influence and popularity were paramount, committed himself strongly to the views of secession promulgated by South Carolina. Senator Davis, and the state delegation to Congress, except Senator Foote, were, almost to a man, secessionists. In the midst of this excitement the famous Nashville Convention assembled, on the action of which so much depended. Chief Justice Sharkey was called on to preside, and by him the resolutions and address were drafted. His patriotic counsels moderated the ardor of the South, restored the discussion to legal limits, and, more than any one cause, prevented the formation of a treasonable Southern Confederacy. While, by his firmness and discretion, he exposed himself to the hostility of the Hotspurs of his own section, he won, by the timely exercise of the same qualities, a place among the statesmen of the Union, by whom the pacification of 1850 was effected.*

The national administration, conscious of these services, and of his abilities, firmness and judgment, has lately appointed him consul at Havana; an office which, from our relations with Cuba and Spain, is one of great delicacy and importance.

The neighboring states of Tennessee and Mississippi have been, from the first, congenial homes for Irishmen. The influence of the Jacksons, Carrolls, Coffees, Brandons, and Sharkeys, has justly rendered the Irish name honorable on this bank of the great river. In the commerce of the South, many emigrants from Ireland have made immense fortunes. The Irish merchants of Baltimore and Charleston have ranked among the foremost for enterprise and probity. In Virginia, the largest fortune ever made by commerce was that of Andrew Beirne, who was as remarkable for his munificence in prosperity, as he had been for his sagacity and industry. In Missouri, the largest fortune was, perhaps, that of Bryan Mullanphy, of St. Louis, whose eccentricities furnish as many anecdotes to that neighborhood, as those of Girard and Astor to Philadelphia and New York. Mr. Mullanphy left one son, a lawyer and judge, who died unmarried, at St. Louis, in 1850. He bequeathed the princely sum of $200,000 for the relief of emigrants entering the Mississippi. At New Orleans, the same year, died John M'Donogh, born in Baltimore, of Irish parents, who, by a long life of penurious and unnatural parsimony, acquired the largest single property in the Southern States. He left an unamiable character, a doubtful will, and legacies which seem more likely to be inherited by the lawyers than those for whom he

---

* " He was nominated a candidate for the Convention called in conformity to an act of the Legislature, and was elected. During the canvass he spoke frequently to immense assemblies, composed of individuals from remote quarters, many of whom declared that, having heard Judge Sharkey's opinion, they would return home without any further doubts on the subject. To no man is the cause of the Union more indebted for the immense majority by which the disunion party was defeated in Mississippi, than to Judge William L. Sharkey."
— *American Whig Review*, May, 1852.

designed them. If mere wealth, unrefined by the graces, and uninspired by the charities of life, was respectable, this man would merit more of our space. But the hardy pioneer, the brave soldier, the close student, and the faithful public servant, are those we can freely honor. All the wealth of John McDonogh cannot purchase him a better name than his life deserved.

A very different character was Daniel Clarke, a wealthy merchant, of Irish birth, who settled at New Orleans, in the year 1795. He acquired immense estates, which he was ever ready to use for the public service. At the time of his migration from the United States to New Orleans, (Louisiana then belonged to France,) he became, or was sent out as, United States consul. In the quasi-French war he offered his entire property for the defence of the Mississippi against the threatened invasion. He died at New Orleans, in 1813, leaving a princely estate, which has also been in great part dissipated through litigation.*

In Arkansas there has been recently some emigration from Ireland, partly induced by the establishment of the diocese of Little Rock, over which the Rt. Rev. Andrew Byrne, a native of Dublin, so worthily presides. A large number of farmers from Wexford county, some three years back, made their homes in that state, under the guidance of their pastor, Father Hoar. The colony, we believe, has not been very successful.

---

* The celebrated "Gaines case," arose from Mrs. Gaines' claims against the property of Daniel Clarke.

CHAPTER XXV.

THE six states carved out of the north-western Indian territories since the beginning of this century, have been the favorite goals of all recent emigration. The facilities of transit offered by the canals and railroads leading from the old Atlantic States westward, and the adaptability of the west for agriculture, attracted and made easy the progress of the Celtic multitude. If, in our own age, this young nation has been able to export its superfluous breadstuffs to the other side of the Atlantic, one of the chief causes is to be found in the constant supply of cheap Irish labor, which, for fifty years, has been poured along all the avenues of the west. If, moreover, Ohio, Michigan, Illinois, Indiana, Wisconsin and Iowa, have done much to increase the wealth and glory of the Union, a large share of the historical honor is due to Irish fugitives from British oppression, and their more fortunate sons, born as freemen.

A glance at the growth of the general population, since the reclamation of the North-west, will enable us to estimate, in one way, its importance to the Union. In 1800, the "Union" counted 5,305,625 souls; in 1810, 7,239,814; in 1820, 9,654,596; in 1830, 12,868,020; in 1840, 17,069,453; in 1850, about 23,250,000. Not only has the increase been mainly in the North-west, but the abundant produce of that fertile region has fed and distended even the older states. For every emigrant who goes up the lakes in spring, an increase of produce, or its price, comes down in harvest. The army of labor makes an annual campaign, and gives a good account of itself in every engagement with the wilderness, and the desolation of ancient barrenness.   The host that unfurled its standard at Bunker's Hill, and took the British colors down at Yorktown, is scarcely more entitled to be called the army of liberation, than this emigrant multitude, who, armed with the implements of labor, smite the forest from the morning until the evening, and plant, in advance of the ages to come, the starry banner of the nation against the frontier skies.

Who constitute this host?   In every case it has been nearly half Irish.   Until 1819, there was, unfortunately, no customs record of emigrant arrivals; until the Atlantic States, within ten years back, appointed local Commissioners of Emigration, we had no exact returns of the classes and origin of those who did arrive.   But the names of men and places, the number of Catholic churches erected in, and the Irish feelings represented by, the public men of the west, enable us to estimate the share of that people in the population of the six new states of that quarter.*

In the United States Senate, Michigan has been represented by Generals Cass and Fitzgerald, both of Irish origin; Ohio was long represented by Mr. Allen, still in the vigor of his public life, — a man of real ability, and not only by blood, but by sympathy, allied to the fatherland of Burke and O'Connell.   Indiana has sent to the

---

* Certainly one half of the recent arrivals from Ireland has been added to the population of the Western States.   How large a proportion these bear to all other settlers, may be conjectured by the following summary of the arrivals at New York alone, which we take from the Annual Reports of the Commissioners of Emigration for that State, for 1848, '49 and '50.

Passengers arriving in New York in the years ending 31st of December, 1848, 1849, *and* 1850, *for whom commutation and hospital money was paid.* (*Americans not included.*)

Countries.	1848.	1849.	1850.
Ireland,	98,061	112,561	117,038
Germany,	51,973	55,705	45,535
England,	23,062	28,321	28,163
Scotland,	6,415	8,840	6,772
France,	2,734	2,683	3,462
Switzerland,	1,622	1,405	2,380
Holland,	1,560	2,447	1,173
Norway,	1,207	3,300	3,150
Wales,	1,054	1,782	1,520

same assembly Edward A. Hannegan, some time minister to Berlin; and Illinois is now represented by James Shields. The popular branch of Congress has also been largely recruited by men, of Irish parentage or birth, from the same region. In the thirty-second Congress there were forty such representatives.

Of the six states, Illinois has been distinguished for the number of its Irish public servants. Not only in the national councils, but in the not less important duties of organizing the finances and establishing the credit of Illinois, some of our emigrants have performed important services to their adopted state. Of these, one, for his industry and abilities, deserves particular mention. In 1842, the late Mr. Ryan, then a very young man, was elected to the State Senate, for the district including La Salle, Grundy, and Kendall counties. The services he rendered are related by an Illinois journal : —

" The election of Mr. Ryan, at this time, as subsequent events have shown, was a fortunate one for our state. At that dark period of her history the state was bankrupt in means and credit. Involved in debt to the amount of about sixteen millions of dollars, there was no hope that she could ever pay any part of that sum unless further means could be obtained to bring the canal, the most available part of her property, into use.

" Mr. Ryan, then, although but twenty-five years of age, was probably as well informed, in regard to the present and prospective resources of the state, as any man in it. Conceiving that it was necessary to complete the canal in order to save the state, and that the money for its completion must be obtained from eastern or foreign capitalists, he justly deemed that it was necessary, in advance of any legislation, to convince those parties that a further advance of money to the state of Illinois was a proper, a prudent measure, on their part. With this view, he, immediately after his election, in August, 1842, proceeded to New York, and so well did he succeed in effecting his object, that, aided by the advice and assistance of Mr. Arthur Bronson, now deceased, Mr.

16

Justin Butterfield, now Commissioner of the General Land
Office, and others, he matured the plan of the canal law
of 1843, for raising the sum of sixteen hundred thousand
dollars for completing the canal.   On his entrance into
the Senate, in December, 1842, he introduced the bill,
which was, during that session, passed into a law.
Strange as it may now seem, the bill was violently
assailed, and it required all the information, talents, and
zeal of Mr. Ryan to secure its passage.

" Upon its becoming a law, Mr. Ryan, who had been
thus instrumental in devising the plan upon which it was
founded, and in carrying it thus far into execution, was
deemed, by common consent, the most proper person to
procure the loan proposed to be raised by the law.
Accordingly he was appointed to this honorable and
responsible agency, by the late Governor Ford, in the
spring of 1843, with Mr. Charles Oakley, who was appointed his colleague.   He proceeded immediately to
England, where, after overcoming many serious obstacles,
they were at length successful in effecting the loan of
$1,600,000, which secured the completion of the canal.

" The mass of information with which Mr. Ryan had
stored his mind, in relation to the resources of Illinois,
together with his powers of argument, contributed largely
to their success.   After having secured the attention of
the foreign capitalists to his facts and arguments, he was
desired to submit to them a written statement of the facts
which had been the subject of their discussion, and was
assured, if Mr. Ryan and Mr. Oakley could verify those
facts to such agents as these parties might send to Illinois, the amount asked for should be furnished.

" In compliance with this arrangement, Governor John
Davis, of Mass., and Captain Swift, one of the present
Canal Trustees, came to Illinois, and, after six weeks'
patient investigation, found themselves able to endorse,
substantially, all the representations that had been made
by Mr. Ryan and Mr. Oakley.

" Soon afterwards, in the latter part of the year 1845,
Mr. Ryan, having thus devoted himself for three years to

the service of the state, with a zeal and vigor that could not be surpassed, and a judgment and discretion that resulted in complete success, felt that some attention to his own business was necessary.

"The supposed mineral riches of the shores of Lake Superior at that time attracted much attention; Mr. Ryan devoted himself to mining, and was engaged in that pursuit, in Pennsylvania, at the time of his death.

"He had just succeeded in his pursuits to such an extent as to be able to turn his eyes towards the prairies of his own beautiful state, with the hope of soon again making them his home, when the inexorable fate which awaits us all interposed her fiat, and terminated his career.

"Thus has Illinois lost, in the prime and vigor of his manhood, one of her most gifted and devoted sons, — rich in every endowment that gives value and dignity to humanity. In intellect, among the first; in goodness of heart, surpassed by none. Elegant and accomplished in his manners, wherever he has been, and in whatever position he has been placed, he has always commanded the respect and admiration of those who knew him. There was a charm in his manners that seemed to possess a mysterious influence over all who approached him. But by those to whom he was best known was he the best beloved. Those only who knew him well could know the full worth of his character."

In Indiana, the families of Gorman, or O'Gorman, the Browns, — two of whose cadets are now in Congress, — were among the pioneers. The family of O'Neils, originally settled in Carolina, and still represented there by the Hon. John Belton O'Neil, a jurist and scholar of high attainments, early branched off into Indiana. Hugh O'Neil, of this stock, was educated in the University of that State, at Bloomington, and studied law at Indianapolis. He is now (1852), in his fortieth year, United States District Attorney for Indiana.

Thomas and John Dowling, of the same state, have long been known, in its local politics, as editors and

legislators.   Thomas is now one of the three trustees of
the state debt; John holds an important office in the
Department for Indian Affairs, at Washington, in which
bureau he was preceded by his countryman, James
Shields, now general and senator.*

Wisconsin, admitted in 1848, has, at this present writing, a numerous and influential Irish population.   Many
of its new towns are almost exclusively occupied and
governed by that class of citizens.   The town of Benton
is of this number, being founded, in 1844, by Mr. Dennis
Murphy, a native of Wexford, who afterwards represented
the county in the State Senate.   In Milwaukie, the Irish
citizens are very numerous, and several of them, as Dr.
James Johnson, are large proprietors of city property.

One of the most honorable reputations made in Wisconsin, is that of the Hon. Timothy Byrne, a native of
Dublin, born in 1819.   His parents settled in New York,
in 1820, from which Mr. Byrne removed, in 1836, to
Wisconsin Territory.   From 1846 to 1849, he was a
member of the Legislature; in 1849 and 1850, he was one
of the commissioners for the improvement of the Fox and
Wisconsin rivers; and in 1851, though his party was
defeated, he was elected lieutenant-governor by a majority of five thousand.   Thus, at the age of thirty-three
years, he fills the second office of his adopted state, without any of the factitious aids of party support.

Iowa, the most recent of the states (except California),
excels them all in her Irish predilections.   In 1851, she
gave the names of Mathew, O'Brien, Mitchel, and Emmett, to four of her newly surveyed counties.   Her State
Legislature has always had Irish members, and her Irish
citizens exercise a controlling influence.   The venerable
pioneer, Patrick Quigley, Judge Corkery (a native of
Cork), and others of the first brigade of emigrants, were

* An obliging friend, long a resident of Indiana, in answer to our inquiries,
writes:—"The truth is, Indiana is full of the descendants of Irishmen.   I
scarcely ever was in a crowd of the old residents, four fifths of whom did not
proudly boast of their Celtic origin.   The first Constitution of the State was
formed by a convention, in which were several natives of the 'old sod.'"

mainly instrumental in producing this gratifying state of feeling in Iowa.

To win respect for a fallen race — to straighten the way of the stranger, and prepare a favorable public opinion to receive him — to watch over the growing passions of a young state — to direct wisely less experienced emigrants who follow — to found churches, towns and reputations — these are the great opportunities of early settlers. Need we add that, to effect all or any of these ends of American life, great judgment, forbearance, and energy are required. No "free-and-easy" philosophy will serve in this undertaking; no living from hand to mouth; no pot-house celebrity, will suffice. For a thousand years — until the population of the South Seas — there will not be such opportunities in the world again as are now open to the Irish in America. In another generation we will be too late, — we will be forestalled and shut out. The continent is being administered, — the dividend of a new world is about to be declared; but those only who are wise, patient and united, can obtain any considerable per centage.

In the older states, many obstacles exist to the successful establishment in life of emigrants. The best farms and trades are all taken up by the native inhabitants, whose capital and connexions give them some facilities denied to the foreigner. But there are not half a dozen states in the whole Union of which this is generally true. Let not indolence plead such an excuse. There are characters, homes and fortunes, still to be made, by honest labor, in America. In what varieties of struggling were not the men engaged whose history we have sketched! What difficulties had not they, in their time, to overcome! Some were sold for a term of years to pay their passage-money; others lived in perpetual apprehension of Indian invasion; almost all were friendless and moneyless, on their first landing on these shores. Do you read this book to gratify vanity, or to furnish food for stump speeches? Alas! if so, friend, you do the book, the writer, and yourself a great wrong. It was written with a far other and far higher object : to make us sensible that we had predecessors in America whose example was instructive, to induce us to compare what they did and were with what we are and ought to do. If it serves not this purpose in a degree, better it never was written or read.

This torrent of emigration from Ireland to America must, in a few years, abate its force; it cannot go on as it has gone. Whatever we can do for ourselves, as a people, in North America, must be done before the close of this century, or the epitaph of our race will be written in the west with the single sentence —

"Too Late !"

CHAPTER XXVI.

THE decennial census, just taken, seems likely, when digested, to show a total population of nearly 24,000,000 in the Union, including an Irish contingent of some 4,000,000, at the close of the year, 1850.

If we are to estimate the influence of this element in the composition of American character, we must not only take its past success on this continent, but the achieve- ments of its emigrants in Europe and South America, into consideration. Especially should we consider their agency of antagonism in the British system.

Edmund Spenser, whose work on Ireland displays many reflections of wonderful originality, gives expression to this very thought. He says he has often thought that Ireland was reserved to be a judgment on England, and that by *her* hand England would be humbled.

For seven hundred years, the Almighty, for his own ends, has kept those two islands in a state of warfare and hostility, England influencing Ireland, and Ireland con- trolling England. Richard the Second's Irish wars pro- duced the wars of "the Roses," which occupied England a century. Bruce, beaten and banished from his own country, finds a shelter in Ireland, and returns from Rathlin to conquer at Bannockburn. Henry VIII. be- comes a reformer and king of Ireland, and it costs his daughter £20,000,000, and, it is said, a broken heart, to subdue the northern chiefs. Ireland fights for the Stuarts who robbed her, and goes into exile, as if for the express purpose of meeting and routing the armies of Britain at

Fontenoy and Dettingen. The Irish emigrate to America, and help to take this continent from England in 1775, as they now help to keep it anti-British in temper and policy.

Is it too much to expect this result from such an element in the great republic ? Before you say " Yes," remember the work of our exiles performed in one generation, when they turned their steps not to the New World beyond the ocean, but to the shores of the Mediterranean.

They were either students in search of schools, or soldiers in search of fighting. The former reckoned on the bourses founded by professors and D.D.'s from home ; and the soldiers, poor fellows, counted on the countenance of those who were gone before them to get them something to do! Both classes worked hard, and both won fame and rank. It is easier to follow the soldier class, who left their mark wherever they went.

Of these, two became Marshals of France (Sarsfield and O'Brien); two Marshals of Austria (Kavanagh and Prince Nugent); five Grandees of Spain (O'Sullivan, Lawless, Gardiner, O'Riley, and O'Donnell); two Marshals in Russia (Lacy and Browne.)

Of general officers, it would be hard to muster the lists. The Irish governors of important posts are more easily enumerated. One Browne was Governor of Deva, for Austria; another, Governor-General of Livonia for Russia; Count Thomond was Commander at Languedoc; Lally was Governor of Pondicherry; one Kavanagh was Governor of Prague; another, of Buda; O'Dwyer was Commander of Belgrade; Lacy, of Riga; and Lawless, Governor of Majorca.

Of the civil offices attained by these emigrants, we find that Kavanagh, Baron Linditz, and Count Nugent, were Aulic Councillors ; Marshal Maurice Kavanagh was Chamberlain of Poland; Colonel Harold, Chamberlain of Bavaria; Sutton, Count of Clonard, Governor of the Dauphin, in France ; the Marquis M'Mahon was one of the first French agents to these states, for which service he received the badge of the Revolutionary Order of Cincinnatus, from Washington and the French Order of St. Louis, from Louis XVI.; Patrick Lawless, Ambassador from Spain to France; Dominick O'Daly, Ambassador from Portugal to France; and Nugent, Minister of Austria at Berlin; and Clarke, Duke de Feltre, Minister of War, in France.

In Spanish America, the Captains General O'Higgins of Chili, O'Donoju of Mexico, and O'Donnell of Cuba; the Supreme Director O'Higgins; the Generals O'Riley, O'Brien, and Devereux; the Colonels McKenna, O'Leary, O'Connor and O'Carroll, were all men of one generation —all Irishmen by birth or parentage.

To North America, within seventy years, we have contributed ten majors general, five commodores, a president, two vice-presidents, six authors of the Constitution, nine signers of the Declaration, upwards of twenty generals of brigade, and an immense amount of minor officers, and rank and file to the army. Considering that till yesterday all education was limited to a caste, in Ireland; considering how the individual is oppressed in the defeat of his nation; considering the more fortunate lot of the self-governing countries, with whose native sons our emigrants have had to compete in the old world and the new, the achievements of her exiles are a glory and a promise, precious to Ireland.

It seems wonderful that so many mere Irishmen, in the same century, should force themselves, by dint of service, into so many important posts, in such old countries, and over the heads of so many native rivals. They all emigrated poor—their land, if they inherited any, being confiscated. They had, as it were, to beg their education, literary and military, and to serve long and hazardous probations, before they attracted the attention of kings. Still, that they did rise, and that they kept the vantage-ground they gained, is apparent as the day.

The Irish emigrants of to-day are the kith and kin of these men of history; and, we think, there are causes working for them, which will produce results not unworthy of the past.

The arrival of a number of educated men, of their own nation, to settle among them, is one such cause. Chiefly barristers and journalists, if they remain true to the cause of their race, (as there is no reason, in any instance, to doubt,) they may exercise an immense influence for good over the general fortunes.[*]

The visit of "Father Mathew" to this country is another source of hope for us. That unwearied preacher of temperance has visited all the districts where the Irish emigrants abound, and in less than two years has pledged over three hundred thousand persons to live sober and peaceful lives.

What a life his has been! Unlike too many modern reformers, who insist on their theories with all the heat of proselytism, and utterly neglect the details of good, his lips have not grown white in theorizing, but in exhorting and blessing multitudes, individual by individual. Those of whom society and the laws despair, — who are often considered as hopelessly beyond the Christian pale, — for these he has, hoping and toiling, worn his life away. Truly may it be said of him, as Grattan said of Kirwan, " in feeding the lamp of charity, he exhausted the lamp of life."

Next to intemperance, ignorance is the emigrant's worst foe. From ignorance, faction, quarrels, partisanship, losses innumerable flow. To found adult schools, circulating libraries, and debating rooms ; to make good use of our newspaper press ; to prepare cheap and suitable books for a neglected people ; these are the solemn obligations resting upon the educated and wealthy of our Irish-American citizens.

Every Celt has an inherent taste for rhetoric and the arts. Witness the long array of poets, artists, and orators, produced even in these latter days of our provincialism. To elevate, purify, and direct wisely these natural tastes, should be the main purpose of all the educational institutions we may create.

---

[*] Of the political refugees of 1848, the great bulk are settled in New York city. There are some, however, in several other states and cities.

The profession of arms has, also, a natural attraction, for this race. In old Ireland, every man was a soldier, but in modern Ireland, England punishes the study of arms as she does felony. We must revive the taste for tactics, wherever, on this continent, there are an hundred of us together.

There are men enough ambitious of command in every city. But, to command, it is necessary to learn; to learn slowly, patiently, practically; to learn through years of service, as the young draper, Ney, and the drummer boy, Bernadotte, learned how to be marshals, and to stand next to Napoleon; to learn to command themselves first and others after; to learn self-control, quick thinking, and ready action; to learn to discriminate wheat men from chaff men—to discover an officer among the privates, and to lift him up to his rank without exciting ill-will in others. In a word, the policy of military life is as essential as the policy of civil life; and men in field and camp, city and congress, are, after all, made of the same identical stuff, and subject to the same kindred defects and passions.

It is said, Irishmen will not serve under Irish officers, though they will under English, French, or American. What is the inference? That the fault is in the Irish officers, not in the men. If it is not to the service, or to officers, as officers, they object, it must be to the particular character of this particular class. If we look long at it, we find that where an Irish captain or colonel is just, firm, and friendly with his men, they obey him as any other officer. In the Mexican war, no Irish soldier but was proud to follow General Shields. Wherever the officer is not obeyed or respected, the explanation will be found to be, that he, not the men, are to blame.

We have now throughout the United States some twenty-five or thirty Irish companies. We have drilled men enough scattered through the militia to make as many more. There are, perhaps, in the several states, 50,000 natives of Ireland who have some smattering of military discipline. In New York City we have an Irish regiment, whose captains refute the imputation that Irish officers are not suited to command Irish soldiers.

To such officers, especially, some degree of military science is essential. No army, no regiment, can be manœuvred without science. England has her Woolwich and other academies; France, her Polytechnique and other military schools; Russia has 200,000 students of military science in her schools of war. Even republican and anti-standing-army America has its West Point. Various works on tactics are easily had in this country, and ought to be had; for it is not marching men through open streets, or defiling by a newspaper office, or presiding over a target excursion, that can alone make good officers. In these things, the merest popinjay might excel General Scott. But it is the reading military books, — the study of the lives of generals and guerillas, — of Washington and Marion, Wellington and Zumalacaregui, that will make an officer in the highest sense of the term. The officers of every Irish company will, we hope, have a small library of such books, well thumbed over.

We desire to see the military spirit of our ancestors revive and flourish among the Irish in America, because it will swallow faction, — because we now want, and will more and more want, all the practical science, military, mechanical and political, we can attain.*

Against the encroachments of landlordism it is necessary also to warn those who live in crowded communities. As no people have suffered from that terrible social despotism so much as ours, so none should resist its spread so resolutely. Every Irish emigrant should consider it the test of his manhood to have a house of his own, — altogether his own.

The frequent reading of the Declaration of Independence, and the Constitution under which we live, is also a duty. We cannot be good citizens, or wise electors,

---

* Oliver Byrne, of New York, the distinguished engineer and mathematician, has done more than any other man to infuse into his emigrant countrymen a military spirit.

unless we refresh our principles at these fountains of American law and liberty. It is unnecessary to urge on our emigrants the importance of going through the forms of naturalization.

It might be improper to refer, in this place, to the most important of all topics, religion. Our emigrants have the benefit of the teachings of an increasing and improving priesthood, who will not suffer them to forget their spiritual obligations.

These wants of character being supplied, our emigrants, as a class, have but one thing more to overcome on this continent, British influence. For, disguise it as men may, that influence, whether exercised through laws, commerce, or books, is fundamentally hostile to all who bear the Irish name, apostates excepted.

The successive British governments never *would* study the Irish nature, and, hence, never *could* govern it. They despised our history, and insisted on it that the caricatures of cockney imagination were true portraits of Irish character. They shipped us laws, ready made, and punished us because we were not patient with the mis-fit. The key to all Ireland's modern wars, sorrows, and agitations, is, that those who had the power to shape her destiny, never had the conscience to study her capabilities.

We must resist every semblance of such conduct on the part of the public men and thinkers on this continent. Every attempt to caricature or proscribe, every effort to exalt the Anglo-Saxon over the other races here undergoing solution, we must resist with reason, argument, and if need be, with well-used suffrages.

All the more generous natures will be easily convinced that it is not a worthy course to judge the vanquished out of the victor's mouth; that, if Ireland has done her part on this soil, she deserves her history to be read here, her genius to be studied, and her national character to be respected. With such men, who compose, perhaps, a majority of this whole people, arguments such as these would generally be found availing: —

17

" There is no observation more true, than that men are the creatures of circumstance. Individual men are, perhaps, less so than nations. Nations are the creatures of their own geography, their history, and their imaginations. In this Union, the idea of sovereignty is the extent of the state. When the individual measures himself against the continent, he feels its sovereign supremacy. In England, the seat of sovereignty is in the sea. In France, the unity of the provinces is the monarchy of all.

" The Irish, also, who settle in America, are creatures of their own antecedents. The Atlantic works no miracle on them. They come to these shores, the production of British power. Disfranchised in their native land, the suffrage is a novelty to them; disarmed, the use of arms is a possession not understood; ruled by a class, they abhor the very semblance of class legislation; untrained to freedom, they make but a poor figure, at first, as freemen.

" The tendency of all class legislation is to obliterate in men the double sense of their rights and their duties. Deny their rights, and you destroy their duties; for rights and duties are two sides of the same medal, and the people that are jealous of their rights must necessarily be true to their duties.

" The naturalized citizen will not only have to cast off his British allegiance, but also to get rid of his British education. The effects of laws are known to remain after the laws have been long abolished; and it is of these enervating, humbling, debasing effects, the emigrant from Ireland has to rid himself.

" In this good work of transition from subjection to citizenship, the natives of free America should be the sponsors and catechists. Being themselves free, nothing is left for them so glorious to do as to impart their freedom to others.

" It is not worthy of this great nation to take its political philosophy at second-hand from any nation. England has endeavored to misrepresent America to Europe, and Europe to America. She tries to be the international intelligencer. She holds up contrary mirrors to opposite states, in which each shows to disadvantage in the eyes of the other. She ' speaks with a double-tongue contradictory languages.' It will not do to trust her as the interpreter of nations, still less as the limner of her own vanquished provinces.

" Whether we may wish it or not, one half of Ireland is here. We grieve that these laborious and obedient men were not possessed of a land of their own; you may regret that they possess already too much of yours. But whether we would alter it, or not, they are here. Here, by the immediate action of British misrule, here by the primal authority of man's first charter, — 'Go forth, and fill the earth and subdue it.' We live in a world of facts, and this is one of its greatest. How, then, shall we deal with this great human force so placed at our disposal? Shall we, who do not suffer the obscurest stream to escape unused to the ocean, disregard what is of infinitely more value, the right use and direction of this moral Niagara, emigration? Physically, our emigrants are well-worked; nor do we underrate their value in that view. But are they not also of use as moral agents? Have they not memory, will, and reason? Have they not imagination, wit, and the desire to please and excel? Are we, democrats of the model republic, to regard men as machines, and to count them by the head, like cattle, rather than by souls, like Christians?

" O, believe me, American reader, ours is a people very teachable by those they love. Deal tenderly with their failings, they are a fallen race. Do not pander to their party prejudices, but appeal to their common sense and love of fair play. Do not make the weak, weaker, and the dependent, more dependent, but endeavor to fit them for equality, as well as liberty, so that the land may rejoice, and be secure in the multitude of its well-instructed children."

" What constitutes a State?
Not high-raised battlements, or labored mound,

> Thick walls, or moated gate;
> Not cities proud, with spires and turrets crowned,
>   Not bays, and broad-armed ports,
> Where, laughing at the storm, rich navies ride;
>   Nor starred and spangled courts,
> Where low-browed baseness wafts perfume to pride.
>   No. MEN, HIGH-MINDED MEN.
>   *   *   *   *   *   *
>   Men who their duties know,
> But know their rights; and knowing, dare maintain;
>   Prevent the long-aimed blow,
> And crush the tyrant, while they rend the chain."

Such a presentation of the case of the recent emigrant, addressed to individuals or societies in America, could not long be made in vain.   British prejudices would fade before it, and while the Irish would become more American, on the disappearance of that hostile influence, America in temperament and policy would become insensibly more Irish.

No people, — not even the natives of New England, — have a greater interest in the preservation of the Union, than the Celts in America.   What we never got from England, we have here, — equal laws and equal justice. And now, if, as seems the fact, our ancient and implacable enemy, through the agencies of corruption and flattery, seeks to undermine this Union, — our refuge, liberation, and relief, — the Irish in America, as a mass, as one man, must choose their place under the Constitution. The Union gives us homes, suffrages, and wages; the Union gives us peace, plenty, and equality; the Union protects our altars, confers our lands, accepts our services in peace and war, and educates our children.   The Union abolished the local persecutions of the Puritans and the Huguenot in Maryland and Massachusetts.   The Union burns no convents, sacks no graves, outrages no rite of religion, nor does it insult any of its sacred teachers. By the Union, therefore, we, too, "stand or fall, survive or perish," and, with Andrew Jackson, our motto as American settlers is, "THE UNION, IT MUST BE PRESERVED."

APPENDIX.

No. I.

THE TRADITION OF SAINT BRENDAN'S VOYAGE TO AMERICA.

THE ancient and wide-spread European tradition of Saint Brendan's voyage is to be gathered from the various sources indicated in the first chapter; that is, from Irish, Danish and Ecclesiastical chronicles, from the popular poems of the middle ages, and the cotemporary legends of the saints. I have thought some illustrations of the references in the text would be desirable : —

Colgan, in his *Acta Sanctorum Hibernia*, makes this mention of St. Brendan's youthful days : "When Brendan was a mere infant, he was placed under her care," (he is speaking of St. Ita, Abbess of *Cluan-Credhuil*, in Limerick,) " and remained with her five years, after which period he was led away by Bishop Ercus, in order to receive from him the more solid instruction necessary for his advancing years. Brendan retained always the greatest respect and affection for his foster mother; and he is represented after his seven years' voyage, as amusing St. Ita with an account of his adventures in the ocean." — *Colgan Acta S. S.*, p. 68, *Louvain*, 1637.

Unfortunately for our better information on this interesting subject, Colgan, who seems to have had the necessary Celtic materials, and who certainly had the requisite learning, did not live to finish his work. It extends only to the end of March, and the festival of St. Brendan being the 16th of May, his biography is not included in Colgan's *Acta.* He incidentally places the birth of St. Brendan in A. D. 485, and his voyage in 545. Dr. Lanigan thinks this latter date incorrect, as St. Brendan was then in his sixtieth year. But Columbus, we know, had passed his fiftieth when he undertook his voyage.

St. Brendan, before his voyage, was Bishop or Abbot of Ardfert and Clonfert, in the present county of Kerry, where the remains of churches, bearing his name, are still visited by tourists. He is honored as the patron of the Diocese of Clonfert.

17*

The Rev. Cæsar Otway, an Irish Episcopalian clergyman and writer of some note, reports the local tradition of the voyage, existing in the west of Ireland, as follows :

"We are informed that Brendan, hearing of the previous voyage of his cousin, Barinthus, in the western ocean, and obtaining an account from him of the happy isles he had landed on in the far west, determined, under the strong desire of winning heathen souls to Christ, to undertake a voyage of discovery himself. And aware that, all along the western coast of Ireland, there were many traditions respecting the existence of a western land, he proceeded to the islands of Arran, and there remained for some time, holding communication with the venerable St. Enda, and obtaining from him much information on what his mind was bent. There can be little doubt that he proceeded northward along the coast of Mayo, and made inquiry, among its bays and islands, of the remnants of the Tuatha Danaan people, that once were so expert in naval affairs, and who acquired from the Milesians, or Scots, that overcame them, the character of being magicians, for their superior knowledge. At Inniskea, then, and Innisgloria, Brendan set up his cross; and, in after times, in his honor were erected those curious remains that still exist. Having prosecuted his inquiries with all diligence, Brendan returned to his native Kerry; and from a bay sheltered by the lofty mountain that is now known by his name, he set sail for the Atlantic land; and, directing his course towards the south-west, in order to meet the summer solstice, or what we would call the tropic, after a long and rough voyage, his little bark being well provisioned, he came to summer seas, where he was carried along, without the aid of sail or oar, for many a long day. This, it is to be presumed, was the great gulf-stream, and which brought his vessel to shore somewhere about the Virginian capes, or where the American coast tends eastward, and forms the New England States. Here landing, he and his companions marched steadily into the interior for fifteen days, and then came to a large river, flowing from east to west; this, evidently, was the river Ohio. And this the holy adventurer was about to cross, when he was accosted by a person of noble presence,—but whether a real or visionary man does not appear,—who told him he had gone far enough; that further discoveries were reserved for other men, who would, in due time, come and Christianize all that pleasant land. The above, when tested by common sense, clearly shows that Brendan landed on a continent, and went a good way into the interior, met a great river running in a different direction from those he heretofore crossed; and here, from the difficulty of transit, or want of provisions, or deterred by increasing difficulties, he turned back; and, no doubt, in a dream, he saw some such vision which embodied his own previous thought, and satisfied him that it was expedient for him to return home. It is said he remained seven years away, and returned to set up a college of three thousand monks, at Clonfert, and he then died in the odor of sanctity."—*Otway's Sketches in Erris and Tyrawley*, note, pp. 98, 99. Dublin, 1845.

The *Codex Kilkeniensis*, in Primate Marsh's Library, Dublin, contains a fragment of an ancient life of St. Brendan, of which, it is possible, the missing parts may be yet recovered by the Irish archeologists.

In England, a version of the voyage was inserted by Capgrave, in his *Nova Legenda*, published in 1516. Wynkyn de Worde, the first English printer, (and a cotemporary of Christopher Columbus,) published the legend, with many adornments, of which we give a specimen : —

" Soon after, as God would, they saw a fair island, full of flowers, herbs, and trees, whereof they thanked God of his good grace ; and anon they went on land, and when they had gone long in this, they found a full fayre well, and thereby stood a fair tree full of boughs, and on every bough sat a fayre bird, and they sat so thick on the tree, that uneath any leaf of the tree might be seen. The number of them was so great, and they sung so merrilie, that it was an heavenlike noise to hear. Whereupon St. Brandon kneeled down on his knees and wept for joy, and made his praises devoutlie to our Lord God, to know what these birds meant. And then anon one of the birds flew from the tree to St. Brandon, and he with the flickering of his wings made a full merrie noise like a fiddle, that him seemed he never heard so joyful a melodie. And then St. Brandon commanded the foule to tell him the cause why they sat so thick on the tree and sang so merrilie. And then the foule said, sometime we were angels in heaven, but when our master, Lucifer, fell down into hell for his high pride, and we fell with him for our offences, some higher and some lower, after the quality of the trespass. And because our trespasse is but little, therefore our Lord hath sent us here, out of all paine, in full great joy and mirthe, after his pleasing, here to serve him on this tree in the best manner we can. The Sundaie is a daie of rest from all worldly occupation, and therefore that daie all we be made as white as any snow, for to praise our Lorde in the best wise we may. And then all the birds began to sing even song so merrilie, that it was an heavenlie noise to hear ; and, after supper, Saint Brandon and his fellows went to bed and slept well. And in the morn they arose by times, and then these foules began mattyns, prime, and hours, and all such service as Christian men used to sing ; and St. Brandon, with his fellows, abode there seven weeks, until Trinity Sunday was passed."

— The "Lyfe of Saynt Brandon" in the Golden Legend.
Published by Wynkyn de Worde.   1483.   Fol. 357.

The voyage was a favorite theme with the early metrical romance
writers, as was to be expected.   It was precisely the subject for
their school.   "Two French versions, as well as the original
Latin," says Mr. McCarthy, "have been published at Paris,"
under the following title, *" La Legende Latine de S. Bran-
daine's avec une traductione en prose et en poesie Romanes.
Publiée par Achille Jubinal,"* 1836.   An English translation
of one of the early French romances, which appeared in *Black-
wood's Edinburgh Magazine,* vol. xxxix., contains the following fine lines : —

> " Right toward the port their course they hold;
> But other dangers, all untold,
> Were there; before the gate keep guard
> Dragons of flaming fire, dread ward !
> Right at the entrance hung a brand
> Unsheathed, turning on either hand
> With innate wisdom ; they might well
> Bear it, for 't was invincible, —
> And iron, stone, ay, adamant,
> Against its edge had strength full scant.
> But, lo! a fair youth came to meet them,
> And with meek courtesy did greet them,
> For he was sent by Heaven's command
> To give them entrance to that land ;
> So sweetly he his message gave,
> And kissed each one, and bade the glaive
> Retain its place; the dragons, too,
> He checked, and led them safely through,
> And bade them rest, now they had come
> At last unto that heavenly home ,
> For they had now, all dangers past,
> To certain glory come at last.
> And now that fair youth leads them on,
> Where paradise in beauty shone ;
> And there they saw the land all full
> Of woods and rivers beautiful,
> And meadows large besprent with flowers,
> And scented shrubs in fadeless bowers,
> And trees with blossoms fair to see,
> And fruit also deliciously
> Hung from the boughs; nor briar, nor thorn,
> Thistle, nor blighted tree forlorn
> With blackened leaf, was there, — for spring
> Held aye a year-long blossoming ;
> And never shed their leaf the trees,
> Nor failed their fruit; and still the breeze
> Blew soft, scent-laden from the fields.
> Full were the woods of venison ;
> The rivers of good fish each one,
> And others flowed with milky tide, —
> No marvel all things fructified.
> The earth gave honey, oozing through
> Its pores, in sweet drops like the dew;

And in the mount was golden ore,
And gems, and treasure wondrous store.
There the clear sun knew no declining,
Nor fog nor mist obscured his shining ;
No cloud across that sky did stray,
Taking the sun's sweet light away;
Nor cutting blast, nor blighting air, —
For bitter winds blew never there;
Nor heat, nor frost, nor pain, nor grief,
Nor hunger, thirst, — for swift relief
From every ill was there; plentie
Of every good, right easily,
Each had according to his will,
And aye they wandered blithely still
In large and pleasant pastures green,
O, such as earth hath never seen !
And glad was Brandon, for their pleasure
So wondrous was, that scant in measure
Their past toils seemed ; nor could they rest,
But wandered aye in joyful quest
Of somewhat fairer, and did go
Hither and thither, to and fro,
For very joyfulness. And now
They climb a mountain's lofty brow,
And see afar a vision rare
Of angels, — I may not declare
What there they saw, for words could ne'er
The meaning tell; and melodie
Of that same heavenly company,
For joy that they beheld them there,
They heard, but could not bear its sweetness,
Unless their natures greater meetness
To that celestial place had borne, —
But they were crushed with joy. 'Return,'
Said they, — 'we may not this sustain.'
Then spoke the youth in gentle strain :
' O Brandon, God unto thine eyes
Hath granted sight of paradise;
But know, it glories hath more bright
Than e'er have dazed thy mortal sight;
One hundred thousand times more fair
Are these abodes ; but thou couldst ne'er
The view sustain, nor the ecstasy
Its meanest joys would yield to thee;
For thou hast in the body come;
But, when the Lord shall call thee home,
Thou, fitted then, a spirit free
From weakness and mortality,
Shalt aye remain, no fleeting guest,
But taking here thine endless rest.
And while thou still remain'st below,
That Heaven's high favor all may know,
Take hence these stones, to teach all eyes
That thou hast been in paradise.'
    Then Brandon worshipped God, and took
Of paradise a farewell look.
The fair youth led them to the gate;
They entered in the ship, and straight
The signal 's made, the wind flows free,
The sails are spread, and o'er the sea

> They bound; but swift and blithe, I trow,
> Their homeward course ; for where was foe,
> Of earth or hell, 'gainst them to rise,
> Who were returned from paradise ? "

It is mentioned among the accomplishments of a troubadour, by old Pierre St. Cloud, that he had many a tale

> " Of Arthur brave or Tristram bold,
> Of Charpel, of St. Brendan old."

Among the more matter-of-fact Flemings, the maritime fame of St. Brendan was not less general than with their French neighbors. Mr. Longfellow assigns their *Reis van Sainte Brandaen*, or "Journey of St. Brendan" to the twelfth century. In his "Poetry of Europe," (p. 372,) he gives the following account of this whimsical Dutch romance : —

"To the same century belongs the wonderful 'Journey of St. Brandaen,' (*Reis van Sainte Brandaen*,)* containing an account of his remarkable adventures by sea and land; how he put to sea with his chaplain and monks, and provisions for nine years; how, after sailing about for a whole year without sight of shore, they landed on what, like Sinbad the sailor, they supposed to be an island, but found to be a great fish; how they all took to their heels, and were no sooner on board than the fish sank and came near swamping their ship; how they were followed by a sea-monster, half woman, half fish, (*half wijf, half visch,*) which the saint sank with a prayer; how they came to a country of scoriæ and cinders, (*drossaerden en schinkers,*) where they suffered from the extremes of heat and cold; how they were driven by a storm into the Leverzee, (the old German *Lebermeer,*) where they saw a mast rise from the water, and heard a mysterious voice, bidding them sail eastward, to avoid the magnetic rocks, that drew to them all that passed too near; how they steered eastward, and saw a beautiful church on a rock, wherein were seven monks, fed with food from paradise by a dove and a raven; how they were driven by a south-west wind into the Wild Sea, in the midst of which they found a man perched on a solitary rock, who informed them he was the king of Pamphylia in Cappadocia, and, having been shipwrecked there ninety-nine years previous, had ever since been sitting alone on that solitary rock; how they came to a fearful whirlpool, called Helleput, or Pit of Hell, where they heard the lamentations of damned souls; how they arrived in Donkerland, a land covered with gold and jewels instead of grass, and watered by

* "This old romance is probably of French origin," says Mr. Longfellow. We see, by the text, that it was originally Irish, but was received in one shape or another in every country of Europe, from Denmark to Italy.

a fountain of oil and honey; how one of the monks stole there a costly bridle, by which afterwards a devil dragged him down to hell; how they came to a goodly castle, at the gate of which sat an old man with a gray beard, and beside him an angel with a flaming sword; how the monks loaded their ship with gold, and a great storm rose, and St. Brandaen prayed, and a demon came with the lost monk on his shoulders, and threw him into the rigging of the ship; how they sailed near the Burning Castle, (*Brandenden Burcht*,) and heard the dialogues of devils; how they came to the Mount of Syoen, and found there a castle whose walls were of crystal, inset with bronze lions and leopards, the dwelling of the *Walschrander*, or rebel angels; how they journeyed further, and found a little man no bigger than one's thumb, trying to bail out the sea; how a mighty serpent wound himself round the ship, and, taking his tail in his mouth, held them prisoners for fourteen days; and, finally, how they came to anchor, and St. Brandaen asked his chaplain, Noe, if he had recorded all these wonders, and the chaplain Noe answered, 'Thank God, the book is written,' (*God danc, lit boec es volscreven.*) And so ends this ancient 'Divina Commedia' of the Flemish school; not unlike, in its general tone and coloring, 'The Vision of Frate Alberico,' or 'The Legend of Barlaam and Josaphat,' and the rest of the ghostly legends of the middle ages, which mingled together monkhood and knight-errantry." *

To conclude this summary of the published versions of the tradition, I cannot refrain from alluding to the noble poem on the same subject, in D. F. McCarthy's "Poems," (Dublin, 1850;) a book which, if we were not such slaves of London criticism as we are, would long ago have been in every library in America. Our readers will thank us for the stanzas descriptive of the outward voyage of St. Brendan : —

I.

At length the long-expected morning came,
    When from the opening arms of that wild bay,
Beneath the hill that bears my humble name,
    Over the waves we took our untracked way :
Sweetly the morn lay on tarn and rill,
    Gladly the waves played in its golden light,
And the proud top of the majestic hill
    Shone in the azure air — serene and bright.

II.

Over the sea we flew that sunny morn,
    Not without natural tears and human sighs,
For who can leave the land where he was born,
    And where, perchance, a buried mother lies ,

* "Oudvlaemsche Gedichten der XII⁰, XIII⁰, en XIV⁰ Eeuwen, nitgegeven door JONKHR. PH. BLOMMAERT. Gent : 1838–41. 8vo."

Where all the friends of riper manhood dwell,
 And where the playmates of his childhood sleep :
Who can depart, and breathe a cold farewell,
 Nor let his eyes their honest tribute weep ?

III.

Our little bark, kissing the dimpled smiles
 On ocean's cheek, flew like a wanton bird,
And then the land, with all its hundred isles,
 Faded away, and yet we spoke no word.
Each silent tongue held converse with the past,
 Each moistened eye looked round the circling wave,
And, save the spot where stood our trembling mast,
 Saw all things hid within one mighty grave.

IV.

We were alone, on the wide, watery waste —
 Nought broke its bright monotony of blue,
Save where the breeze the flying billows chased,
 Or where the clouds their purple shadows threw
We were alone — the pilgrims of the sea —
 One boundless azure desert round us spread ;
No hope — no trust — no strength, except in THEE,
 Father, who once the pilgrim-people led.

V.

And when the bright-faced sun resigned his throne
 Unto the Ethiop queen, who rules the night, —
Who, with her pearly crown and starry zone,
 Fills the dark dome of heaven with silvery light, —
As on we sailed, beneath her milder sway,
 And felt within our hearts her holier power,
We ceased from toil, and humbly knelt to pray,
 And hailed with vesper hymns the tranquil hour '

VI.

For then, indeed, the vaulted heavens appeared
 A fitting shrine to hear their Maker's praise,
Such as no human architect has reared,
 Where gems, and gold, and precious marbles blaze.
What earthly temple such a roof can boast ? —
 What flickering lamp with the rich star-light vies,
When the round moon rests, like the sacred Host,
 Upon the azure altar of the skies ?

VII.

We breathed aloud the Christian's filial prayer,
 Which makes us brothers even with the Lord ;
" Our Father," cried we, in the midnight air,
 " In heaven and earth be thy great name adored •
May thy bright kingdom, where the angels are,
 Replace this fleeting world, so dark and dim."
And then, with eyes fixed on some glorious star,
 We sang the Virgin-Mother's vesper hymn !

VIII.

" Hail, brightest star ! that o'er life's troubled sea
  Shines pitying down from heaven's elysian blue !
Mother and maid, we fondly look to thee,
  Fair gate of bliss, where Heaven beams brightly through.
Star of the morning ! guide our youthful days,
  Shine on our infant steps in life's long race ;
Star of the evening ! with thy tranquil rays,
  Gladden the aged eyes that seek thy face.

IX.

" Hail, sacred maid ! thou brighter, better Eve,
  Take from our eyes the blinding scales of sin ;
Within our hearts no selfish poison leave,
  For thou the heavenly antidote canst win.
O sacred Mother ! 't is to thee we run —
  Poor children, from this world's oppressive strife ;
Ask all we need from thy immortal Son,
  Who drank of death, that we might taste of life.

X.

" Hail, spotless Virgin ! mildest, meekest maid —
  Hail ! purest Pearl that time's great sea hath borne —
May our white souls, in purity arrayed,
  Shine, as if they thy vestal robes had worn ;
Make our hearts pure, as thou thyself art pure —
  Make safe the rugged pathway of our lives,
And make us pass to joys that *will* endure
  When the dark term of mortal life arrives."

XI.

'T was thus, in hymns, and prayers, and holy psalms,
  Day tracking day, and night succeeding night,
Now driven by tempests, now delayed by calms,
  Along the sea we winged our varied flight.
O ! how we longed and pined for sight of land !
  O ! how we sighed for the green, pleasant fields !
Compared with the cold waves, the barest strand —
  The bleakest rock — a crop of comfort yields.

XII.

Sometimes, indeed, when the exhausted gale,
  In search of rest, beneath the waves would flee,
Like some poor wretch, who, when his strength doth fail,
  Sinks in the smooth and unsupporting sea,
Then would the Brothers draw from memory's store
  Some chapter of life's misery or bliss —
Some trial that some saintly spirit bore —
  Or else some tale of passion, such as this.

18

No. II.

MANY anecdotes of the early Irish settlers and the Indians might be given in this place, if the graver facts of a history too long neglected did not press for precedence. One or two points of chapter IV. will, nevertheless, be the better for some slight illustration.

It appears that Irish pedlers, or traders, were the most successful in dealing with the Indian tribes. In Western Pennsylvania, "McKee's Place" and "Mahoney" were founded by two traders. In 1763, we find mention of an Irish trader, "named Tracey, killed in the massacre" at Michilimackinac. In a dramatic piece called, "Ponteach, or the Savages in America," published at London in 1766, (republished at Boston, in Drake's "Tragedies of the Wilderness,") we find the Irish traders introduced among the *dramatis personæ*. The piece opens with — "Act I. Scene I. An Indian trading house; enter McDole (McDowell?) and Murphy, two Indian traders, and their servants." Dr. Parkman judges, from the actual knowledge of the wilderness displayed in this piece, "that Major Rogers," the famous pioneer, "had a hand in it." * Messrs. McDole and Murphy are plentifully supplied with rum, by administering a preparation of which, they make excellent bargains for furs with the intoxicated red men, — too true a picture of the times, we fear.

It is possible that the Irish traders being Catholics, as many of the Indians visited by the Jesuits were also, that, therefore, a peaceable intimacy was more easily established between them. There seems to have been something in an Irish education particularly suited to make Indian traders, interpreters, and allies. The Irish in the valleys of the Susquehanna and Juniata, at first, managed their savage neighbors very well. Afterwards, like the other inhabitants of the Sylvania, they were, in the middle of the last century, divided into two parties, for and against extermination. Colonel Stewart, of Donegal, was one of the leaders of the party for exterminating the reds; O'Hara, an alderman of Philadelphia, was at the head of the opposite one. In a satiric poem, in the Hudibras style, called "the Paxtoniade," published at Philadelphia in 1764, one of O'Hara's philanthropic speeches is travestied with some humor. Charles Thompson, who was, of course, of the humane party, published at London, in 1759, his "Causes of the Alienation of the Delaware and Shawnee Indians from the British Interest." In the border wars of Pennsylvania, we find the

---

* "Conspiracy of Pontiac," Appendix, p. 581. Boston, 1852.

brothers Croghan and McCulloch, whose cotemporary narratives are still accessible.

In the insurrection under Pontiac, which lasted from 1763 to 1769, and was the most formidable attempt ever made by the red race, many Irish lives were lost. This formidable league was crushed by William Johnson, "a young Irishman, who came to New York" in 1734, in 1754 was made a major-general, and created a baronet, for his services. He died, on his plantation in western New York, in 1774. His life is a curious and instructive story, hardly inferior in interest to Clive's or Hastings'. In a cotemporaneous poem upon the Pontiac War, published at Philadelphia, the author informs his readers that he "received his education in the great city of Dublin." If he did not fight better than he wrote, he could have been no great hero.*

In Mrs. Ellet's interesting memoirs of the "Women of the American Revolution," (New York, Baker and Scribner, 1849,) there are some capital anecdotes of the intrepidity displayed by the wives, sisters, and daughters of Irish settlers, against the armed Indians, and their worthy allies, the savage old Tories. Many others are scattered through old local histories.

Of the interpreters employed in the Indian territories, several were Irishmen; Henry Conner, long the interpreter at Detroit, is mentioned with commendation by Mr. Cass and Dr. Parkman.† He is quoted by all writers on the history of the north-western tribes.

Indian fighting seems to have come as naturally to our versatile predecessors as trading or translating. More than one Irishman of education was naturalized in the forest, like Stark and Houston, and obeyed as chiefs. Of the number was the strange character known as Tiger Roche, at one time the friend of Chesterfield, and the idol of Dublin drawing-rooms; at another, the tattooed leader of an Iroquois war-party. A Dublin barrister at law, and a Fermanagh landlord, went through similar scenes and adventures, some of which furnished Lever with the hints for his best character in "The Knight of Gwyne." Jackson and Harrison well knew the aptitude of Irishmen for Indian warfare, and we find them promoting many of them for valuable services and daring expeditions.‡ Perhaps, on the whole, our account of good and ill with the poor Indian is nearly balanced; but there should have been some credit on our side.

* Parkman's Conspiracy of Pontiac, p. 543.   † Ibid, p. 591.
‡ Butler, in his "History of Kentucky," gives us the following glimpse at one of Harrison's bivouacs :
"The general, seated round a small fire, with his staff, wrapped in his cloak, and taking the rain as it fell, directed one of his officers to sing an Irish glee. The humor of this song, and the determination which seemed to exist at *head-*

No. III.

THE only "History of the United States Navy," that has much reputation, is the late Fennimore Cooper's, which is somewhat compendious and inexact. A few points, in relation to distinguished Irishmen in the American service, are here supplied:

The first naval capture made in the name of the United Colonies, was that of the British store-ship Margaritta, in Machias Bay, in June, 1775. This bold attempt was made and effected by five brothers, the sons of Maurice O'Brien, a native of Cork, who then resided at Machias. Two British vessels, the Tapnaquish and Diligence, sent against the rebel village, were captured by the same brave men and their friends. A small squadron, consisting of a frigate, a twenty-gun corvette, a brig of sixteen guns, and several schooners, was next sent from Halifax, but, by the skill and bravery of the O'Briens, and Colonel Foster, was beaten off. An attack by land was decided on; but, on the second day's march from Passamaquoddy, the British troops returned to Halifax, despairing of effecting a passage through the woods.

" This affair," says Cooper, " was the Lexington of the seas; for, like that celebrated conflict, it was the rising of the people against a regular force,— was characterized by a long chase, a bloody struggle, and a victory. It was also *the first blow* struck on the water after the war of the American Revolution had actually commenced." *

The aged father of these heroic brothers could hardly be prevented from accompanying their expedition. After their first success, three of them made the sea their profession. Jeremiah was appointed to command "The Liberty," the armed schooner with which his first capture was made; his brother, William, served as his first lieutenant. John O'Brien served under Captain Lambert, as first lieutenant of "The Diligence." " For two years they did good service on the northern coast, affording protection to our navigation, after which they were laid up."† Jeremiah, with others, fitted out a twenty-gun letter-of-marque, called the Hannibal, manned by one hundred and thirty men. She took several small prizes; but, falling in with two British frigates, after a chase

quarters to put circumstances at defiance, soon produced cheerfulness and good-humor throughout the camp.

" The general was afterwards joined by a Kentucky officer, who sung a glee beginning with —

　　　　' Now 's the time for mirth and glee,
　　　　　Sing and dance and laugh with me.' "

* Cooper's Naval History.　　　† C. P. Ilsley, Portland Eclectic for 1851.

of forty-eight hours, the Hannibal was captured. O'Brien was imprisoned in "The Jersey" guard-ship, for six months, and then sent to Mill Prison, England, from which he escaped, after nearly a year's confinement. He retired, after the war, to Brunswick, in Maine, where, at the age of over four-score, he furnished the simple details of his famous beginning, to a generation that had shamefully forgotten him and them. *

Of John O'Brien, we find, in the history of the town where he died, at a ripe old age, some thirty years back, the following notice : " From a journal, kept by Captain John O'Brien, I make a few extracts. On June ninth, 1779, he sailed in the armed schooner Hibernia. On June twenty-first, took an English brig, and sent her in. On June twenty-fifth, had an engagement with a ship of sixteen guns, from three till five o'clock, P. M., when the Hibernia left her, having had three men killed, and several wounded, and was then chased by a frigate till twelve o'clock. On July seventh, took a schooner, and sent her to Newburyport. July tenth, in company with Captain Leach, of Salem, took a ship carrying thirteen four pounders, and on the same day took a brig, and then a schooner, laden with molasses. July eleventh, took an hermaphrodite brig, in ballast; and, having a number of prisoners on board, gave them the brig, and gave chase to another brig that was in sight, and took her. He concludes by saying, that ' if Captain Leach and he had not parted in the fog, they could have taken the whole fleet.' Captain O'Brien was engaged in many enterprises and battles, but was never taken."†

Of Lieutenant William O'Brien, I have found no further notice. He probably was killed at sea, or died in prison.

Of particular officers of the navy, except those of the first class, it is difficult to get any full information. Among the first commissions issued by Congress, December 22d, 1775, we find the names of Captains John Fanning, Daniel Vaughan, and John Barry. On the peace establishment, previous to 1801, we find Captains Barry, McNeil, Barron, Mullowney, and James Barron; Lieutenants Ross, McElroy, McRea, O'Driscoll, Byrne, Somers, McCutchen, and McClelland; Midshipmen McDonough, Roach, Carroll, Magrath, Fleming, Hartigan, Hennessy, Dunn, O'Brien, Walsh, Blakely, T. McDonough, T. Moore, C. Moore, Rossitter, McConnell, Blake, Kearney, and Casey,— all Irish, by birth or parentage. Of these, such as rose to high rank in the war of 1812, are specially mentioned in the fourteenth chapter. Those who perished in battle or the storm have also passed away from memory.

The United States Navy, for many years, owed much to the abilities of the late John Boyle, chief of the naval bureau at

---

* Historical Coll. of Maine, vol. I.   † Coffin's Newburyport, p. 407.

Washington, from 1813 to 1839.   Mr. Boyle was a United Irishman in his youth, and lost his fortune in that good cause.   Landing. in 1801, unknown and friendless, at Philadelphia, he earned
his first dollar by laboring as a coal-porter in discharging a ship.
He afterwards was employed by a merchant in Baltimore, where
he married Catherine, great-granddaughter of Ulick Burke, one of
Lord Baltimore's Irish settlers, and "the first proprietor of a brick
house in the colony."   Mr. Boyle obtained a professorship in St.
Mary's College, from which he passed, in 1813, to the naval
bureau, where, for nearly thirty years, he was the soul of the
department.   He often acted as Secretary of the Navy, and was
generally respected for his talents, judgment, and character.   He
resigned in 1839, and died at Washington, March 23, 1849, aged
seventy-two years.   He is worthily represented by his son, Dr.
Boyle, a resident at Washington.

The following authentic anecdote of the gallant McDonough,
which I find straying about, may aptly close these addenda:

"When McDonough was first lieutenant of the Siren, under the
command of Captain Smith, a circumstance occurred in the harbor
of Gibraltar indicative of the firmness and decision of his character.
An American merchant brig came to anchor near the United States
vessel.   McDonough, in the absence of Capt. Smith, saw a boat
from a British frigate board the brig, and take from her a man.
He instantly manned and armed his gig, and pursued the British
boat, which he overtook just as it reached the frigate, and without
ceremony took the impressed man into his own boat.   The frigate's
boat was twice the force of his own, but the act was so bold as to
astonish the lieutenant who commanded the press-gang, and so no
resistance was offered.   When the affair was made known to the
British captain, he came on board the Siren, in a great rage, and
inquired how he dared to take a man from his boat.   McDonough
replied that the man was an American seaman, and under the
protection of the flag of the United States, and it was his duty to
protect him.   The captain, with a volley of oaths, swore he would
bring his frigate alongside the Siren, and sink her.

" 'That you may do,' said McDonough; 'but while she swims,
the man you will not have.'

"The English captain told McDonough that he was a young hair-
brained fellow, and would repent of his rashness.   'Supposing,
sir,' said he, 'I had been in that boat; would you have dared to
have committed such an act?'

" 'I should have made the attempt, at all hazards,' was the
reply.

" 'What, sir!' said the captain, 'would you venture to interfere
if I were to impress men from that brig?'

" ' You can try it, sir,' was the reply of McDonough.

"The British captain returned to his vessel, manned a boat, and steered for the brig. McDonough did the same; but here the matter ended. The English captain took a circuitous route, and returned to his vessel. There was such a calmness in the conduct of Lieutenant McDonough, such a solemnity in his language, such a politeness in his manner, that the British officer saw that he had to deal with no ordinary man, and that it was best not to put him on his metal."

No. IV.

PARTICULARS OF SOME IRISH SETTLERS IN PENNSYLVANIA.

THE following letter, given *verbatim*, will be found suggestive of many useful reflections to our readers :—

"York, Pa., March 29th, 1852.

"SIR :— With the hope of being able to send you some *facts* for your History, I made an examination of the local history of York county, and hasten to send you the result of my ' labor of love.' I am the more anxious to see the names of our brave countrymen rescued from the obscurity of the grave, on account of the base ingratitude with which they have been neglected; for I believe that York, above all other counties in the state, is the most negligent in doing justice to her illustrious dead. The reason of this is obvious. Many parts of the county were settled by Irish families as early as 1734; towns were founded, and Celtic names given to them; but the Germans, who form, at present, the majority of the population, succeeded, in the course of time, in making themselves masters of these Irish settlements, and they now talk about us as if we were the outcasts of the earth, despised by God and man. Hanover, which was founded by an Irishman, whose name it bore for many years, has now a German name and German masters. What is the reason, sir, that the Irishman loses so much ground when brought into *practical* competition with his German neighbor ?

"It would be a tedious undertaking were I to give you an account of *all* the men of Irish birth and parentage who figured conspicuously in York county; the names of those whom I regard as particularly deserving of notice, are James Smith, ' the signer,' John Clark, Richard McAllister, and David Grier.

"JAMES SMITH is too well known for me to say much concerning him; yet there is not a record, in manuscript or in print, that gives a full biography of this distinguished Irishman. In Sanderson's 'Lives of the Signers' is the best account of him that has been published. The author came to York before he wrote it, and had an interview with James Johnston (Smith's son-in-law), and procured all the information that could be had respecting him.

"Thinking that I might be able to learn something of his life, I went to Mr. D. G. Barnitz, the executor of his estate (for there is not one of his descendants living), and learned from him that an accident, which happened in 1805, shut out from the world forever the possibility of procuring a detailed history of his services in the Revolution. In the destruction of his office by fire, his books and papers of business, which were on the lower floor, were saved; but all his numerous private papers, which were in the upper part of the building, were destroyed. Among these were the records of the family, manuscripts of his own, connected with the history of his times, and numerous letters from Franklin, Adams, and many other distinguished men of the Revolution. Mr. Smith died, in York, on the 11th of July, 1806. His monument, in the Presbyterian churchyard, states that he was ninety-three years old at the time of his death. I have been informed, by those who knew him, that he would never tell his age to his most intimate friends; there is, therefore, no small difference of opinion with regard to it. Some of his friends say that he was not so old by many years as is represented. There is one thing certain, that he must have been a member of the bar between sixty and sixty-five years. He was the first who raised a company of volunteers in this state, in opposition to the law of England.

"JOHN CLARK was born in Lancaster county, Pa., in 1751. His grandfather was an Irish weaver; but at what time the family came to this country, I am not informed. He had just commenced the practice of the law when the Revolution broke out; he relinquished it, and entered the service of his country, being then twenty-four years old. He proved himself no ordinary man. Attracting the attention of Congress, he was shortly commissioned as major, and was appointed aide-de-camp to Greene. In this capacity he rendered important service to the cause of liberty. He was confidential agent to Washington, and often procured him the most valuable information concerning the motions of the enemy. On one of his daring reconnoitring expeditions he fell into the hands of the British, and would have lost his life had he not effected his escape, which he did by the assistance of an English officer, who was a brother freemason. On another occasion, he took a party of the enemy prisoners, and marched them into Washington's camp. When the young officer in scarlet gave up his sword, the keen eye of Clark perceived some masonic devices on the scabbard, and asked permission to return it to the owner as a present; being refused by Washington, he kept the sword and standard, and left them to his children as reliques of the war. I have seen these, and many other memorials of his bravery, which are preserved by his daughters, three of whom are yet alive, in this place. Some years before his death, he was offered two hundred pounds if he would return the standard to the British government: he rejected the proposal with scorn.

"In 1776, he marched his detachment to join Washington on the Delaware. 'I crossed the river in the night, and lay, under a tree, with only a blanket over me,' are his own words, in a letter, which is now before me, containing also instructions how to avoid the Hessians, in the handwriting of Gen. Greene. Though surrounded on all sides by the enemy, he joined his beloved commander at Trenton, and gained his confidence so much that he was afterwards employed by him in duties for which no one would have been selected who was not true as steel.

"He continued to serve in the field until January, 1779. Previous to this period, he had accidentally received a dangerous wound from a pistol, which went off at the moment his servant was taking it up to put it in his holsters. The disability resulting from the effects of this wound had made him ineligible for active field service, and, on the tenth of the above-named month, he was appointed Auditor of Accounts for the army, in which capacity he acted until the first of November following, when the feebleness of his health compelled him, reluctantly, to quit the service; and he thus lost the benefits of pay, bounty, land, and commutation; and, though disabled by a severe wound, he had not, until the pension act of 1818, the benefit of a pension.

"In 1819, the committee of the United States Senate reported on his claim, but would not recognize a depreciation account at that time. His daughters are very indignant, and I think justly so, at the treatment they have received from Congress. They are very old, and have not wherewith to place a slab over the mortal remains of their heroic father.

"After the close of the Revolutionary War, Gen. Clark resumed the practice of the law, and continued in it until the time of his death. On the 27th of December, 1819, he attended court as usual, in good health, and returned home in the evening, and retired about half-past eight o'clock; at nine, on the same evening, he was dead. Thus ended the earthly career of as brave a man as ever drew a sword in the cause of liberty. He was sixty-eight years of age when he died. His remains are resting in the Episcopalian graveyard, without even a headstone to mark the grave of the brave soldier; but his epitaph is written on the hearts of all who knew him, and will not be effaced so long as man can appreciate true greatness and exalted virtue.

"General Clark's papers are now in my possession. I send you two letters, carefully copied from the original, as written by Washington,—one to Congress, the other to Clark while on one of his expeditions. While on his dangerous missions, the gallant Col. Fitzgerald was often the bearer of despatches to him from Washington : this shows what confidence the father of his country had in these men.

[WASHINGTON TO GENERAL CLARK.]

'Head-quarters, *Nov.* 10th, 1777.

'DEAR SIR :—I am favored with yours of this date, and send you fifty dollars for the purposes you mention. I beg I may have the most instant intelligence of any accounts that you may obtain, because I believe that some move of consequence is in agitation among the enemy. I shall, for that reason, be obliged to you for remaining a few days longer at your present station, as I can put more dependence upon having any accounts regularly and expeditiously forwarded by you than by any other in that quarter. I shall, with pleasure, give you that character to Congress which I think your services deserve; and am, dear sir, your most obedient servant,

'G. WASHINGTON.'

[WASHINGTON TO CONGRESS, INTRODUCING CLARK.]

'Head-quarters, *Valley Forge, Jan.* 2d, 1778.

'I take the liberty of introducing Gen. John Clark, the bearer of this, to your notice. He entered the service at the commencement of the war, and has for some time past acted as aide-de-camp to Major-General Greene. He is active, sensible, and enterprising, and has rendered me very great service, since the army has been in Pennsylvania, by procuring me constant and certain intelligence of the motions and intentions of the enemy. It is somewhat uncertain whether the state of his health will admit of his remaining in the military line : if it should, I shall, perhaps, have occasion to recommend him in a more particular manner to the favor of Congress, at a future time. At present, I can assure you, that if you should, while he remains in York, have any occasion for his services, you will find him not only willing, but very capable of executing any of your commands.

'Respectfully,   GEO. WASHINGTON.'

"RICHARD MCALLISTER was born in Ireland, in 1725, and came to this country when he was young. The first account of him that I can find in the records of this county, is in 1749, when he was elected Sheriff. In 1764 he founded the town of Hanover (a flourishing borough in this county). It was called McAllister's Town for many years before the Germans got it. The statute, by which it was erected into a borough, in 1815, says that it 'shall be comprised within the tract of land of Richard McAllister, deceased.' The only one of his descendants, at present living there, saws wood for his daily bread ! •Richard entered the army at an early period. In 1776, he was colonel of the second battalion of York County Volunteers, which marched to New Jersey, and was embodied with the 'Flying Camp,' ordered to be raised, by Congress, on the 3d of June in that year. This second battalion was mostly commanded by Irishmen. David Kennedy was lieutenant colonel, John Clark was major, and there were Captains McCarter and McCloskey. They all fought like heroes at Fort Washington, where Capt. McCarter received his death-wound, and died on the fifth day. He was twenty-two years old when he thus offered his life upon the altar of his country's freedom.

"Col. McAllister was a member of the Provincial Conference of Committees, which met at Philadelphia on the 18th of June, 1776; so was Col. Kennedy, Col. McPherson, and James Smith,— all Irishmen. He was also a member of the Council of Censors, which met on the 10th of November, 1783. After a life devoted to the service of his adopted country, he died, in Hanover, on the 7th of September, 1795, aged seventy years. His son, Archibald McAllister, was a captain in the eleventh regiment of the Pennsylvania line.

"I have thus endeavored to give you a brief sketch of those brave men. I have received, from Mr. D. G. Barnitz, a short memoir of David Grier, which I transcribe here:

"'Lieut. Col. DAVID GRIER was born at Braeke, Romelton, near Londonderry, county Donegal, Ireland, on the 27th of June, 1741, o. s. He emigrated to this country at an early period, and studied law with Mr. Bowie, and was admitted as a practising attorney of York county on the 23d April, 1771. He was commissioned a captain of a Pennsylvania Company, by Congress, on January 9, 1776, and afterwards commissioned major of the sixth battalion of Pennsylvanians, on the 1st June, 1776. He was finally commissioned, on the 12th January, 1777, lieutenant colonel of 'the seventh battalion of Pennsylvania, in the army of the United States.' He was wounded at the battle of Paoli, in the fall of 1777; and, returning to York, was employed in the War Department,— being unable, from the severity of the wound, to be actively engaged in the field. At the close of the war, in 1783, he resumed the practice of the law, and continued to be ranked as one of the ablest lawyers of Pennsylvania until 1790, when he finally died, from consumption, the effect of his wound. He left to survive him a widow and four daughters; three of these died unmarried, and the fourth was married to Hon. C. A. Barnitz, who was a distinguished attorney, and represented York county both in the state and national councils.   DANL. G. BARNITZ,

('Grandson of Lieut. Col. Grier.')

"I am informed by Major Emmett, a worthy citizen of this place, that his grand-uncle, who came to this country about the year 1730, was the founder of Emmettsburg, in Frederick county, Md. I believe his name was Abraham Emmett. Perhaps some of your readers in that place can give you a fuller account of him.

McSherrystown, in Adams county, was founded by the grandfather of James McSherry, the historian of Maryland. Gettysburg was founded by Major Getty, also an Irishman. I intend, God willing, to visit Adams county next summer, and, if I find anything of interest, I shall send it on to you. I think I risk nothing in saying that you can rely with certainty upon all that I have written. Wishing you success, I remain your obedient servant,

"MICHAEL McLAUGHLIN."

No. V.

IRISH SERVICES TO EDUCATION AND SCIENCE.

THE chapter treating upon the "Services of Irishmen to Education and Science in America," might have been much enlarged if the design had been to make a big book and a dear one. A few additional names and particulars may be useful, as indicating where further facts can be found.

Among historical works, we find Butler's Kentucky, Ramsay's South Carolina, Burke's Virginia, Edmund Burke's European Settlements in America, McMahon's Maryland, McSherry's Maryland, Dwyer's Buffalo, O'Reilly's Rochester, O'Callaghan's Documentary History of New York, Sullivan's Maine, Browne's Jamaica, Walsh's Jamaica, Madden's Cuba, Breen's St. Lucia, Warburton's Conquest of Canada, Bishop Burke's tracts on Nova Scotia. All these are the writings of Irishmen on American historical subjects.

In imaginative literature, our race has given less to America, than, from its tendencies, would be expected. In 1728, Thomas Makin's Latin poems appeared at Philadelphia; the poem on the Pontiac war, before alluded to, appeared thirty years after. With these exceptions, and the poems of the late John A. Shea, Mr. Gallagher, of Cincinnati, the Misses Carey, Miss Anna C. Lynch, daughter of an United Irishman, W. Mulchinock, and some other writers, we are not fully represented in this department.

In theology and politics we have done most. Bishop England's works; the several Catholic Controversies of Boston, New York, Philadelphia and Cincinnati; the learned Works of the Kendricks, brothers and archbishops; the Political Essays of Charles Thompson, Matthew Carey,* and William Sampson; the Speeches of

------

* A friend has furnished us the following condensed note of the Irish antecedents of that excellent and able man, the late Matthew Carey : —
   "He was established in the printing and publishing business in the city of Dublin, Ireland, as long ago as 1777. Two years later, having written and

Calhoun and of Emmett; the Lectures and Essays of Henry Giles; the Letters and Lectures of Archbishop Hughes; the various journals written by Irish hands; all these make up a fair contribution to American literature of this class. In political economy, we have furnished Henry C. Carey, certainly the most able and original American writer on that subject.

Yet, summing up all, it seems certain that, until the present, the Irish in America, in proportion to their numbers, have not done their share towards founding an American literature.

In science, so long as we have Robert Fulton, Colles, Adrain, and Oliver Byrne, we fear no comparison. In the application of science to practical objects, De Witt Clinton, in New York, and James Sullivan, in Massachusetts, from their high official position, were mainly instrumental in the "canal-ization" of their respective states. The introduction of the cotton manufacture, and the first railroad in Massachusetts, were also effected chiefly by the energy of another Irish American, PATRICK TRACEY JACKSON, born at Newburyport, August 14th, 1780. "His maternal grandfather," says his biographer, "from whom he derived his name, was Patrick Tracey, an opulent merchant of Newburyport, — an Irishman by birth, who, coming to this country, at an early age, poor and friendless, had raised himself, by his own exertions, to a position which his character, universally esteemed by his fellow-citizens, enabled him adequately to sustain." * When Arnold's expedition against Canada, by way of Maine, was quartered at Newbury, we find that on September 19th, 1775, the officers "dined at Mr. Nathaniel Tracey's," and on the 18th, "at Mr. Tristram Dalton's," another Irish merchant of Newbury. Writing from Fort Western, September 28th, Arnold returns his thanks "for the many favors received from" Mr. Nathaniel Tracey, at Newburyport, and desires his best respects to "Mrs. Tracey, your brother, and Mr. Jackson."† This Mr. Jackson, afterwards a member of Congress, married Pat-

---

published a patriotic political pamphlet, he was obliged to leave that country. He went to Paris, and was there employed in the office of Dr. Franklin, who was at that time the American envoy to the French court. In the course of a year afterwards, he returned to Ireland and commenced the publication of the 'Freeman's Journal.' In 1784, being then editor and proprietor of 'The Volunteer's Journal,' a paper which had called into existence the 'Volunteers of Ireland,' he was arrested and underwent a trial before the English House of Commons.

"On being discharged, he resolved to settle in America, and in January of the following year he established, in Philadelphia, a paper called 'The Pennsylvania Herald.' This was followed by the 'American Museum,' a periodical which, to the present day, is regarded by students of American history as an invaluable book of reference.

"Mr. Carey subsequently commenced the publication of books, and became one of the principal publishers in the country."

* Memoir of Patrick Tracey Jackson, Merchants' Magazine for 1848.
† Coffin's History of Newbury, p. 249.

rick Tracey's daughter, of whom the distinguished citizen of Massachusetts just mentioned, was born. After visiting India and the Cape, young Jackson went into the India trade at Boston, which, in 1812, he gave up for manufacturing. The beginnings of his cotton speculations are worthy of some detailed notice. His biographer says : —

"The first object to be accomplished was to procure a power-loom. To obtain one from England, was, of course, impracticable; and, although there were many patents for such machines in our patent office, not one had yet exhibited sufficient merit to be adopted into use. Under these circumstances, but one resource remained — to invent one themselves ; and this these earnest men at once set about. Unacquainted as they were with machinery, in practice, they dared, nevertheless, to attempt the solution of a problem that had baffled the most ingenious mechanicians. In England, the power-loom had been invented by a clergyman, and why not here by a merchant ? After numerous experiments and failures, they at last succeeded, in the autumn of 1812, in producing a model which they thought so well of, as to be willing to make preparations for putting up a mill for the weaving of cotton cloth. It was now necessary to procure the assistance of a practical mechanic, to aid in the construction of the machinery ; and the friends had the good fortune to secure the services of Mr. Paul Moody, afterwards so well known as the head of the machine-shop at Lowell.

"They found, as might naturally be expected, many defects in their model loom; but these were gradually remedied. The project hitherto had been exclusively for a weaving-mill, to do by power what had before been done by hand-looms. But it was ascertained, on inquiry, that it would be more economical to spin the twist, rather than to buy it; and they put up a mill for about one thousand seven hundred spindles, which was completed late in 1813. It will probably strike the reader with some astonishment, to be told that this mill, still in operation at Waltham, was probably the first one in the world that combined all the operations necessary for converting the raw cotton into finished cloth. Such, however, is the fact, as far as we are informed on the subject. The mills in this country — Slater's, for example, in Rhode Island — were spinning-mills only ; and in England, though the power-loom had been introduced, it was used in separate establishments, by persons who bought, as the hand-weavers had always done, their twist of the spinners.

"Great difficulty was at first experienced at Waltham, for the want of a proper preparation (sizing) of the warps. They procured from England a drawing of Horrock's dressing machine, which, with some essential improvements, they adopted, producing the dresser now in use at Lowell, and elsewhere. No method was, however, indicated in this drawing for winding the threads from the bobbins on to the beam; and, to supply this deficiency, Mr. Moody invented the very ingenious machine called the warper. Having obtained these, there was no further difficulty in weaving by power-looms."

In 1820, he was the founder of the city of Lowell, which he called for his relative and partner, Francis C. Lowell. From the sketch already quoted, we extract Mr. John A. Lowell's account of the event : —

"Ever prompt to act whenever his judgment was convinced, he began, as early as 1820, to look around for some locality where the business might be extended, after the limited capabilities of Charles river should be exhausted.

"In 1821, Mr. Ezra Worthen, who had formerly been a partner with Mr. Moody, and who had applied to Mr. Jackson for employment, suggested that the Pawtucket canal, at Chelmsford, would afford a fine location for large manufacturing establishments; and that probably a privilege might be purchased of its proprietors. To Mr. Jackson's mind, the hint suggested a much more stupendous project, — nothing less than to possess himself of the whole power of the Merrimack river, at that place. Aware of the necessity of secrecy of action, to secure this property at any reasonable price, he undertook it single-handed. It was necessary to purchase not only the stock in the canal, but all the farms on both sides of the river, which controlled the water-power, or which might be necessary for the future extension of the business. No long series of years had tested the extent and profit of such enterprises; the great capitalists of our land had not yet become converts to the safety of such investments. Relying on his own talent and resolution, without even consulting his confidential advisers, he set about this task at his own individual risk; and it was not until he had accomplished all that was material for his purpose, that he offered a share in the project to a few of his former colleagues. Such was the beginning of Lowell; a city which he lived to see, as it were, completed. If all honor is to be paid to the enterprise and sagacity of those men who, in our day, with the advantage of great capital and longer experience, have bid a new city spring up from the forest on the borders of the same stream, accomplishing almost in a day what is in the course of nature the slow growth of centuries, what shall we say of the forecast and energy of that man who could contemplate and execute the same gigantic task at that early period, and alone ?"

Another service to his state was the introduction of the first railroad,— the Boston and Lowell. His biographer says : —

" In 1830, the interests of Lowell induced Mr. Jackson to enter into a business new to himself and others. This was the building of the Boston and Lowell railroad. For some years, the practicability of constructing roads, in which the friction should be materially lessened by laying down iron bars, or trams, had engaged the attention of practical engineers in England. At first, it was contemplated that the service of such roads should be performed by horses; and it was not until the brilliant experiments of Mr. Stephenson, on the Liverpool and Manchester railroad, that the possibility of using locomotive engines was fully established. It will be well remembered that all the first estimates for railroads in this country were based upon a road-track adapted to horse-power, and horses were actually used on all the earlier roads. The necessity of a better communication between Boston and Lowell had been the subject of frequent conversation between Mr. Boott and Mr. Jackson. Estimates had been made, and a line surveyed for a Macadamized road. The travel between the two places was rapidly increasing; and the transportation of merchandise, slowly performed in summer by the Middlesex Canal, was done at great cost, and over bad roads, in winter, by wagons.

" At this moment, the success of Mr. Stephenson's experiments decided Mr. Jackson. He saw, at once, the prodigious revolution that the introduction of steam would make in the business of internal communication. Men were, as yet, incredulous. The cost and the danger attending the use of the new machines were exaggerated; and even if feasible in England, with a city of one hundred and fifty thousand souls at each of the termini, such a project, it was argued, was Quixotical here, with our more limited means and sparser population. Mr. Jackson took a different view of the matter; and when, after much delay and difficulty, the stock of the road was subscribed for, he undertook to superintend its construction, with the especial object that it might be in every way adapted to the use of steam-power, and to that increase of travel and transportation which few had, like him, the sagacity to anticipate.

" Mr. Jackson was not an engineer; but, full of confidence in his own energy, and in the power he always possessed of eliciting and directing the talent of others, he entered on the task, so new to every one in this country, with the same boldness that he had evinced twenty years before, in the erection of the first weaving-mill.

" The moment was an anxious one. He was not accustomed to waste time in any of his undertakings. The public looked with eagerness for the road, and he was anxious to begin and to finish it. But he was too wise a man to allow his own impatience, or that of others, to hurry him into action before his plans should be

maturely digested. There were, indeed, many points to be attended to, and many preliminary steps to be taken. A charter was to be obtained, and, as yet, no charter for a railroad had been granted in New England. The terms of the charter, and its conditions, were to be carefully considered. The experiment was deemed to be so desirable, and, at the same time, so hazardous, that the Legislature were prepared to grant almost any terms that should be asked for. Mr. Jackson, on the other hand, whose faith in the success of the new mode of locomotion never faltered, was not disposed to ask for any privileges that would not be deemed moderate after the fullest success had been obtained; at the same time, the recent example of the Charles River Bridge showed the necessity of guarding, by careful provisions, the chartered rights of the stockholders.

"With respect to the road itself, nearly everything was to be learned. Mr. Jackson established a correspondence with the most distinguished engineers of this country and of Europe; and it was not until he had deliberately and satisfactorily solved all the doubts that arose in his own mind, or were suggested by others, that he would allow any step to be decided on. In this way, although more time was consumed than on other roads, a more satisfactory result was obtained. The road was graded for a double track; the grades reduced to a level of ten feet to the mile; all curves, but those of very large radius, avoided; and every part constructed with a degree of strength nowhere else, at that time, considered necessary. A distinguished foreigner, Mr. Charles Chevalier, has spoken of the work on this road as truly 'Cyclopean.' Every measure adopted shows conclusively how clearly Mr. Jackson foresaw the extension and capabilities of the railroad.

"It required no small degree of moral firmness to conceive and carry out these plans. Few persons realize the difficulties of the undertaking, or the magnitude of the results. The shareholders were restless under increased assessments and delayed income. It is not too much to say that no one but Mr. Jackson, in Boston, could, at that time, have commanded the confidence necessary to enable him to pursue his work so deliberately and so thoroughly.

"The road was opened for travel in 1835, and experience soon justified the wisdom of his anticipations. Its completion and successful operation was a great relief to Mr. Jackson. For several years it had engrossed his time and attention, and at times deprived him of sleep. He felt it to be a public trust, the responsibility of which was of a nature quite different from that which had attended his previous enterprises.

"One difficulty that he had encountered in the prosecution of this work led him into a new undertaking, the completion of which occupied him a year or two longer. He felt the great advantage

19*

of making the terminus of the road in Boston, and not, as was done in other instances, on the other side of the river.   The obstacles appeared, at first sight, insurmountable.   No land was to be procured in that densely populated part of the city, except at very high prices; and it was not then the public policy to allow the passage of trains through the streets.   A mere site for a passenger depot could, indeed, be obtained ; and this seemed, to most persons, all that was essential.   Such narrow policy did not suit Mr. Jackson's anticipations.   It occurred to him that, by an extensive purchase of the flats, then unoccupied, the object might be obtained. The excavations making by the railroad at Winter Hill, and elsewhere, within a few miles of Boston, much exceeded the embankments, and would supply the gravel necessary to fill up these flats. Such a speculation not being within the powers of the corporation, a new company was created for the purpose.   The land was made, to the extent of about ten acres ; and what was not needed for depots was sold at advantageous prices.   It has since been found that even the large provision made by Mr. Jackson is inadequate to the daily increasing business of the railroad."

In the summer of 1847, this remarkable man, who had enriched almost every citizen in the state more than himself, by the improvements he introduced, died at Beverly, Massachusetts, of dysentery. If he had another Christian name, we would have monuments to his memory.   As yet the trump of fame in the east refuses to sound the pre nomen PATRICK !   Poor human nature !

No. VI.

THE UNITED IRISHMEN IN AMERICA.

IN Chapter XIII. there is a sketch of the public life of the principal United Irishmen, who, with the consent of the British government, exiled themselves to the United States.   Some interesting facts, concerning other members of that party, both before and after the insurrection, may not improperly be added to those already given.

Among those who were obliged to fly Ireland before the year 1798, Archibald Hamilton Rowan was, on many accounts, one of the most remarkable.   He inherited a fine fortune, was a graduate of Cambridge, and had led an eventful life, before he joined the United Irishmen ; having been, in succession, secretary to the last colonial governor of South Carolina, major in the Irish Volunteers, colonel in the Portuguese army, a devotee of Marie Antoinette, and, lastly, an ally of Wolfe Tone.   Having escaped from Newgate, where he had been sent on a charge of seditious writings, he fled from Dublin to France, from whence he emigrated to Philadelphia in 1795. That city was then the seat of government, and Washington was president. Rowan lodged in the same house with John Adams ánd Andrew Jackson. "It had been my intention," he writes in his *Autobiography*, "to have waited on the president, but being informed that Washington had refused to receive Talleyrand, I gave up that idea; and, having determined on removing to some country situation, I fixed upon Wilmington, in the state of Delaware." Soon after this removal he was joined by three of his old associates in patriotism, Tone and Tandy, and Dr. Reynolds, the same whose name is mixed up in the federal riots. "It was a singular rencontre," says Tone, "and our several escapes from an ignominious death seemed little short of a miracle. We communicated our adventures since our last interview, which took place in the jail of Newgate, in Dublin, fourteen months before." "Mr. Tone," Rowan writes in August, 1795, "has bought an hundred acres of ground. The situation is pleasant, and within two or three miles of Princeton, where there is a college, and some good society. Tandy arrived here about a fortnight or three weeks since; he has got a lodging in the same house with me, and, of course, we mess together." News from Ireland and from France, by the end of the year, induced Tone to devote himself to the design of a French-Irish alliance, with which object he sailed from New York on New Year's day, 1796, and, on arriving in Paris, found a friend and adviser in James Monroe, the American ambassador, and, in after years, president. Tandy followed Tone's example, and returned to France. Both attained rank as general officers in that country, where Tandy died at an old age. Dr. Reynolds remained at Philadelphia. Mr. Rowan resided in America till the year 1800, when he was permitted to return home. During this time, as he could not induce his family to emigrate, he took no steps to become an American citizen. At first he writes his wife — "One wants me to remain in Philadelphia, and another 'to buy a small farm in a settled country. But I will do neither; I will go to the woods, but I will not kill Indians or keep slaves." He seems to have been thoroughly disgusted with Philadelphia politics, as they then were. In 1796, he writes, "I assure you, except on general topics, I scarcely open my lips." His familiar associates were the Butler family, Dickinson, (author of "The Farmer's Letters,") and Cæsar Rodney; but, even with them, he seldom talked on American affairs. His prudence, in this respect, was admirable, when we consider his temperament. He speaks, in 1797, of "the imprudent interference of some of my own countrymen in their politics, which it is almost impossible to avoid." In the same year he started a calico printing establishment at Wilmington, which he abandoned the next, as an unfit speculation for one of his habits. In 1798, he was fiercely attacked by Cobbett, then editing the *Porcupine Gazette* at Philadelphia, on the ground of being an avowed "antifederalist." This statement Mr. Rowan corrected, declaring, in accordance with all his previous views, that, "not being a citizen, (he) studiously avoided mingling in the politics of the country." The only events of his residence, which had any historical interest, were his acquaintance with Kosciusko, and his participation in the obsequies of Washington. After his return to his native land, he lived in honor and in peace, until February, 1834. During this time he kept up a kindly intercourse with those of his old associates who remained upon this side of the sea. The following letters, given in his AUTOBIOGRAPHY, belong to this part of our subject : —

"New York, January 8th, 1827.
"My Dear Old Friend, —

"For, as I am feeling the advances of age, I presume you have not remained *in statu quo* for the last five and twenty years, — I received your letter by Mr. Macready, and thank you for it. Many circumstances prevented my answering it until now, which it is impossible to detail on paper; but, be assured, no indifference or coldness of feeling towards you had any share in causing the delay. Mr. Macready is a gentleman whose talents and worth have gained him very high consideration here, and who has entirely justified the warm recommendations he was the bearer of from Europe.

"I dare not write to you about Ireland, though probably, if we were together, we should talk of little else. I remember the day when I fancied letters might be intercepted; if such a thing could happen now, a letter from T. A. E. to A. H. R., filled with Irish politics, would be a *bonne bouche* for a secretary. America is not what you saw it, nor what even your sanguine mind could anticipate; it has shot up in strength and prosperity beyond the most visionary calculation. It has great destinies, and I have no doubt will ameliorate the condition of man throughout the world. When you were here, party raged with a fiend-like violence, which may lead you to misjudge of what you may occasionally meet with in an American newspaper, should you ever look in one. Whether the demon be absolutely and forever laid, I cannot undertake to say; but there is at present no more party controversy than ought to be expected, and perhaps ought to exist in so free a country; and sure I am it does not interfere with the general welfare and happiness; indeed, I think it never can, their roots are struck so deep. Of myself and family I need only say we are all extremely well. I have succeeded better than I thought possible, when I set foot on this shore. I still enjoy my health and faculties. The companion of my youth and of my sufferings does the same. We are surrounded by eight children and twelve grand-children, with the prospect of steady and progressive increase in the American ratio.

"I pray God you have had your share of the happiness of this life.

"Your sincere and affectionate friend,

"THOMAS ADDIS EMMET.

"ARCHIBALD HAMILTON ROWAN, Esq."

Mr. Emmet did not long survive the date of this letter. In 1829 Mr. Rowan received from William Sampson, the well-known Irish exile, an epistle, in which, after expatiating on Mr. Rowan's "honorable principles," on Mrs. Rowan's kindness to his wife, and on the state of Irish politics, he continues thus : —

"You have, I presume, heard of the death of Thomas Addis Emmet, and probably of the extraordinary honors paid to his memory ; how a monument was voted by the bar of New York, which has since been established in the court-room where he 'fell. A eulogy was also voted, which De Witt Clinton, governor of this state, had undertaken to deliver ; and by the same resolutions I was requested, as an incentive to the younger members of the profession, and as a model for their imitation, to write a history of his life. I could not refuse a task so honorable, and I accepted of it. But I was soon after seized with an aguish complaint, which returned from time to time, and so far debilitated me that I was unable to make any strenuous exertion. I had besides the affliction of losing my son-in-law, Captain Tone, son of one that you knew well, and husband of my daughter, now my only surviving child. This obliged me to lay aside the work, but, with returning health, I have now resumed it.

"I was greatly disappointed, also, in applying to the family of my deceased friend, in finding that I could have not the least assistance from any of them. Mrs. Emmet, who loved her husband most tenderly, and did him honor whilst he lived, was affected by his death in such a manner that she cannot speak upon the subject of his early life, and his children were too young to know anything of it ; several of them, indeed, were born here. That portion of Emmet's life past in this city affords little incident. It was entirely absorbed in the duties of his profession, and in a course of unexampled industry. He was looked upon with admiration for his abilities, learning, and eloquence, and universally beloved for his virtues and his manner of living ; and, great as was the tribute paid to him, he deserved it all. He was a shining honor to his country. There exists amongst all here the greatest curiosity to know the particulars of his former life, and, indeed, everything concerning him. I have been trying to make arrangements for the publication of the work in London. You were one of the men Emmet most esteemed, and now that the events of those days are matters of past and useful history, I should request of you to assist me with some account of him and his family, his father, his brother Temple, his early studies, travels, first entry into public life, and to point me out where such details are to be looked for. You, it is true, had nothing to do with the *rebellion* in Ireland, nor do I expect anything of that kind from you; but any letters of his, however trivial or familiar the subject, may go to satisfy the friends under whose commission I act. I shall, if I can find one, send you a copy of a eulogy upon him by Dr. Mitchell, whose name, probably whose person, you must know. Mr. De Witt Clinton, late governor of this state, one of the most distinguished of our statesmen, had undertaken to fulfil the vote of the bar, and would have delivered a eulogy upon him, but he was called upon to pay his great debt before the day appointed; and it is urgent with me to discharge this duty before a similar casualty should put a bar to my performance forever. I owe much on my own account to my professional brethren here, as you will see by an article which I forward to you, containing their kind and affectionate adieus when, some years ago, after the marriage of my daughter, I went to reside in Georgetown, D. C. Since my son-in-law's death I have again fixed my residence in this city. I have seen a book advertised, called the History of the Leaders of the Rebellion in 1798. Is there anything in it that could help me in the biography of Emmet? There never yet was fair play nor justice shown to the sufferers in that unhappy struggle. I often wonder how I myself, and other men given to peace entirely, should have been driven from less to more, by mere feeling for others, to desperation, and almost to self-devotion; for I was always among the least sanguine and backward, till no neutrality was left, and then, even then, there was nothing to warrant any part of what was done to me latterly.

"I had, indeed, taken my ground; but if law was to be had, and I was willing to chicane, I should have as good actions of false imprisonment as ever man had. But now I am for truth, and no other revenge. It is so long since I have encountered any hostility or ill office, or envious or angry words from any man, that I may truly say I live in charity with all mankind, in which blessed spirit, &c., as they say at the end of all sermons, may we all live.

"Your sincere and obliged friend,
"W. SAMPSON.

"New York, April 29th, 1829."*

* Autobiography of Archibald H. Rowan, p. 469. Dublin: Tegg & Co., 1840.

Unfortunately Sampson's health never entirely recovered, and the projected biography never appeared. Of the accomplishments and vivacity of this excellent man, the daughter of his dearest friend, Dr. McNeven, has given a pleasant sketch. Writing to Dr. Madden, she says : —

"At the period of Mr. Emmet's death I was too young to have many personal recollections of him; but of Mr. Sampson I have the most vivid and affectionate remembrance. His family and ours have ever been united in the warmest friendship, and when I look back, the pleasantest of our past recollections are connected with him. He possessed, more than any one I ever knew, the power of creating enjoyment; it was impossible that any company could be dull of which he was a part. His brilliant wit and pleasant fancy enlivened and adorned the conversation, whether grave or gay. I wish it were in my power to describe, as I remember it, the delightful social intercourse between our families.

"My grandfather, Mr. Riker, a descendant of the early Dutch settlers, resided on his farm, on the shore of a beautiful bay, about eight miles from the city. He had served his country through her revolutionary struggle, and afterwards as a representative in Congress; and had a mind and heart to appreciate and understand men like my father and Mr. Sampson, whose society he greatly enjoyed. Mr. Sampson, to the great qualities of his mind, added a refinement, I may say a poetry of feeling, which enabled him to relish keenly the beauties of nature, and to tinge even the commonplace realities of life with a bright and pleasing coloring. He had always great delight in boating, and, during his years of health and vigor, was never without a boat large enough to hold himself, his friends and their families; and it was one of his greatest pleasures to collect them together, and make excursions up the river, to visit the Rikers, his friends at Bowery Bay. The sail from New York up the East river is one of much variety and beauty, with just sufficient peril in passing through the narrow passage, called Hellgate, to give it a romantic interest; but Mr. Sampson was a master of boat-craft, and used safely to conduct his little vessel through all dangers, until it entered the smooth waters of the bay, when he would give notice of his approach, by playing an air on his flute, always his companion, and he was greeted by a hearty welcome before his boat could reach the shore. Sometimes the sound of his flute might be heard at the quiet farm-house, of a moonlight night, as late as eleven or twelve o'clock. The doors were immediately thrown open to receive the party, and after passing an hour or two in cheerful conversation, he and his friends would take the turn of the tide and sail gayly back to the city. I have often, in thinking of these scenes, contrasted the peaceful serenity and pure pleasures of the exiled lives of my father and his friends, with the stormy and painful ordeal they had encountered in their native land." *

Sampson died in 1836, and McNeven so recently as 1841. A recent writer thus gracefully closes the best notice of their lives that has appeared in America : —

" A few miles from New York, in a small grave-yard, overlooking the waters of the Sound, rest Sampson and McNeven, two as brave hearts as ever lived or died for any country. The Protestant and the Catholic sleep side by side, as if to carry out even in the grave the principles of the United Irishmen. ' They were lovely and pleasant in their lives, and in death they were not divided.' A rose-bush, planted on this spot, has grown till it now covers it with beauty and fragrance. Not many months ago an Irish heart, led by sympathy to the spot, discovered that a little bird had built its nest over the graves. Was this the spirit of some Irish exile, which had come to pour its lament over the dust of the benefactors of his country ?" †

No. VII.

CONCLUSION.

SUITABLY to close this record of the Irish race in America, it only remains to append some statistics of the actual position of that holy religion which they have been so widely instrumental in establishing. Other races have contributed forms of speech and of law; but that which, in the lifetime of a nation, wears well and wears longest, is the religion which dictates the use of the one and restrains the abuse of the other.

While we write these supplementary pages, in the month of May, 1852, the second National Council of the Catholic Church in the United States has just closed, at Baltimore. It assembled at the residence of the Ab-legate, the Most Reverend and Illustrious Francis Patrick Kendrick, Archbishop of Baltimore, on Sunday, the ninth day of this month, and proceeded to the cathedral, where the council was formally opened. Eight Archbishops, twenty-six Bishops, and one mitred Abbot, accompanied by their several Doctors of Theology, attended ; and the city was so crowded with lay spectators, that it was with some difficulty the procession could proceed to and from the cathedral. ‡ How different, in the

---

* The Irish Confederates and the Rebellion of 1798, by Henry M. Field. pp 344. New York, Harper & Brothers, 1851.   † Ibid., p. 347.
; ‡ The following is a list of the prelates in attendance at the National Council, with the dates of their several consecrations, so far as ascertained : —

numbers and cares, was this holy assembly from that which in 1791 the then Bishop Carroll convened in the same city! Then one Bishop, three Vicars, the President of the St. Sulpice's, and sixteen priests, made the Catholic Council of these States. In 1829, one Archbishop and five Bishops composed the first Provincial Council; in 1833, the number of Bishops had increased to nine; in 1837, it was the same; in 1840, at the fourth Provincial Council, there were with the Archbishop twelve Bishops; at the fifth Provincial Council, in 1843, there were fifteen Bishops, and one Vicar; at the sixth, in 1846, there were twenty-two Bishops with the Archbishop.

Province of Baltimore. — Most Rev. Francis Patrick Kendrick, D. D., Archbishop of Baltimore, consecrated June 6, 1830; Right. Rev. Ignatius Reynolds, D. D., Bishop of Charleston, consecrated March 19, 1844; Right Rev. John McGill, D. D., Bishop of Richmond, consecrated Nov. 10, 1850; Right Rev. Michael O'Conner, D. D., Bishop of Pittsburg, consecrated August 15, 1843; Right Rev. Richard V. Whelan, D. D., Bishop of Wheeling, consecrated March 21, 1841; Right Rev. Francis X. Gartland, D. D., Bishop of Savannah, consecrated Nov. 10, 1850; Right Rev. John Nepomucene Neumann, D. D., Bishop of Philadelphia, consecrated March 28, 1852.

Province of New Orleans. — Most Rev. Anthony Blanc, D. D., Archbishop of New Orleans, consecrated Nov. 22, 1835; Right Rev. Michael Portier, D. D., Bishop of Mobile, consecrated Nov. 5, 1826; Right Rev. John J. Chanche, D. D., Bishop of Natchez, consecrated March 14, 1841; Right Rev. John M. Odin, D. D., Bishop of Galveston, consecrated March 6, 1842; Right Rev. Andrew Byrne, D. D., Bishop of Little Rock, consecrated March 10, 1844.

Province of New York. — Most Rev. John Hughes, D. D., Archbishop of New York, consecrated Jan. 7, 1838; Right Rev. John McCloskey, D. D., Bishop of Albany, consecrated March 10, 1844, Right Rev. John Fitzpatrick, D. D., Bishop of Boston, consecrated March 24, 1844; Right Rev. John Timon, D. D., Bishop of Buffalo, consecrated Oct. 17, 1847; Right Rev. Bernard O'Reilly, Bishop of Hartford, consecrated Nov. 10, 1850.

Province of Cincinnati. — Most Rev. John B. Purcell, D. D., Archbishop of Cincinnati, consecrated Oct. 13, 1833; Right Rev. Martin J. Spalding, D. D., Bishop of Louisville, consecrated Sept. 10, 1848; Right Rev. P. P. Lefevre, D. D., Bishop of Zela, in part, coadjutor and administrator of Detroit, consecrated Nov. 21, 1841; Right Rev. Amendeus Rappe, D. D., Bishop of Cleveland, consecrated Oct. 10, 1847.

Province of St. Louis. — Most Rev. Peter Richard Kenrick, D. D., Archbishop of St. Louis, consecrated Nov. 30, 1841; Right Rev. Mathias Loras, D. D., Bishop of Dubuque, consecrated July 28, 1837; Right Rev. Richard P. Miles, D. D., Bishop of Nashville, consecrated Sept. 16, 1838; Right Rev. John P. Henni, D. D., Bishop of Milwaukie, consecrated March 19, 1844; Right Rev. James O. Vandevelde, D. D., Bishop of Chicago, consecrated Feb. 11, 1849; Right Rev. Joseph Cretin, D. D., Bishop of St. Paul's, consecrated Jan. 26, 1851.

Province of Oregon City. — Most Rev. Francis N. Blanchet, D. D., Archbishop of Oregon City, consecrated in 1845; Right Rev. Magloire Blanchet, D. D., Bishop of Walla Walla, consecrated Sept. 27, 1849. The See of Nesqualy, administered by Archbishop Blanchet, and those of Fort Hall and Colville, administered by Bishop Blanchet, are now vacant.

Diocese of Monterey. — Right Rev. Joseph Alemany, D. D., Bishop of Monterey, consecrated 1850.

Apostolic Vicariate of New Mexico. — Right Rev. John Lamy, D. D., Vicar Apostolic of New Mexico.

Apostolic Vicariate of Indian Territory. — Right Rev. John Miege, D. D., Vicar Apostolic of the territory east of the Rocky Mountains.

20

In this interval of little more than half a century, the number of Bishops had increased over twenty-fold, and the number of pastors and churches had proportionately multiplied. The number of the faithful must have increased more than a hundred-fold, from Bishop Carroll's conjectural census of 1785, when he (erroneously, as we think) placed them at twenty-five thousand. Exceedingly difficult it is to form a correct estimate of the total Catholic population in the Union at any given time, even the present.* The clergy and bishops return only the numbers as they appear on their registries of births or marriages, and we have no proof that these registries are quite correct, or are kept by every missionary priest. With some personal experience of the most densely settled province of the American church, we venture to state that it is almost impossible to obtain a near approximation to the true aggregate of Catholics. At the present writing, we have no hesitation in declaring our own estimate to be nearer four than three millions. This, of course, includes a large number of minors, born and baptized abroad, and a considerable number of nominal Catholics, whose negligent lives leave no record of the faith behind, except a hurried death-bed repentance.

By direction of his Holiness Pope Pius IX., the first National Council was convened, by Archbishop Eccleston, at Baltimore, on Sunday, May 6th, 1849. The Archbishop of St. Louis, Most Rev. Peter Richard Kendrick, and twenty-four Bishops, assembled on this occasion. Archbishop Eccleston presided, for the fourth and last time, over his august peers,† in that most important conclave. The fathers there assembled recommended, in their wisdom, the division of the church in the United States into six provinces, namely, those of Baltimore, New Orleans, New York, Cincinnati, St. Louis, and Oregon city. The following year this division was approved of by the Holy Father, and, as will be seen from the list of the second Council, four Archbishoprics were created, in addition to those of Baltimore and St. Louis. Under this religious government exists a numerous and active clergy, whose numbers are, however, incommensurate to the numbers of the laity, everywhere

---

* The total stated in the Metropolitan Catholic Almanac for 1852 — 1,980,000 — is about one half of the true total! It was made up from the data described in the text, and therefore shows the number returned to the editor, rather than the actual whole. The compiler of that most useful almanac is, therefore, free from all blame in this respect. In 1836, the Right Rev. Dr. England, in a report to the Propaganda, says, on this subject: — "Of the population acquired by immigration and by cession (of territory), we may estimate at least one half to have been Catholics; and supposing the children to have adhered to the religion of their parents, if there were no loss, we should have at least four millions of Catholics from these sources, without regarding the portion which was Catholic fifty years ago, and its natural increase, and the many converts and their descendants."

† He died at Georgetown, D. C., April 22d, 1851.

scattered. A notice of each Catholic province will enable the reader to judge of the diffuse multitude of the faithful :

I. "The Province of Baltimore" has for its suffragan sees Philadelphia, Pittsburg, Charleston, Savannah, Richmond, and Wheeling. It contains three fourths of a million of Catholics, has about three hundred churches, and an equal number of clergymen. In educational and charitable institutions it is, perhaps, the richest province, that of New York not excepted. It is governed by the Archbishop Kendrick, translated to Baltimore, from Philadelphia, in 1851. The present suffragans, in the order of the sees given above, are Bishops Neumann, O'Connor, Reynolds, Gartland, McGill, and Whelan.

II. "The Province of New York" comes next in point of influence and institutions, while it exceeds that of Baltimore in numbers. Its suffragan sees are Boston, Albany, Buffalo, and Hartford. It contains, at least, one million of Catholics, has three hundred and fifty churches, and about the same number of clergymen. It is governed by Archbishop Hughes, consecrated in 1838, whose suffragans are Bishops Fitzpatrick, McCloskey, Timon, and O'Reilly.

III. "The Province of Cincinnati," whose missionary state makes its exact statistics more variable than those of the two just mentioned. It contains six or seven hundred thousand, has over three hundred churches, a somewhat less number of clergymen,— but has a hundred clerical students in its colleges. Its suffragan sees are Louisville, Detroit, Vincennes, and Cleveland. It is governed by Archbishop Purcell, consecrated in 1833, whose suffragans are Bishops Spalding, Lefevre, St. Palais, and Rappe. One third, or, perhaps, more nearly one half, of its Catholics are French or German, and have clergymen who speak familiarly their own languages.

IV. "The Province of St. Louis," like Cincinnati, is difficult to estimate. It may be set down at four hundred and fifty thousand. It has two hundred and sixty churches, and an equal number of clergymen, and many well-endowed institutions. Its suffragan sees are Nashville, Dubuque, St. Paul's, Chicago, and Milwaukie. The Archbishop Peter Richard Kenrick was consecrated in 1841. The Bishops are Loris, Miles, Henni, Vandevelde, and Cretin. It has also a large proportion of German and French Catholics.

V. "The Province of New Orleans" contains about three hundred thousand; it has above a hundred and fifty churches and clergymen. Its suffragan sees are Mobile, Natchez, Little Rock, and Galveston, of which the respective Bishops are Most Rev. Anthony Blanc, and Right Reverends M. M. Portier, Chance, Byrne, and Odin. Nearly one half of the Catholics in this province are of French and Spanish origin.

VI. "The Province of Oregon City" is divided into the diocese of that name, of Nesqualy, Walla Walla, Fort Hall, and Colville. The Most Rev. Francis N. Blanchet, and the Right Rev. Magloire Blanchet, are the only Bishops at present. The whole province, as is to be expected in so primitive a country, is in a missionary condition. There are thirty churches, and forty clergymen at present employed there.

An important addition to the church in the United States is the new diocese and probable province of California, at present under the first Bishop of Monterey, Right Rev. Joseph Alemanny. There are forty thousand Catholics, and the number is rapidly increasing. Forty churches and as many clergymen administer to the wants of this population, chiefly old Spanish settlers and Irish miners. The clergy are nearly all from the regular orders, Jesuits, Franciscans, or Dominicans. The Bishop, consecrated in 1850, was himself of the order of St. Dominick. There is a Diocesan college at Santa Ynez, a Jesuit college at Santa Clara, a Catholic school at Los Angelos, under the direction of the Brothers of the Sacred Heart; at St. Catherine's, a female school, under the Sisters of St. Dominic, and another at the Pueblo San Jose, under the direction of the Sisters of Notre Dame. There are also eight day schools in the diocese. The recent emigration of Irishmen to California has, of course, much increased the resources of the diocese. Judging from the support they have given to their Bishop, and the fervor with which they celebrated the festival of St. Patrick, they seem to be truly zealous and steadfast in their faith.

In addition to these statistics of the number and government of the Catholics in the United States, a few words may be said as to their position, public duties, and prospects. They are certainly rising in respectability and influence in proportion to their numbers. They have newspapers at Boston, New York, Philadelphia, Baltimore, Buffalo, Chicago, Pittsburg, St. Louis, and New Orleans. There are extensive Catholic publishing-houses in Baltimore, Philadelphia, New York, and Boston. At present, the Catholic press is very active, chiefly in reprinting London publications, or translations from foreign languages. Each of these publishing-houses has, within a few years back, issued several editions of the Holy Scriptures, in admirable typography.

Catholics of the old Maryland colony, of French, Spanish, or German origin, are, perhaps, less exposed to temptations, and, in the education of their children, more favored, by their isolation, than Irish Catholics are. The hardest labor of the Irish settler is not in the woods or the mines, but in forming the character of his children. A busy materialist state of society, a country without traditions, the demand for more labor, which imposes the responsibilities of life upon the merest youth, are all so many obstacles and distractions in the labor of Catholic education.

A few reflections on the relations of the first and second Irish generations in America are very respectfully submitted to the Catholic reader who is, or may be, the parent of children born in the United States : —

The first Irish generation in America can be traced very easily from the side of the emigrant-ship to the interior. In every six-house hamlet, in every town and city, we find them. They can be told by their faces, habits, speech, and old religion; for, wherever they are, the cross is the sign under which they conquer. But their children, born twenty and thirty years ago, in this land, where are they? If we look for them in our churches, we do not find them. If any Catholic clergyman, of thirty years' standing, will take up his old register, and call out the names of the baptized, how many will rise in the congregation to answer him, or claim their places? Few, very few, we fear.

In our patriotic societies, in our public undertakings as a class, they are absent from us. They are where they ought not to be; but where they should be, there they are not to be found.

It must be a proper subject of inquiry to know where the second generation breaks off from the first, why they break off, and where they go after they leave us.

We know a family, of which the parents were born, reared, and married in Ireland, and the sons and daughters born, reared, and married in the United States. We must consider the circumstances that formed and fashioned the parents, and those under which the children are to grow and live, marry, and be given in marriage. The case of that family is the whole subject. Every one knows some such family.

Ireland is a country with two thousand years of history; America is but two hundred years old. Ireland has been three hundred years under the yoke of the heretical kings of England; America laid the foundations of her freedom with those of her population. This country and its constitution have grown up together, and here all forms of faith are free.

These are the apparent political differences; the points of social contrast are finer and more numerous. The new continent is not more unlike the old island than this state of society is unlike the other.

In an old crowded island, population rises class above class. One man owns the fee of the soil, another leases it, a third cultivates it. A few thousand proprietors own Ireland, and its people have existed recently by sufferance upon that soil. Property and power naturally went together, and the laws as well as the land

20*

were absolutely controlled by the will and interest of this privileged Protestant minority.

The middle-men, of course, looked up to "their betters," and imitated their example. The rich farmer aspired to be "a gentleman." He hoarded up his money and educated his children to that especial end. The trader, who made a few thousands, bought a pigeon-box in the country, and learned to write "J. P." after his name. The middle class, seldom or never recruited from below, was thus vitiated from above, leaving Ireland an inclined plane, with the central parts cut out and cleared away.

The poor, the people, governed absolutely by their gentry, were deprived of any general system of public instruction. Up to 1834, there were no national schools open to the children of the poor. This class, therefore, seventy-five per cent. of the whole, grew up in a wild, untutored state of nature. There was but one place where, and one party from whom, they received instruction; the place was the parish chapel, the party the parish priest. By the sign of the cross we were saved from savagery. It was the star in our sky and the spring in our soil. Oppression such as our nation has endured would have made us thorough savages, if religion had not kept the souls stirring and alive in the breasts of our fathers and ourselves.

Even that holy religion has been made a source of additional oppression to us. Henry VIII. was elected King of Ireland in 1541. He is the first of our English line of sovereigns. (The usual supposition that Henry II. was so is a gross historical error.) From his days until Lord John Russell, no generation of Irish Catholics has enjoyed the exercise of its religion in peace.

If, therefore, young friends, you should at any time wonder why your parents are so rigid in their faith,— if the zeal of the old and poor, who travel through storm and snow to the early morning mass, astonishes you,— if their hatred of all the forms of Protestantism surprises you,— remember that for three hundred years all Ireland has been leading a life of martyrdom. Lands, suffrages, power, we might have had, if we only apostatized; we chose poverty, famine, and flight, but we kept — thank God, we kept ! — the teachings of our saints unviolated and entire.

But not alone did the clergy keep the people Catholic; everything in the island conspired to the same end. Imagine yourself upon a hill in Ireland, with the mists rolling from the scene. Look down; at your feet bubbles a holy well, which was once a primitive baptismal fount. Look up; a round tower points its index finger to the sky; to the left a Celtic cross, with the circle, emblem of eternity, uniting its arms, stands by the wayside; to the right is a churchyard, where an emigrant family kneel in prayer above the dead, before they turn their faces to the far west, never, never to return!

From this island, this garden girdled by the blue ring fence of ocean, where the air broods with a holy heaviness, and the land weeps man's perverse inhumanity,— from this solemn and prolific nursery of men, your ancestors have swarmed out upon the world. Ah! young men, be not too quick to jest or gibe at their antique terms of thought or speech. When America is two thousand years old, she may make a comparison. It is not wise, it is not manly, it certainly is not noble, to mock the weakness of our patriarchs, the American founders of our race.

Suddenly thrust out of the bottom of an ancient society, by political pressure, Irish men and women awake, and find themselves in America. The cry of "land" calls them all on deck. Land! what land is this? Its parti-colored forest trees, its shining new houses, its steaming harbors, its busy trading-people, with pale, care-knit brows, and lips compressed like oyster-shells,— how strange, how wonderful is all this to the man who whistled to his wooden plough along an Irish field, or the girl accustomed to gather her cows behind the hawthorn, and fill the evening air with " MA COLLEEN D'HAS CRUITHA N'MA BHO!" while she filled her pail with milk!

The wonder wears away, and knowledge comes painfully, and in bits, through experience. It is a hard school, this school of emigrant experience. It may be likened to a crowded corridor, in which there is no turning back. From the front to the back door, from manhood to death, there is no pause, no return. The vanishing backs of our predecessors before us, the eager faces of our cotemporaries round us, are all we see, or can see. Some in this crowd may have their pockets picked, or their ribs broken, or their corns trampled; but on they must go, with ribs broken or whole, pockets full or empty. The rich and poor, the weak and strong, the native and the stranger, are all thrown mercilessly upon themselves, in the common school of American experience.

But for the inexperienced emigrant large allowance should be made by all the rest. He starts with no stock of native traditions. He was not reared in the neighborhood. His knowledge, such as it is, being suited only to a totally different latitude, is rather a burden than a benefit to him. An East Indian suddenly left on a cape of Labrador would not pass more visibly from one condition of being to another, than the Irish emigrant who finds himself new landed in America.

With us, Catholics, there can be no doubt that the family is everywhere, and under all circumstances, an institution of Divine origin. Its laws are part of the sacred Scriptures,— its bond and warrant is a sacrament of our holy religion. But, as a matter of fact, there is equally no doubt that the family ties are weaker in America than they are in Ireland.

In Ireland, every son was "a boy," and every daughter "a girl," till he or she was married. We have all known "boys" and "girls" of five-and-forty. There was a meaning in this, absurd as it looks : they were considered subject to their parents till they became parents themselves; their allegiance was due to "the heads" of the old house until they were called to preside over the fortunes of "houses of their own."

In America, in consequence of the newness of the soil, and the demands of enterprise, boys are men at sixteen. There are, in fact, no CHILDREN in America. They are all little old men and women, cut down or abridged. They seem like some pigmy generation of the past, come back to criticize the present. They all work for themselves, and pay their own board. They either live with the "boss," "governor," or "old man," or elsewhere, as they please. They may have respect, — they must have some natural deference for parents; but the abstract Irish reverence for old age is not yet naturalized in America.

Over half a dozen of these keen, hard, worldly young Yankees, an Irish father is to preside. They are born, they are doctored, they go to the public school. They are called "Paddies," perhaps, by Darius, and Cyrus, and Habakkuk, of the Plymouth rock dynasty. They come home, and they want explanations. Yes, they want explanations; and here is, precisely, where the second generation breaks off from the first. If the first can explain itself to satisfy the second, the second will naturally stick to its pedigree; but if not, the family tie is snapt, and our children become our opponents, and sometimes our worst enemies.

You have seen two equals attempt an explanation. If it is not full, frank, and satisfactory, they part worse friends than before. They explain, and are enemies ever after. So with the American child of Irish parents; in the word "explanation" are included disobedience, sorrow, apostasy and death !

Many emigrants do not know the extent of this responsibility. While they are talking disrespectfully of Ireland or their Irish neighbors, their children are swallowing every word. They are holding a grand inquest upon them, in the corner ! Take care of what you say. They are taking notes of it, in tenacious young memories, from which it never, never will be effaced !

We ask parents to think of three things which cannot be too well remembered by a people situated as we are in the United States : —

One is, never to laugh or approve of "the smartness," as it is called, which your children pick up in the streets. Another, never to refuse them an explanation connected with your religion and your country : the third, never to speak lightly, before them, of what you wish them to respect or to practise.

The "smartness" of the streets consists in a few out-worn phrases, in a certain impertinent self-assurance, in swearing, smoking cabbage cigars, and still worse dissipations. If you applaud the first signs of such smartness, how can you tell where it will stop ? If you applaud it, how can you hope to escape the consequence of your own folly ? Many an Irish father and mother began to observe these things in laughter, who lived to weep heart-wrung tears of tribulation over them in the end.

Again : try to give them or get them reasons to justify yourselves, your religion and your country. Beg, borrow, or steal, explanations. For example, your boy is called by this young Puritan, Darius, "a Paddy." He wants to know what a Paddy is. Tell him; tell him all you know. Tell him of that great Saint, whose festival is our national holiday; of how, from a shepherd and a slave, he became the founder of a kingdom of souls ; how mountains, cathedrals and cities, have rejoiced in his name ; how, not to mention earlier celebrities, Patrick Sarsfield and Patrick Henry, the Irish soldier and the Virginia orator, were proud to bear it. Send him into the world well armed with facts, strong in his faith, proud of his principles, above every cowardly compromise, and from that sacred struggle bid him return, as the Spartan mother bid her son return,—" Come back victorious, or come back no more ! "

On the third topic, of unguarded speaking before children, it is needless to enlarge.

We meet every day the apostate children of Irish parents, sons of emigrants, and themselves the worst enemies of emigrants. We see them afraid to profess their religion, because they do not know its doctrine and its history, its sanctity and its glory ; ashamed of their origin, because ignorant of Ireland and of themselves. We see them marry strange wives, and wed their beliefs or no beliefs into the bargain ; we see them desert the eternal portals of God's church, to trim and temporize among the schismatical spawn of yesterday, to ally themselves to sects that swarm in the spring like gad-flies, and die annually out. Why do we see these sights ? Admit that evil grows wild, while good needs cultivation ; admit that good parents will sometimes have bad children, does that account for all — all ?

This generation of Catholics will not probably lose many of its members. We have now in our midst churches, a clergy, and a hierarchy. We have some useful institutions, the effects of which are entirely conservative of the ancient faith.

Sooner than we suspect, a severe test may be put to our principles. In Europe and America the men of this age are fast dividing into two universal parties, or two camps. Those who were neutral last year are decided now; those who are neutral now will be enlisted next year. The modern mind has been filled with a new morality, and new theories of duty, which it is inclined to put into operation. It thinks it can do without pope and property, executive and obedience. It proposes to erect new institutions on the shifting basis of aggregate private judgment; to confiscate and distribute property; to elect and inspire its teachers from the plenitude of its own untaught fancies. All who are not besotted beyond redemption, with these theories, must choose the other side, the conservative side of this contest. The debatable land is being rapidly narrowed; their pickets drive in ours, and, it is to be feared, a great contest is at hand throughout the nations, now so closely connected as to present the appearance of a coöperative populace, and a close federation of parties, naturally foreign to each other. No one can contemplate the approach of this contest without anxiety, for much suffering and much evil will be transacted in its progress. But if it must come,—if the christianized Celts, who resisted and overcame barbarism a thousand years ago, and resisted and repelled the Lutheran schism three hundred years ago,—if the christianized Celts of Italy, Spain, France, Ireland and America, must arise and arm once more for the law of God and the deliverance of men, the second Irish generation in America will not be wanting in the hour of need.

· Now and then there is a part for us to perform, from which none, not even the church itself, can release us. There is an education of the pulpit, an education of the schools, and an education of the fireside. To teach our children reverence in an irreverent age, this is the great task for Irishmen in America.

It matters little if you leave them houses or land, if you leave them not reverence. If they devour books and digest them, they will sink into mere materialists, or empty sceptics, without reverence. Get yourselves in positions in which you can command respect,—be citizens, and good ones,—be Catholics, and good ones; and then you will command the homage of your children, and be to them fit teachers of sacred reverence.

We have brought into America great numbers, much poverty, willing spirits, able arms, and the Catholic faith. The last census found us to be above three millions. The second generation are, at least, as many more. Men of our nation have, from the beginning, helped to plant the free institutions which keep this an open country for us. We are no intruders here; we are not here by the tolerance of any party; by the laws of the land, and by virtue of our own labors, and those of our nation, we stand free and equal among the favored inhabitants of this confederacy.

Let us understand our duty and our position in America. The clearance of this continent, partly effected by Irish hands, is the greatest work of these latter days. It is the only new feature in the world's face. Wonderful revolutions and inventions we have had enough; but the most lasting change among men is the apparition of a new world in the western waters. Felling forests and planting men, scattering cities through a continent, and covering savage seas, rivers and lakes, with navigated ships, this is the great transpiring act of human enterprise. We live in the times of our Theseus and Hercules, in the golden and adventurous age of the West. Two great families of men are in the American field, the Teutons and the Celts. The English and Germans are of Teuton origin; the Spanish, Irish, French and Scotch, of Celtic origin. Each, after its own peculiar genius, is doing its share of the New World's work.

Numerically the Irish are increasing upon all the other divisions of the population; morally and religiously, also, they are beginning to grow upon the earlier emigrants. We have only to be true to our creed, our country, and our children, and the European legend, which called America *Ireland it Mikla*, will be translated from the realm of legends into the world of realities.

Gentlemen "of the second generation," do not accept English accounts of the country of your ancestors. Do not mistake every miserable *Farceur* for a representative of Irish character. Read the history of your ancestral island, by McGeoghegan; study its present character in Banim, Griffin, or Carlton, in the "Collegians," or "the Poor Scholar;" study its music in Moore; study its creed here where it has raised its altars. If you want to know what education has made of the men of your race, look at Burke, Curran, and O'Connell; if you want to know what oppression may bring to it, read the police reports of any great city. Cast up the account of your fathers with the world, set forth what they owe it and what it owes them, and tell me, do you not find a balance in their favor? You are heirs to their history; you are concerned in their character; you have no choice but to acknowledge and stand by us, or to pass through apostasy to a cheerless and unprincipled prosperity.

Youth is the age of generous resolutions, and, in the filial duties, its inclinations are generally right. If the first generation will be wise and gentle and exemplary, the second will be dutiful, faithful, and honorable; the first must *be* right, if it would have the second *do* right; the first generation must use its citizenship, and live up to its religion, if it would have the second made up of good men and women, good sons and daughters, good citizens, and good Catholics.

If this book should chance to fall into the hands of one who has withdrawn himself, in youth, from filial obedience, and has grown up in a selfish separation from the interests of his race, to him we say, there is no character but a common character for so marked a people as ours. A jay in the dove-cot, or a red rose among violets, is not more strongly contrasted than a Celt, even of the second generation, among the children of the Teutons. He is at war with nature who is at war with his own kindred. He stands in an unsafe place; he is trying the impossible experiment of a separate existence. Let him pause and examine; and when his mind has surveyed the past of our people in its brightness and its darkness, its degradation and its heroism, without doubt he too will feel that it is a proud privilege to be ranked among the laborious missionaries of Providence, THE IRISH IN AMERICA.